*The story of Toronto*

UNIVERSITY OF TORONTO PRESS

# The story of Toronto

G. P. deT. GLAZEBROOK

© University of Toronto Press 1971
Toronto and Buffalo

Printed in Canada
ISBN 0–8020–1791–6
Microfiche ISBN 0–8020–0108–4
LC 78–163815

# *Preface*

The purpose of this book is to tell the story of Toronto from its earliest days to the present: to describe its character at each stage of growth, how it changed, and why. The first chapters are chronological, an arrangement possible when describing a small and simple society. For the later ones it seemed best to adopt a compromise between chronology and themes.

The bibliography lists most of the manuscript collections and certain reference and other basic publications, but not all the specialized items mentioned in the footnotes.

My warm thanks go to the many men and women who have helped me in my task. Professor D. C. MacGregor, Professor J. M. S. Careless, and Miss Edith Firth read the whole draft and made helpful suggestions. I am indebted to Miss Firth, too, for her volumes of documents on the Town of York, and for the assistance of herself and her colleagues in the Canadian History and Manuscript Section of the Metropolitan Toronto Central Library who found answers to my endless questions. I am grateful, too, to members of the staffs of the Ontario Archives, the City of Toronto Archives, the library of the University of Toronto, the Metropolitan Toronto Business and Municipal Reference Library, the Metropolitan Toronto Planning Board, the City of Toronto Planning Board, the Bureau of Municipal Research, the Metropolitan Toronto Industrial Commission, the Ontario Department of Municipal Affairs, the Bell Telephone Company, and the Dominion Bureau of Statistics.

Miss Jean Houston, executive editor at the University of Toronto Press, gave wise advice as the chapters emerged, and Mr G. Hallowell has carefully and sympathetically edited the whole.

G.P. deT.G.

Toronto, 1971

# Contents

# Illustrations

*The story of Toronto*

# I ∎

# A place in search of a purpose

This is the story of a town dropped by the hand of government into the midst of a virgin forest. For the site chosen no record exists of earlier habitation although small groups of Indians may at one time have lived not far from it. To the extent that Toronto has any history before 1793 it is to be found further west, near the mouth of the Humber River. In this sense it differs from its elder brother, Kingston, the location of which remained constant from the time of its foundation in the seventeenth century. But neither Kingston nor Niagara could in the French régime have been called a town. Each was a fort and a service establishment for trade in furs; the populations were transient and wholly male. Any civil activities peculiar to a town were either for the maintenance of the garrison and the traders or, as in shipbuilding, for the furtherance of the trade. Such places resembled the posts of the Hudson's Bay Company; and, indeed, until after the American revolution the country of the lower lakes was not settled at all. It was part of the *pays d'en haut*, the wild fur trade area west of the farms and towns of the St Lawrence Valley.

In both the French and the early British régimes Montreal was the base for the fur trade, and from it the western routes fanned out, the one by the Ottawa River and the other by the lower lakes. The first, with its many portages, was laborious and could be followed only in canoes with their limited capacity for freight; but it was direct and well away from the English colonies or the later United States. The other was by way of the St Lawrence River to Lake Ontario, over the Niagara portage to Lake Erie, and so on past Detroit to Michilimackinac. It was longer but allowed for the use of sailing vessels. On this second thoroughfare supporting posts were required at strategic points. When Count Frontenac founded at Kingston in 1673 the fort first named after him he made the inevitable choice. At the junction of the St Lawrence and Lake Ontario and with a

3

natural harbour for sailing ships it could readily be made into a military and commercial centre. The second fort followed not long after the first and at an equally obvious place. The French Fort Niagara, on the east bank of the river, was another port for sailing vessels, and the starting point for the combined river and portage system that led to Lake Erie. In addition to being staging posts these two strongholds were essential to the local trade of the districts in which they were placed.

The main-travelled routes and principal posts were supplemented by minor ones. It was possible to proceed northwestward out of Lake Ontario by the Trent River and Kawartha Lakes or by the Rouge River, but few canoes went by either way. The Don River was also navigable but seldom followed. It is a curious anomaly that the Humber River, although evidently not navigable, should have attracted more travellers. There are a few references to the use of the portage beside it from the early seventeenth century, and in the 1680s a more positive though only outline account occurs. La Salle, the great explorer, travelled between Georgian Bay and Lake Ontario in both directions. Northbound in 1681 he apparently spent two weeks (although this seems incredible) transporting his canoes and goods overland from the lake to near Lake Simcoe. Unfortunately he left no record of the starting point or of the nature of the portage.

The course of the carrying place can be identified, if not in detail, throughout.[1] It ran close to the east bank of the Humber, crossed the east branch of that river at the later village of King Creek, followed over the height of land, and so to the Holland River where the canoes could at last be launched. From there they would be paddled into Lake Simcoe, across it and Lake Couchiching, and by way of the Severn River (with about seven portages) into Georgian Bay. The length of the Toronto portage was about thirty miles, and it must seem strange that no use was apparently made of the Humber itself. Were no stretches ever navigable?

No description has been found of the river as it was in the seventeenth and early eighteenth centuries, but one would expect it to have had more water before the forests were cut down. Yet what little evidence there is points to an uninterrupted carry as far as the Holland River. La Salle had Indians with him when he went that way, and if it had been Indian practice to paddle parts of the distance surely they would have objected to bearing everything on their backs? Long portages were always unpopular with the personnel of the fur trade. The Grand Portage, past the Pigeon River at the west end of Lake Superior, caused incessant grumbling and it was only nine miles. Portaging was not only slow and irritating but it was also expensive. Why bypass a river? One quite probable explanation is that the Humber, like some other rivers flowing into Lake Ontario, was blocked by beaver dams which no one, apparently, was ready to break. In 1788 an official surveyor concluded that 'it is impossible to pass with large canoes on account of the rapids and difficult carrying-places.' The banks, he understood were rocky. It is frustrating not to know whether he meant that small canoes could be and were used in places; but all in all one must conclude that at least for fur trade craft the Humber was simply not navigable.

In terms of miles the route to Michilimackinac by way of Toronto was appreciably shorter than that by Detroit, but it is a question how far that was offset by the amount of land travel. Unfortunately little light can be thrown on how much the former was used or on the volume of traffic it carried in comparison with the Ottawa or Great Lakes routes. Neither the French traders, the British from Albany, nor the later British firms at Montreal left such tidy records as did the Hudson's Bay Company. Probably all that can be said of the use of the portage is that it was part of a minor route and may have been used more by individual Indians than by organized trading concerns.

Activity close to the mouth of the Humber should not be measured only by the volume of traffic over the portage, even if that were known. Sporadic trading on a small scale was undoubtedly conducted near the lake over a long period, some of the furs being brought from nearby and others – increasingly – from greater distances. Like a number of other places on the north shore of Lake Ontario this was the site of a village established by a group of Iroquois after the defeat and dispersal of the Hurons in the mid-seventeenth century. The supply of fur-bearing animals to the south of the lake being exhausted these Indians collected skins near their new homes and traded them to the Dutch from New York and Albany. Early records of Teiaiagon, the Seneca village on the east bank of the Humber and near its mouth, are, however, sketchy and not informative. After their strength declined in the early eighteenth century the Iroquois had left the north shore of the lake and the Mississaugas moved south and took their place.

The fur trade on and through Lake Ontario was a highly competitive business. Without constant vigilance the French must expect to see the best of it slip southward into the hands of the British from the Hudson, whose own enterprise was aided not only by Indians but by those private French traders who sought to turn a penny through illicit trade. To strengthen their position the French authorities restored Fort Frontenac, neglected for some years, and rebuilt Fort Niagara. A small post was set up, probably in 1720, at a point near the mouth of the Humber. Records show that trade goods were sent there in the subsequent few years and the terms on which the post was leased; but exactly where it was, how large, and with what personnel are not known. It was a dependency of Niagara which, with Frontenac, was the principal instrument for meeting English competition on the lower lakes. So little emphasis was placed on the Toronto

An early French post

post, however, that it was allowed to lapse in about 1730. Trade did not disappear completely, for visits were certainly made by French traders and probably by English ones no less often.

It was not until the middle of the century that the post was reopened, the decision to do so being specifically related to the successful competition from the English post at Oswego, diagonally across the lake. By the time that the small building party arrived in the spring of 1750 the Mississauga village had been moved, probably nearer the lake. A small wooden fort was erected on the east bank of the Humber – too small as it proved when a brisk trade developed. A few months later work began on a more commodious one, named Fort Rouillé after the minister of marine but more commonly known as Fort Toronto. It was in a new location three miles to the eastward, at the foot of Dufferin Street and on the grounds of the Canadian National Exhibition.

Built of squared logs the fort occupied an area of some 180 feet each way. It contained dwellings for the commandant and the garrison and had a store, a bakery, and a blacksmith's shop. The garrison varied in size but was never large. In 1754 one officer, three sergeants, four soldiers, and a storekeeper made up the complement. A few boatmen and labourers lived in or near the fort. Finished in 1751, Fort Rouillé offered no life of luxury. Illness plagued the personnel, and cannot have been helped by the diet provided in the rations. Trade goods ran short at times. No exact figures of trade seem to have survived, but an estimate for 1757 was 150 bales of furs as compared with 250 to 300 for Niagara. That was not insignificant. But the new post had a brief life. Neither the construction of the fort nor the number of soldiers in it was designed to withstand any serious attack and the commandant's standing orders were that in case of emergency he was to burn the buildings and destroy everything of value to the enemy. Fort Frontenac fell to British forces in 1758, and when Niagara suffered the same fate in July 1759 the commandant carried out his instructions. He and his men – a party of fifteen in all – retreated toward Montreal as the falling ashes foretold the collapse of the French empire in North America.

When Britain, with limited enthusiasm, acquired all Canada under the treaty of 1763 the area west of the Ottawa River was wholly undeveloped, except for the settlements at and near Detroit, designed as a means of supplying food to the western forts. Although His Majesty's old subjects were, by royal proclamation in 1763, invited to settle on the conquered land, few took advantage of the opportunity other than merchants who hastened to Montreal, hoping to inherit such part of the fur trade as had been conducted from there. Other immigrants were rare and no land-hungry peasants stepped forward in the St Lawrence Valley. For the time being, then, the western country remained the realm of the Indian, the trader, and the diminishing beaver upon which so much unwanted attention was heaped.

For another twenty-five years the Toronto district is on the record only to the extent that fur trading was done there, and that was on a minor scale. Several independent traders were reported, being conspicuous chiefly for the large amounts of rum that they had brought with them. The fur trade was badly dislocated first by the Indian uprising under Pontiac and then by the war of the American revolution – Toronto suffering in common with other commercial sites. Two men from the Indian Department had for a time a house of sorts, while Jean Rousseau from Montreal, who in 1770 secured a licence to trade, built a house on the east bank of the Humber not far from the lake, and was ready to welcome the Simcoes when they later arrived.

The first applications for land were made in connection with the Toronto portage as part of a long-distance route for the fur trade. Shaken by the curtailment of their area by the boundary settlement of 1783 and in fierce competition with the Hudson's Bay Company, the North West Company – principal agents of the trade centred on Montreal – were concerned about the rising cost of transportation, the distances becoming greater as the beaver receded. Writing to Governor Haldimand in 1784 the company described the Ottawa 'inland navigation' as 'perhaps the most expensive in the known world'; but as the argument was leading up to a claim to exclusive rights of trade in the northwest, and as they continued to use the Ottawa, their case cannot be regarded as wholly disinterested.[2]

Transport by sailing ships on the Great Lakes was, the traders asserted, handicapped by a requirement that only the king's ships, the Provincial Marine, were allowed to operate. The reason for this rule was probably sound enough: that the masters of private ships might sneak down to enemy or ex-enemy ports for profitable sales. It was exactly the same situation as the French had faced earlier in the century. From the point of view of honest (or even dishonest) merchants, however, the service provided by the king's ships was unsatisfactory. Serious delays added to the difficulties in a business that at best was never easy. After the war the restrictions were progressively reduced. The first step was to allow private ships to be built under a permit from the governor general, and then in 1788 the provincial Inland Navigation Act withdrew the royal monopoly altogether and put in its place a code of control to govern unofficial shipping.

That helped, but the situation in other respects was still far from satisfactory. The voyage by the Niagara portage and Detroit was roundabout, and in years of alternate war and tension proximity to the American border was dangerous. Under such circumstances, and given the cost of the Ottawa River canoe route, could some other way be found from Lake Ontario to the upper lakes? In 1784 Benjamin Frobisher and his brother Joseph explored the possibilities on behalf of the North West Company. They turned down the Trent Valley as impractical but reported favourably on the Toronto portage. They admitted to be going only on hearsay, which indicates that the Nor'Westers had no direct experience of travel over it. The company, however, was sufficiently impressed by what it could learn to apply for a strip of land from Lake Ontario to Georgian Bay.

Nothing came of the proposal at the time but a similar one was made in 1785, and more formally in 1787, by a private individual, Philippe, Chevalier de Rocheblave, on the strength of his loyal services and losses during the American revolution. He asked for a thousand acres of land running back from the lake between the mouth of the Humber and a point to the east of it that is not clearly identified. He also sought what was evidently intended as a monopoly contract to carry governmental and commercial freight from Lake Ontario to Lake Simcoe. Transport was to be by wheeled vehicles, so that the Humber trail could not be used as it was. He spoke of a new road to be cut, but whether he had in mind a particular location for it is not clear. It could be, and probably was, somewhere to the east of the river. He based his proposed tariff on that of the contractor at the Niagara portage (who had a highly profitable business), increasing the charges because of the greater distance. The officials who considered the proposition looked for comments by the merchants, which, if ever made, have not been found.

8

Meanwhile events dictated that southern Ontario should become more than a passageway for the trade in furs. The development was as rapid as it was unexpected, arising out of the American revolution: what Lord Dorchester in his first term of office had described as 'a catastrophe shocking to think of' was the one cause which would bring to Canada people of other than French origin. The arrival of political exiles, the defeated Tories of the revolution (later named United Empire Loyalists), created an entirely new situation for it spelled the beginning of settlement on the upper St Lawrence and the Great Lakes. Other immigrants, from both the United States and Great Britain, followed. As early as 1764 the British authorities had established a precedent by buying, through treaty, land from the Indians. Two principles were followed, both intended to protect the interests of the tribes: that any land inhabited by Indians belonged to them, and that such land could be acquired only by the crown, which could then, if it wished, sell or grant portions to individuals or groups.

The purchase of 1764 was of a small district in the vicinity of Fort Niagara, and it was only when the Loyalists arrived that large areas were needed. A further treaty of 1781 with the Mississauga and Chippewa Indians added to the first Niagara purchase the equivalent of four townships. Kingston was the other main centre of settlement, so that three purchases were made in 1781 which together embraced a wide strip along the river and lake all the way from Cornwall to a point not far short of Toronto. It was in the course of this process that the Toronto purchase was effected. It was, Dorchester wrote to the deputy surveyor general, 'expedient to join the settlements of the Loyalists near to Niagara, to those west of Cataraqui.' In 1787 an agreement was made with the Mississaugas and was later clarified and extended. The specific boundaries are, however, of no particular significance since the whole north shore of Lake Ontario was being taken over piecemeal.[3]

The way was clear for the Toronto area to be opened and settled, but for a time it remained almost untenanted between the Kingston and Niagara districts. The number of immigrants was small in relation to the amount of land available on the river and lake, and it is not surprising that Niagara and Kingston became the first hubs of settlement. They were established centres in the French régime, chosen because of their situations on water communication; and for the same reason they were attractive to the new order. Toronto, however, also had a natural harbour. By the 1780s it seems to have been used little if at all. Lord Dorchester, who returned as governor general in 1786, early had his eye on it. One or more ports were needed as naval bases but they must not be too vulnerable to enemy attack; for the problem of defence was very much to the fore from the end of the revolutionary war to the second outbreak of hostilities in 1812. Moreover, Toronto had what Niagara and Kingston lacked, what Dorchester referred to in a letter as 'the proposed communication from Toronto to Lake Huron.' What he meant by 'Toronto' is not evident, but he was aware of Rocheblave's scheme for a new road; and if that were to be sufficiently to the east the new portage would run from the harbour.

On the other hand the Humber portage continued to be examined if only to show that the river was not navigable and that the land track would hardly justify a town near its southern extremity. The harbour, the deputy surveyor general, John Collins, reported in 1788 was 'capacious, safe and well sheltered,' but handicapped by the fact that the only entrance was from the west, so that sailing ships had to beat out against the prevailing wind. Collins did not raise the question of the harbour as the terminus of a route to the north.[4] None of this was very encouraging, but Dorchester intended to go ahead with the establishment of a town on the bay, and for that he had plans drawn. How much weight he placed on the way to the north is not certain, but it was undoubtedly an element. The applications of Rocheblave and of others who asked for smaller grants were approved. However, they never went into effect. Moving slowly through the official mill they lapsed in the new jurisdiction.

When the old Province of Quebec was divided in 1791 the lieutenant governor of Upper Canada proved to have different opinions, and the fact that his relations with the governor general were less than cordial made him the less ready to defer to the latter's views. John Graves Simcoe was a soldier of the American revolutionary war, a landowner, and a recent member of parliament. Dorchester was a veteran of both the Seven Years' War and the revolution, and in the second had not been on good terms with Simcoe. That these two men should have had to share responsibility was an unfortunate coincidence but one that had little effect on the history of Toronto. At least they were in agreement that a town should be established there.

In the months between his appointment and his arrival in Canada Simcoe devoted his time to the study of his new realm.[5] It must have a capital, but where? From the point of view of established settlements Kingston would be best and Niagara next, but he ruled out both as exposed to American attack. Looking at the colony from across the Atlantic he saw its body as 'that great peninsula between the Lakes Huron, Erie, and Ontario' and reached the determination, from which he never departed, 'to establish a capital in the very heart of the Country, upon the River la Tranche [Thames], which is navigable for 150 miles – and near to where the Grand River which falls into Lake Erie, and others that communicate with Huron and Ontario, almost interlock.' Richard Cartwright thought the idea absurd – unless that uninhabited district could be reached by balloon. Cartwright, as a leading merchant of Kingston, was undoubtedly biased, but even Simcoe considered that what he variously called Georgina and New London would have to wait.

A temporary capital then had to be chosen. It must be accessible, which in practice meant somewhere on the lower lakes. With the aid of maps Simcoe went over the possibilities again and again, both before and after his arrival in Canada. Niagara, although 'the most important Possession in the country,' he found dangerously close to the United States, even if with the same breath he designated it as one of the three strong points for defence (the other two being Long Point on Lake Erie and Toronto). He viewed with some alarm the fact that Kingston was the refitting port for shipping on Lake Ontario. It was 'absolutely indefensible' in winter when invaders could cross the river on the ice. From this point of view Toronto was much preferable. 'I propose,' he wrote, 'that the winter Station of the Fleet, and its refitting Port, and such Naval Buildings as may be wanting, be at York – the Port is at a great distance from the foreign shore, is capable of being easily defended, and [in] the Grants of Land having been made by the present Government, sufficient care has been taken, that great reservations of timber should be made for naval purposes.' All types of ships that might be needed could be built there.

On this matter, as on others, the two soldier-administrators disagreed. Dorchester was convinced that the naval base should be on the St Lawrence, as near to Lake Ontario as possible. Toronto was too far out of the way. Simcoe retorted that it was the very fact of distance that might ensure its preservation. He was of the opinion that York 'ought to be the refitting port and winter deposit of all Naval & Military Stores under existing circumstances – That it must hereafter become the permanent Naval Arsenal of [Lake] Ontario, and in some respects of Upper Canada, I believe, will not be controverted.'

It could be controverted and was, but on other reasons for establishing a town at Toronto opinion was less divided. Because of the bay some kind of village would in any case have grown there, as happened at many points on Lake Ontario where harbours were less good. Simcoe's choice of Toronto as the site for a temporary capital, however, hastened the process, greatly facilitated it, and stamped a character on the town that was built. Simcoe admitted that Toronto was a long way from a source of supplies, either to the west or to the east, but noted correctly that the nearby country was suitable for agriculture so that part of the difficulty would disappear as settlers started to grow crops. How far either Dorchester or Simcoe was influenced by the Toronto portage, old or new style, is impossible to say. Toronto was not selected for that reason alone or primarily, and it is probably safe to say that the site would have been picked even if there had been no prospect – and it was prospect rather than past experience – of a way to the north and west. Perhaps the portage can best be described as a makeweight, and one of some significance for economic and military reasons.

All this, however, is speculative. What is known is that Simcoe, like Dorchester before him, was determined to create a town on the harbour of Toronto. This, then, is the origin of Toronto as an urban community of men, women, and children rather than as a series of minor and temporary trading posts scattered throughout the neighbourhood. There was nothing to go on: no people, no buildings, hardly any cleared land and none cultivated. All that had happened in the past was preliminary, and largely, as it proved, irrelevant.

# 2 ■■

# The birth of a town

Boom of cannon and rattle of muskets broke the silence of the lakeside woods to celebrate a military victory in Holland by the Duke of York and to mark the bestowal of his name on a town yet to be built. Some twelve and eighteen pounders that Simcoe had picked up here and there, a firing party from the Queen's Rangers, the muskets of a few Indians, and the guns of the ships in harbour were brought into play for this improvised ceremony. The audience was small: Mrs Simcoe, ready as ever to support her husband; their young son, Francis, held in the arms of an old Indian and delighted with the loud noise; and a few squaws.

It was late August of 1793. An advance party of the Rangers had been there for some weeks, cutting down trees to make huts for the regiment near what is now old Fort York. The Simcoes had come toward the end of July, full of enthusiasm and ready to face anything. They brought with them a 'canvas house' that had once belonged to Captain Cook. Set near the military camp, it was placed on a wooden floor, fitted with doors and windows, and encased in an outer wall of boards. It was more like a pre-fabricated cottage than a tent but was viewed with marked distaste by officials and their wives who were clinging to what now seemed comfort in the temporary capital at Niagara-on-the-Lake. Nor did they care for the restless energy of the Simcoes. He was now at Niagara, now at York, bustling about to get his town started. Mrs Simcoe was exploring on foot, by boat, and on horseback; jumping her horse over logs and racing on the sands of the peninsula. Wherever she went she noted the species of trees, birds, and wildflowers.[1]

The town was to be somewhere between the Don and the Humber rivers, and certainly on the great natural harbour which had been seen as one of the main assets of the location. The stretch along the bay was flat, backed by land rising to a moderate height before dropping again in the

York Harbour, 1793, a water colour by Mrs Simcoe

Huts of the Queen's Rangers, erected 1793–4, from a drawing by Mrs Simcoe

watershed of Lake Simcoe. To the west was low ground as far as the head of the lake, but on the other side, beyond the Don, the Scarborough Bluffs broke the monotony. Some signs of French clearing remained but the general appearance was of forest untouched by human hand. Anything that may have been left of Fort Rouillé after it was burned in 1759 had disappeared, perhaps removed by the few Indians who lived not far away. That persistent fur trader, Jean Rousseau, had his house by the Humber, and his knowledge of local navigation and other conditions was useful. East of the Don and a few miles north one or two settlers were moving on to their lands. They were the forerunners of the farming population of York County.

Several early town plans were already on file but the one adopted was drawn up by a surveyor, Alexander Aitkin, in 1793. It called for a simple grid of ten blocks and, using modern names, was placed east of Yonge Street and bounded by George, Berkeley, Front, and Duke streets. This came to be called the 'old town' when a 'new town' was added to its west in 1797. The result of the extension was that the limits were pushed to Peter Street, that is, to the edge of the Garrison or Military Reserve. A large square space between old and new was reserved for public purposes: a hospital, church, school, gaol, and residences for the persons connected with them. The northern boundary of the town was at the same time moved up to Queen (then Lot) Street where for many years it rested.

Lot Street was also the base survey line. Between that and the next (second) concession, which was later named Bloor Street, was the standard distance of one and one-quarter miles. The land between was divided into hundred-acre parcels, 'park lots' as they were called. On the southern extremity it was intended that a strip should be reserved for public use between the bay and the first row of houses, which would have an uninterrupted view of the water and the peninsula. Such were the blueprints, uninhibited by previous construction or commitments, but with more respect for symmetry than topography. Having designed the town the next step was to people it.

Who would want to live in this wholly undeveloped place having the name but none of the characteristics of a town? Whoever came must of necessity be new to York and in most cases to Upper Canada. What the whole province needed was inhabitants, and what it had to offer was crown land – thousands and thousands of acres of it. For the time being land had little if any commercial value but it could, after clearing, be put to immediate use for agriculture or held for later increment. It seemed logical, then, to give land away subject only to fees (waived for United Empire Loyalists), but not to do so indiscriminately. Loyal and hard working people were welcome. Group settlement was encouraged and very large grants were made to organizers. The officials concerned made honest efforts to exclude absentee landowners but could accomplish little in the face of contradictions within the system itself. For those near the top of the tree – army officers, judges, government officials, and other prominent men – grants were in thousands of acres, and it could hardly be pretended that the recipients of such favours could or would take steps to develop their holdings. Most of them thought only of selling at future and higher values.

At the time when the town was founded it was in an area only thinly spotted with people. The first waves of Loyalist immigrants had stopped short of it or passed it by. There were some – probably very few – grants to Loyalists not far from York. Mrs William Jarvis referred briefly in a letter of October 1792 to her uncle who expected to go to Toronto 'to settle of Loyalists,' and by 'Toronto' she would mean that area. Unlike Kingston and Niagara, York itself was not a distinctively Loyalist town. An analysis of the first list of inhabitants, that of 1797, has shown that the Loyalists made up about one-quarter of the total, and after that the proportion decreased.[2]

One group of people who came to York did so from necessity, because it was to be the temporary capital. These were the officials of government and those who were to administer justice. All colonial posts were filled by patronage, but in the eighteenth and early nineteenth centuries it would be a rare appointee who expected his emoluments to be confined to salary or fees. Nearly all demanded that they should be enabled to live in the style to which they were accustomed or to which their positions gave claim. It was a point of view generally endorsed by the British government and its representatives in the colonies, taking concrete form in award of the best locations in the town and near it. Somewhat illogically in the case of those who had solicited appointment the officials liked to think that they were unselfishly carrying the burden of empire; yet it was a state of mind that increased their sense of responsibility and therefore their effectiveness in performing their duties.

They were new to York but not all to North America. John Elmsley, the first chief justice resident in York, was an English lawyer, and so was the attorney general, John White. William Dummer Powell, born in Boston, came to Montreal in 1779 after a short stay in England. He practised law for a time and in 1794 was made a puisne justice of the Court of King's Bench in Upper Canada. He had already been granted a front lot in York. Peter Russell, receiver general, was an Irishman who had been in and out of the army and in more than out of debt. He had long sought preferment and in 1780 was made assistant secretary to the commander-in-chief in America. The civil secretary, William Jarvis, and the commissary of stores, John McGill, had both served under Simcoe in the Queen's Rangers. The solicitor general was R. I. D. Gray whose family had come to Canada in 1776. D. W. Smith, a recent arrival from

England and a member of the legislative assembly, was surveyor general. In this latter work he was assisted by William Chewett, earlier from England, and Thomas Ridout, who had migrated from Dorset to Maryland. John Small, recently from Gloucestershire, was clerk of the executive council. On Simcoe's immediate staff Major E. B. Littlehales was military secretary and Thomas Talbot, later famous for his empire on Lake Erie, was for a short time private secretary. Simcoe brought with him a Scottish regimental surgeon, James Macaulay.

They were, as Jarvis put it, 'a roving tribe of Israelites.'[3] The executive council first met in the comparatively developed town of Kingston but were soon dragged – Jarvis' word – to Niagara (or Newark as it came to be called). This again was to be temporary. The legislature met there; courts and offices were improvised; and Simcoe divided his time between the old and new capitals, with the executive council (in practice three or four men) meeting at one or the other. The officials who visited York were not attracted by what they saw. The simple life could be overdone. Had they not, at great discomfort and expense, established themselves at Niagara? And now they were told to give that up and start over again in the wilds. The transfer was set for the spring of 1796 but not completed until after Simcoe had gone to England, never to return. One by one the officials, reluctant pioneers, were torn from their moorings. Russell held out for some time but as administrator of the province at last resigned himself to York, for which he exhibited a new-found enthusiasm. Elmsley, who had invested in an expensive house in Newark in spite of knowing that he would have to leave it, put up the maximum resistance but was in the end detached from his comforts.

Some of the group that has been mentioned stayed for only a short time but others remained to establish families long prominent in Toronto. Because for a time York was noteworthy only as a capital the senior government officials loomed large; but before long other men and families came who added to those who were to dominate the town economically or socially, and sometimes both. John Scadding, father of the historian of Toronto, was Simcoe's estate manager in Devonshire; he came to Upper Canada with the lieutenant governor and returned to England when he did. Some years later, however, he came back to live on the land granted to him east of the River Don, where he was close to the farm carved out by Mrs Ashbridge and her sons, immigrants from Philadelphia. John Denison, a Yorkshireman, had a somewhat similar career as he moved to York in 1796 and managed Russell's farm. Two families from Ireland came to be closely allied: William Willcocks was in York by 1797, and William Warren Baldwin married his daughter. D'Arcy Boulton was an early arrival from England and so was Stephen Heward. James Baby, son of a Detroit family, spent much of his time in York and all of it after 1816.

Christopher Robinson, from a leading family in Virginia, arrived in York in 1798.

Enterprising merchants were in York from early days. William Allan, a Scot, had been in Montreal for some years before he moved to York. Alexander Wood was Scottish too, and Joseph Cawthra was from Yorkshire. Laurent Quetton de St George, a French royalist, arrived in 1798 but returned to France in 1815. John Cameron was a merchant but better known as editor of York's only newspaper, the *York Gazette*.

Much less is known about the humbler folk of York but they were no less essential to the growth of the town. Government in those days did not have serried ranks of civil servants but did have some clerks. Carpenters and bricklayers were much in demand for a town without buildings of any kind. Some of those who came were young bachelors from the United States attracted by rumours of high wages and ready employment. Labourers, carters, and shop assistants came too. Total population statistics may not be exact but are near enough. The first recorded figure for the town itself is 241 people in 1797. The rise was slow: 432 in 1804, 577 in 1809. York was still a village in all but name. Immigration in the first two decades was small but according to Elizabeth Russell, half-sister and heiress of the former administrator, the birth-rate was high. Writing in 1811 she remarked:

The women in this country are in general very prolific. I am intimately acquainted with a lady who lives in this place that has five pairs of twins four pairs of which are now living also two more children that she has had in single births – and has buried several besides. I think it is sixteen she has had in all. And she is now only about seven and thirty years of age ... They marry very young here many girls not more than 13 or 14 years old.[4]

Although the population in early years was not large it did increase rapidly in the sense that it started from zero; so that York grew suddenly and problems arose faster than experience. Allocation of land and placing of buildings were not haphazard for broad plans existed, even if they never worked out exactly as intended. Land to the westward and just outside the town was reserved for the garrison. Here the Queen's Rangers had built their huts of round logs. Near Garrison Creek, which ran through the reserve, was a blockhouse. Beyond that military installations were minimal. Another blockhouse stood near the Don; and at Gibraltar Point on the peninsula (Hanlan's Point of later days) were two storehouses with loopholes in the upper storeys. The garrison was small and changing. In 1802 the Queen's Rangers, who had literally built parts of York, were disbanded. That York was a garrison town was more evident in its social life than in military capacity.

The extreme southeastern corner of the town was set aside as the abode of civil government. Simcoe began construction at the foot of Berkeley Street of two plain brick buildings to house the provincial legislature and the courts. It was intended that these should be the wings of a block of which the central structure would be Government House, residence of the lieutenant governor. When Russell found, however, that the main building would cost £10,000 he wisely did not proceed with its construction. Lieutenant Governor Hunter, who was a general and the commander-in-chief, built a square one-storey residence on the west side of Garrison Creek, which lasted until it was damaged during the American occupation. As it turned out both the parliament buildings and Government House were placed in the western part of the town at a later date. The post office was housed on the property of the postmaster, William Allan, who, in another of his many capacities, was also customs officer and examined goods coming in from the United States in what he called 'my Stone House on the water edge.'

The large area between the old and new towns, kept free for public purposes, was in part used in that way. The first and only church of the period before 1812, St James', was built on the lot at King and Church streets in 1807. In long discussions which preceded construction suggestions were made that the church be of brick or stone, but financial resources proved to be sufficient only for a simple frame structure of forty by fifty feet. The one state school, the District Grammar School, was on King Street east of Yonge. A hospital came later but the gaol could not be postponed. In 1798 Russell authorized construction 'of a small log building to be erected of sufficient strength and size to secure three separate Prisoners, and accommodate the Keeper.' It was situated on the south side of King Street at the corner of Leader Lane. After some delay a market came into being in 1803. Five and one-half acres were assigned, with Market (Wellington) Street as the southern boundary, New (Jarvis) Street as the eastern, and King Street as the northern. It was 'set apart ... for exposing publicly for Sale, Cattle, Sheep, Poultry, and other Provisions, Goods and Merchandize, brought by Merchants, Farmers and others, for the necessary supply of the ... TOWN of YORK.'

Business in its many forms was scattered about the lower part of the town, particularly at the eastern end. Hotels came and went. Jordan's York Hotel on King near Princes Street (later misspelled Princess) had in these years a good reputation. Several members of the legislature stayed there during sessions and it had accommodation for public dinners and private dances. At one time it had been intended to set aside eighteen half-lots for certain named trades (tinsmith, blacksmith, saddler, wheelwright, cooper, shoemaker, and baker) but the idea was dropped; and in practice one of the characteristics of York, though not peculiar to it, was that

Berkeley House, southwest corner of Berkeley and King streets, first part of
the house built about 1794 by John Small

commercial and residential buildings were interspersed. This was a condition found in most American cities, but one specific reason for it in the
case of York was the dual role of the waterfront, which was at once commercially important because of the harbour and attractive as a residential
area. In these early years the first did not interfere with the second.

The 'front lots' had originally the highest priority and were granted to
judges, senior officials, army officers, and other favoured persons. By no
means all the recipients held the lots or built on them; if they had done
so the peopling of York would be simpler to describe. Some of them moved
away from the town and sold out; others built elsewhere in York. At one
part of the waterfront, on Palace Street (the eastern extension of Front
Street), Peter Russell and his half-sister lived in Russell Abbey, a pleasant
one-storey house with wings attached to a central block. Immediately
westward were the houses of William Allan, W. W. Baldwin, and Duncan
Cameron. Other early houses were also chiefly in the eastern section. John
Small built Berkeley House on King Street East, beyond Princes Street.
In its original form it was a more modest affair than its name suggests.
William Jarvis' first house was at the corner of Duke and Sherbourne
streets, built for him by William Smith who himself started with a log

house at the corner of King and Sherbourne streets, replacing it in 1794 with a frame building.

Wood was the material chiefly used. Round logs were the simplest and squared logs, which were much better, could be procured without difficulty. Boards were often in short supply. An early step was to place a sawmill on the Humber, erected by the government and leased to a private operator; but it could not keep up with the demand and was supplemented by private mills on the Don, the other nearby source of waterpower. Bricks were made locally but little used, and stone hardly at all. Most of the hardware had to be imported.

In types the houses of York varied all the way from crude cabins of round logs to spacious residences of some distinction. The executive council of the province followed in detail the planning of the town and endeavoured to make it as attractive as possible. Simcoe urged his council 'to adjust such regulations as may be expedient to give an architectural uniformity to the town, an object of great importance in a New Province.'[5] They placed emphasis on the front lots, widening them from sixty-six to eighty-eight feet, and had visions of a row of mansions, to be seen by those who entered the harbour, each faced with a line of pillars in the classical manner. Unfortunately for their plans the owners did not respond, and the nearest thing to a Grecian temple (as Mrs Simcoe described it) was Castle Frank, the Simcoe's country retreat, which had pine trees as pillars.

D. W. Smith's Maryville Lodge was of medium size, well proportioned, and, like many of the houses of York, set in the midst of large gardens. Probably the house and certainly the gardens were not as perfect as contemporary drawings show, since these were done in connection with Smith's efforts to sell his house and large land holdings in concessions just north of York. Quetton St George built at the corner of King and Frederick streets, in 1807, a substantial house which he used also for his store. It was of two storeys and probably the first brick house in York. Its simple and dignified style was followed in several other houses then and later. 'You have heard no doubt,' George Ridout wrote to John Macaulay, 'of Mr. St. George's famous house as Mr. Cameron has taken great care to proclaim it in the Gazette. D'Arcy Boulton is building one of the same materials though in miniature.'[6]

Normally the choice was between squared logs and frame, and the comparison is well illustrated by plans which William Jarvis had drawn for him while he was still living at Newark. One was for a log house with a cellar. The size is not recorded but as it was to have four chimneys it must have been quite large. The price was £256–8–0. The other was for a two-storey frame house 'according to the Ionic order' and shown by the drawing as of some charm. It was to be fifty feet square and the estimate, without hardware and paint which Jarvis was to import from the United States, was £1,453-1-0.[7] Few other houses, or intended houses, are described in detail. The advertisements seldom went beyond the stock remark that a house was 'commodious,' explaining that it was too well known to need any description; and in a town of a hundred houses that was reasonable enough. An exception was an advertisement in 1801 of a house 'fit for residence of a gentleman, merchant or tavern-keeper.' It was of two storeys, frame, and measured forty-six by thirty-five feet – and was placed on an acre of land with a view of the bay and the lake.

That outlook, indeed, was pleasant when there were no railways or factories in the way. Furthermore, at a time when it was not easy to get about and space was ample in the southern part of the town, convenience dictated that both houses and business establishments should be there. According to a description of houses in York before 1812,[8] one of uncertain accuracy, only one building stood on Queen Street. North of that, however, were the so-called 'park lots,' some of which were shaping into large family holdings. Each was a hundred chains long, from Queen Street to Bloor Street, and ten chains wide. Like the front lots on the bay they were granted to persons of rank and influence. Numbered 1 to 32 westward from the Don River they skirted the Garrison Reserve and reached a point beyond the present Lansdowne Avenue.

Simcoe followed a common way of accumulating land by granting to his young son the top halves of numbers 1 and 2, the southern sections being held for a government centre and park which never eventuated. It was on Francis' land that Castle Frank was built to meet the obligation resting on a grantee. After Francis was killed in 1810 during the Peninsular War the land passed through the Scaddings to a firm of brewers who later sold part of it to the churchwardens of St James' for a cemetery. Moss Park originated out of the purchase of lot number 5 (from George to Mutual Street) by William Allan. The next lot, number 6, was granted to William Jarvis and held by the family. By an arrangement made with his neighbour, John Elmsley owned the top halves of lots numbers 9 and 10 (the two together running from Yonge Street to the modern University Avenue), and to that he added number 11 by purchase. On his property Elmsley established a farm and built a house, Clover Hill, just east of Queen's Park.

The Baldwin estate developed out of a series of circumstances. Peter Russell, in a strong position to acquire land, was granted (by himself, as was noted at the time) lot number 14 to which he later added number 16. He had also been granted four hundred acres in the second concession (north from Bloor Street) and in the third concession (north from St Clair Avenue). At his death all this went by will to his half-sister who in turn left it to her cousins, the daughters of William Willcocks. One of these girls, Phoebe, was married to W. W. Baldwin, and this pair also inherited the share of the sister who was unmarried. To that substantial total was added the park lot in between, number 15, which had been granted to Willcocks. The Denison lands were less extensive but still large. George Taylor Denison secured lot number 17 and half of 18. But that was not the end, for between them the Denisons bought number 25, half of 26, and all of 27. They thus had a very large property. Like Elmsley and Russell, George Crookshank, who was in the commissary department, had a farm; he held half of lot number 18. Bathurst Street, the approach to it, was long known as Crookshank's Lane.

Thus a number of large estates emerged from the granting, willing, and buying of park lots. The prices were in some cases quite high but they varied wildly. For example, number 18 was sold in 1816 for £160 and half of it went in the next year for £375. Elmsley's widow sold number 11 to Alexander Wood for £184 and three years later Wood sold half of it to J. B. Robinson for £1,000. In another three years Robinson sold six acres to the Law Society for the same amount as he had paid for the whole fifty acres. It was on this ground that Osgoode Hall was built.

The dominating factor in early York was that it was the seat of the provincial government, and consequently that the administrators and judges lived there. They were the men who held much of the land, created a demand for goods and services, and set the tone of society. The legislature – parliament as contemporaries liked to call it – met in York as soon as it could be moved from Newark. The upper house, the legislative council, was a small appointed body which in personnel so overlapped the executive council that it reflected more the views of the government than of the public. The assembly, elected on a wide franchise, drew to York men from all settled parts of the province. The less conservative element in it was coming to adopt an independent and critical attitude and to claim for the House power greater than the Tories thought proper. The people of York could watch and participate in political debates within the assembly and outside it, and at the same time broaden their horizon by meeting representatives of other areas.

The early planning of York was entirely the responsibility of provincial authorities who retained jurisdiction in questions of policy, but continued administration was necessarily in other hands. In the absence of municipal institutions local government was made up of two unrelated processes. One was the 'town' meeting, the word usually meaning township as in some contexts it still does. Under a provincial statute of 1793 (33 Geo. III, c. 2) such meetings were to be called by constables once a year under the authority of warrants issued by two justices of the peace. They elected town clerks, assessors, collectors, overseers of highways, pound keepers, and town wardens. There their authority ended. They had no control over the officials they had elected and almost no means of raising revenue.

Real power was in the hands of the men variously known as justices of the peace and magistrates who were appointed by the lieutenant governor for each District or group of counties. York was in the Home District, a part of which had briefly laboured under the inappropriate name of Nassau. Some fees accrued to a justice of the peace but his position was unsalaried. Men prominent in the community were ready to accept appointment partly from a sense of responsibility, partly for added prestige. In each District the magistrates met together in the Court of General Quarter Sessions of the Peace and soon found it necessary to have special as well as quarterly meetings. Such a group of magistrates met, as the name suggests, as a court of law and handled a great volume and variety of cases, both civil and criminal. They also, however, had the real responsibility for local government, in town and country. They appointed a number of local officials and directed the activities of those elected by town meetings. In general they performed most of the tasks later attached to elected municipal bodies. The Court of Quarter Sessions for the District always met in York.

The revenue available for local expenditure, drawn from District taxation, was consistently inadequate even for the most essential purposes and could not be stretched to salaries for new officials. From the top to the bottom of the local government ladder emoluments were, with few exceptions, in the form of fees, whether for issuing a solemn legal document or examining the line and adequacy of a fence. That method of payment was acceptable to magistrates and to some extent to high constables; but lesser officials so often sought to evade appointment that they evidently found the fees poor compensation for interruption of their normal occupations. All of them, high or low, devoted only spare time to duties in local government, just as many township officials have done ever since.

The call for a change in local government began early and grew louder as York increased in size and complexity; but in the first decades of its history the peculiarities of the old order were not as great as they first appear. Being a District organization the Court of Quarter Sessions could devote only a portion of its time to the town. On the other hand the magistrates who attended the sessions were men who lived in York and were fully conversant with local conditions. Some were employees of the provincial government, such as William Jarvis and William Chewett; but the merchants were well represented too, as in the persons of William Allan and Alexander Wood. Although such men were not typical of the community as a whole they took their duties seriously and were no respecters of persons. On several occasions the records show stern treatment of eminent citizens who were held to be in default on road work or assessment returns.

24

The public services for which the justices of the peace were responsible were far less comprehensive than those of modern times, for piped water, gas, electricity, public transport, and collection of garbage were either anachronic or impractical; but what remained was enough to tax the time of the justices and the resources of the town. Particular attention had to be given to the prevention or extinguishing of fires. Wooden houses with open fireplaces, stables full of hay, and bonfires of rubbish constituted invitations to fire, and in addition there was the danger of forest fires in a town only partially out of the bush. Attempts were made both to reduce the risks and to organize means of putting out fires which did start. On the suggestion of a grand jury the Court of Quarter Sessions ordered that joiners were to burn their shavings only on Wednesdays and Saturdays at about sunset (when there would normally be least wind). In 1801 the court ordered that every householder should

provide and keep Two Buckets for carrying water, when any House shall happen to be on Fire, which buckets shall be made of Wood, Leather or Canvas, painted on the outside and covered with pitch on the inside, and shall hold, at least, two Gallons of water; and the said Bucketts shall be marked with the Christian and Sirname of the Housekeeper to whose House they belong, and shall not be used for any other purpose than the extinguishing of fires.

Ordered, also

That every House Keeper in the said Town, do keep two Ladders, the one to reach from the Ground to the Eaves of the House, and the other to be properly secured and fixed with Hooks or Bolts on the roof near the Chimney.

Inspection teams were sent around by the magistrates and penalties provided in case of infraction of the order: five shillings for anyone who failed to provide the buckets and ladders and forty shillings for those whose houses, not so protected, caught fire.[9] Mechanization began when the lieutenant governor presented a fire engine to the town, but the volunteer fire brigades of later days were not yet in existence. It was assumed that everyone nearby would lend a hand in what could quickly become a threat to a whole section of the town. For long the main problem for the firefighters was the supply of water. It could be brought in carts or buckets from the bay or from one of the rivers or streams, but that was a slow process and doubly difficult in winter. Some householders had wells or storage tanks but the first public well was not dug until the 1820s. Fire insurance was available through the agents of British or American companies.

The fire regulation that has been quoted was under the authority of a provincial act. The first statute of Upper Canada, in 1792, introduced English civil law (with the express exception of the poor laws) into the province. English criminal law remained as before. The courts sat in York, using one of the two brick government buildings that have been mentioned. In its judicial capacity the Court of Quarter Sessions dealt with minor cases, of which the largest number involved charges of assault and battery, with burglary and theft coming next. Those found guilty of assault were fined from one shilling to £5 or given gaol sentences. One condition tacked on to a fine and recognizance to keep the peace was that the convicted person 'shall not gamble or play at Billiards or any unlawful games of Chance or other, nor wager any sum of money upon any game.' In that age billiards were regarded with particular suspicion, but this poor man was debarred from a wide field of entertainment. Trial was by jury although it was not always easy to find enough jurors. The statutory requirement was for service once a year but most of the men on the sheriff's list served two or three times. Another problem is indicated by the statement of the foreman of a grand jury that one of the jurors was too drunk for the others 'to enter upon business with him.' In spite of difficulties, however, consistent efforts were made to keep the court's proceedings dignified and just.

For enforcement of the law each District had a high constable, just as each English county still has a chief constable, who received a nominal salary of £10 a year (reduced from £20), but the office never had the prestige that it enjoyed in England. Every town or township had a number of constables. York averaged about a dozen at any one time. All were appointed in quarter sessions and frequently against their will: so much so that stiff fines for refusing office were considered necessary. By an ingenious arrangement each tavern keeper was called upon to act as a constable on his own premises, thus both authorizing and requiring him to maintain order. His duty was clear enough but that of the regular constables, if it was ever written down, is not now known. Magistrates gave them individual orders and presumably they took action when they saw or were notified of breaches of the peace. No indication exists that they made regular patrols, day or night, and, indeed, complaints were made that they did not. Whether anyone was in immediate charge, what supervision the chief constable maintained, or whether there were any regular hours of duty are all mysteries in the absence of any preserved regulations.

Collectively the constables bore little resemblance to a modern police force but contemporary comparisons are more relevant. In England it was to be another generation before Sir Robert Peel created the Metropolitan Police for London and other English cities were not quick in following that example. In at least some American cities night watches were manned at ten o'clock by men who had already done a day's work in a factory or elsewhere. The first daytime patrol in the United States was initiated in New York in 1837.

Small as it was York offered many problems for local travel. Some roads stopped at natural obstacles, rivers or valleys. Others came to an end at the edge of a private property which somehow had been allowed to block the grid of streets. Some were unusable because they were no more than bogs. Even the best were a misery. Responsibility for the construction and repair of roads was divided between the Court of Quarter Sessions, which dealt with policy and large projects, and the pathmasters who superintended particular operations. The workers were drawn in through the obligation to statutory labour or as substitutes paid by those who did not wish to perform the tasks personally. Those who evaded responsibility could be fined at the rate of five shillings a day, the estimated value of statute labour. Unusual projects such as the improvement of Yonge Street or construction of larger bridges were undertaken by private subscription. In spite of all these arrangements the roads were on the whole very bad indeed and not improved by the illegitimate use made of them. An official admonition of 1800 reads:

Whereas the streets in the Town of York, are frequently obstructed and made dangerous to passengers, by piles of WOOD and STONES placed in them, as well as PITS dug in several places,

It is notified, by Order of the Magistrates in quarter sessions assembled, That whoever shall leave any Wood or Stone, or suffer any nuisance to remain in the said street, opposite their respective premises, after the 12th day of May next, will be prosecuted as the law directs.

Stray pigs were picked up by the elected poundkeepers, but horses only if they were trespassing on private property. Sanitary regulations were minimal and the streets were liable to be covered with rubbish of all kinds. Butchers were required to bury or remove offal and no doubt some people buried or burned their garbage; but it may be that the wandering pig did not receive his just deserts as a volunteer street cleaner.

For the ferries over the Don and the Humber tolls were set by the court. As population in the west brought increased use of the ferry the current charges were criticized with the result that they were reduced in 1807 and again in 1810. A floating bridge was placed on the Don in 1806 but it was not to be used for loaded waggons, presumably because it would sink under their weight. According to a notice in the *Gazette* it was to enable people to get to the island, there to take the air or watch horse races. The island (it was commonly called that although at the time it was a peninsula) was a place of resort offering open space and, so the tradition went, salubrious air.

In a more serious vein, education was partly in public and partly in private hands. In York, as in other Upper Canadian towns, the pioneers of primary education were small private schools, each conducted in the

27

house of the single teacher. Sometimes they were the result of individual enterprise, sometimes encouraged and supported by groups of parents. Most of them went little beyond the three R's but occasionally a teacher turned up who was himself well educated and could carry his small class much further. 'Dames' schools' were for little children. Most of these schools were ephemeral. They had weaknesses but they filled a gap and pointed the way to the more elaborate private schools of the future.

The first step taken by the provincial legislature in accepting responsibility for education came in 1797 when a petition to the king asked that crown lands be set aside for grammar schools and for a college or university. A large amount of land was in consequence appropriated but no further action was taken until an act was passed in 1807 providing for the establishment of a grammar school in each District. It might seem ill-advised to begin with secondary rather than primary education, but the second already existed in some form and the first probably not at all. In practice, moreover, the grammar school in York had pupils, boys and girls, from six to nineteen years of age. The teacher was George Okill Stuart.

Religion also overlapped the governmental and private domains. The Church of England was never technically established in Upper Canada, but it had official blessing and financial support, as did some other churches in lesser degree. Nothing like accurate figures exist as to the numbers of adherents of the various churches, but it is known that the Church of England had in early years a large majority in York. Peter Russell was worried by the absence of clergy: how, he wondered, could one expect moral standards in a godless society? He had great hopes of the first Anglican incumbent, Thomas Raddish, who took up residence in 1797. Unfortunately Raddish proved to be no hero of the gospel. After amassing 4,700 acres of land he withdrew from the rigours of the new world. G. O. Stuart, who succeeded him after an interval, complained that his emoluments (from the colonial government and the Society for the Propagation of the Gospel in Foreign Parts) were insufficient, but he stuck to his job, until he was transferred to Kingston in 1811, and saw the opening of St James' in 1807. Methodist, Presbyterian, and Congregationalist preachers visited York and held services wherever they could; but the first, so active in rural districts, were slow to establish themselves in this hive of Anglicanism. It is agreeable to find that dissenters and Roman Catholics alike attended St James' when it was the only church.

Even before sabbatarianism was stiffened by a greater proportion of noncomformists it had some support from authority. In 1802 a grand jury made the proposal, approved by the justices in quarter sessions, that it would be 'proper to direct the wardens appointed for the Town of York to visit the several Keepers of Houses of Public Entertainment therein and represent to them the indecency and impropriety of allowing people to drink intoxicating liquors and be guilty of disorderly behaviour during the hours of Divine Service, and generally on the Sabbath days.'

The place of government in health and welfare was in no country large and in York it was further narrowed by lack of funds and facilities. The main burden was carried by private charity. Little is known about forms and extent of illness. The complaint most frequently mentioned was 'ague,' sometimes called malaria as in some cases at least it certainly was. More often at the time it was attributed to mists from swamps than to the mosquitoes that throve in them. York was low-lying and for that reason could be accused of fostering ague, but in fact there is more mention of it in Niagara. Smallpox was not uncommon, for although vaccination was early available it was not universally accepted. Cuts and broken bones, consumption, heart attacks, and the whole gamut of human frailties took their toll. It was not until the epidemic of cholera in the 1830s that serious attention was directed to the filthy condition of the town (a characteristic which it shared with most other communities in North America and elsewhere). It is a reasonable guess that the water in the bay was becoming polluted and that some of the dug wells were impure. From that one would deduce the existence of typhoid fever.

There was no public hospital. The mentally ill could be sent to the District gaol, a cold, miserable, and ill-equipped place, or be put in charge of a family indemnified out of public funds. Some doctors had come to York. Dr James Macaulay, like many of the army surgeons, gave a hand to civilians now and then. The first non-military physician was Dr W. W. Baldwin, a graduate of Edinburgh; but he found so few patients that he became a lawyer as well. In 1807 Dr J. Glenner advertised his presence, his training in Europe, and his readiness to accept patients. Quacks, too, were found in York as elsewhere in Upper Canada. Specifics for anything and everything were advertised and commonly used. Some were drawn from traditional herbal formulas; others depended more on superstition than chemistry; and too many in the patent medicine class contained alcohol, opium, or laudanum. These made people feel better but did nothing for their afflictions – more likely the opposite.

Little could be done for those in financial distress. The English poor laws were not introduced into Upper Canada, probably because they could not have been financed, but no workable alternative was available. A child who was an orphan or deserted by his parents could be apprenticed to someone who would feed, clothe, and perhaps teach him a little. In 1800 a town warden reported to quarter sessions that a woman and her two children were poverty-stricken but the court held that it had no authority to intervene. In the case of a family near York the magistrates could think of no better course than to order their cattle to be sold and the money spent on food and other necessities.

What Simcoe ceremonially christened 'York' was no more than a small slice out of the endless forest. To make it more than that was an adventure in pioneering, one of many such in a pioneer province. The economy is to be seen first in this setting. Trees had to be cut down and tracks – they could hardly be called roads – laid out. Houses, government buildings, and commercial buildings came next. Particularly in these early stages labour was urgently needed, in an age in which mechanization was hardly known. For long after the lists of inhabitants were to show 'labourers' – broadly, unskilled workers – in large proportion of the whole. Carpenters were also numerous, followed by other artisans such as bricklayers, painters, and stonemasons. At times the supply of workers was inadequate and building was held up. In the opinion of contemporaries labour was not only scarce but expensive. To pay $1.50 a day to an artisan provoked employers to indignation.

The blacksmiths who shoed horses and did simple iron work were essential. Chairmakers and cabinetmakers came to the town. Advertisements appeared of men and women who offered personal services: hairdressers, tailors, seamstresses, and shoemakers. Domestic servants were found with difficulty. Clerks were required in limited numbers in government offices and in shops. Carters and wheelwrights became available. Employment in industry was negligible since for many years manufacturing hardly existed. Outside the town, on the Humber and the Don, sawmills and grist mills were erected. No town, it seemed, could get on without beer, but the breweries were small and employed few hands. One of them did some tanning on the side. Though it is one that never can be told, the story of how all these men and women, with and without particular skills, came to the new town would be a fascinating one.

The occupations so far mentioned, when added together, account for the greater part of the population. It was far from constant, for people came and went, but the people in these types of work tended to stay in them. Exceptions were possible. The occasional cabinetmaker might expand his business into something more like a furniture factory, or the enterprising blacksmith's shop become a small foundry. But it was rather in the professional and executive categories that individuals found versatility both necessary and possible. Few builders and no architects devoted all their time to those skills, and it is perhaps for that reason that too little attention has been paid to those who designed and constructed buildings. On occasion the builder, with or without the aid of the owner, was the architect. Surveyors and officers of the Royal Engineers might turn their hands to architecture. As in later years the results were sometimes good, sometimes not.

Leaving aside government and the judiciary, specialization was not general for the middle class, partly because, in a very small place, the

30

market was not broad enough. Another, if more nebulous, explanation is that enterprising persons found opportunities in a situation in which so many things were to be originated. A case that is often quoted is that of W. W. Baldwin. Coming to York as a physician he found that the little community did not produce enough patients. He therefore added a second profession, that of lawyer; and, not content with those, he dabbled in teaching and architecture. Most of the school teachers were part-time and transient. Some at least of the lawyers confined themselves to that field or combined it with politics. Some of them had the further alternative of going on the Bench, as in the case of D'Arcy Boulton who came to Upper Canada from England in 1797. G. O. Stuart supplemented his thin Anglican living by teaching. William Allan combined in a remarkable way versatility with opportunism. A Scot from Aberdeenshire, he started a shop, built a wharf, was collector of customs, inspector of stills and taverns, postmaster of York, and treasurer of the Home District. When banks and railways came on the scene he took an active part in them.

The earliest road to wealth was in retail trade. Small shops came and went, but the few that grew and prospered played a leading part in the economy. One such was owned by Allan in partnership with Alexander Wood, another native of Aberdeenshire; and when the two parted company Wood continued as a successful merchant. Laurent Quetton de St George, after fighting in royalist forces for some years of the French revolution, came to Canada with the Comte de Puisaye's exiles and received land as one of them. Finding pioneer farming not rewarding, he turned to the fur trade and then, in addition, to shopkeeping. Owning shops not only in York but also in Queenston, Fort Erie, Lundy's Lane, Dundas, Amherstburg, Kingston, and Niagara he might well be credited with the initiation of chain stores in Ontario. The large shops were general or department stores and had for sale a wide range of goods including some of quality. In a single shop could be found liquor and groceries; hardware, paints, and china; watches and jewellery; boots and shoes; stationery and books; hats and clothes; perfumes, drugs, and soap. Amongst these and other commodities – including, perhaps, guns and violins – were items which seem to be luxuries, of a kind not appropriate to a bush town. But even if York was small and in some ways primitive some of its residents could and did maintain a standard far removed from pioneer life. The larger general stores were the ones that catered to such customers, for it was not until later that speciality shops were for a time successful in drawing the carriage trade away from them.[10]

If some of the shopkeepers did well it was not because they were free of problems. Shop-lifting belongs to all ages, but the financial arrangements of the time were unusually difficult. Credit was prominent both in buying and selling but no banks existed to discount notes, hold funds, or make loans. Currency was not uniform. Calculations were made in Spanish dollars, pounds sterling, and in the imaginary Halifax or (New) York currencies which were no more than ratings of the dollar and not represented by paper or coins. One can only admire the ability to understand accounts drawn up in an unexplained mixture of dollars, sterling, and the two so-called currencies.[11] Partly because of the scarcity of actual currency, partly because farmers ordinarily had little cash, barter was common. Shopkeepers accepted agricultural products in exchange for groceries, hardware, and other goods; and were then obliged to sell the grain or eggs or meat in which they had been paid.

Like any other urban centre at any other time York was a place of trade, not a self-contained area for mutual buying and selling. The York merchant bought where he could find what he needed, sold in as wide a market as he could command, moved goods by whatever means of transport existed. Apart from a limited range of farm products (most of which were sold in the market rather than in the shops), leather, and a few other things that could be produced locally or nearby, merchandise was all imported. Some of it was brought in from Montreal and in that case the York shopkeeper was dealing with the equivalent of wholesalers. Orders could be by mail or personal selection. In 1804, for example, Quetton de St George went to Montreal to buy crockery, hats, and carpets from dealers there. The York shops increasingly bought direct from Britain although that was a slow process. Goods ordered in the autumn would not be delivered until the middle of the following summer. Purchases were also made in New York, again by mail or personal choice, but in that case some of them would be subject to customs duties, unlike those imported directly or indirectly from Britain.

Delivery of anything to what the Earl of Selkirk described in 1803 as 'an insulated spot almost detached from both ends of the province' was never easy. Contemporaries agreed that travel by land should be avoided as much as possible, which for the moment meant dependence for all or part of a journey on sailing vessels. It was no accident that York had been placed on a large natural harbour, one usually given high marks by observers. It had some disadvantages. The single entrance was difficult because of sandbars and prevailing west winds. Nevertheless the harbour was a good one and the entrance was made safer by the erection of a lighthouse at Gibraltar Point in 1809. Built of stone it has defied the years. The first wharf of any kind was built in 1793 or 1794 at the mouth of Garrison Creek, close to the entrance to the harbour and near the old fort. It was used for unloading stores for the troops and was probably very small. In any case it was a long way from the town. The first wharf constructed for civil purposes was William Allan's, dated about 1801. This also was small. There is no record of other wharves until after the war of 1812.

Gibraltar Point lighthouse, completed in 1809

It was not easy to entice shipping into the harbour, not because of difficulties of navigation but because return cargoes were uncertain and only a few ships sailed the lake at the turn of the century. The government decided that it was necessary to have a ship that would be under its control and arranged for the yacht *Toronto* to be built on the Humber. Launched in 1799 the *Toronto* was described with some enthusiasm but unfortunately became one of the victims of the sandbar off Gibraltar Point not many years later. The only other vessel built at York before 1812, *Bella Gore*, ran to Kingston, but it too was wrecked. The casualty rate was high. The *Speedy*, a faithful visitor to York, was lost with a distinguished passenger list in 1804. The York newspaper announced a coming weekly service to the head of the lake, but a serious deficiency of shipping handicapped business. Shops published embarrassed notices that goods had not arrived and in 1807 the *Gazette*, printed on inferior blue paper, remarked plaintively that the usual supply of white paper had not come from Niagara.

Unsatisfactory as lake transport was, even in the season of navigation, no one suggested that it could be replaced by that overland. On the other hand land travel was essential to meet certain needs. The plans of the provincial government for roads and the aspirations of the people of York overlapped but were not identical. Decision rested with the provincial authorities who alone could undertake any construction. The latter saw three principal requirements. In days of uncertain relations with the United States facilities were needed for the movement of troops and military supplies. To people the province access must be provided for immigrants and means for their necessary travel after they were settled. The third objective was to encourage commerce: within the province, and with the United States and Britain. The difficulties encountered by the British Post Office in carrying mail may have been kept in mind but they would be automatically overcome to the extent that roads were opened.

To the people of York, too, it was of the utmost importance that immigration be encouraged and in particular that the hinterland of the town be peopled. A source of foodstuffs was the first consideration. As Peter Russell put it in 1798 the head must not grow too big for the body lest provisions be scarce and dear. And as settlers moved in to Scarborough, Etobicoke, and townships to the north roads must be cut to allow them to bring in their goods for sale in the shops and market, with the surplus, as it developed, for export by ship. Those coming to the town to sell would also be buyers of goods and services: clothes, hardware, and groceries; visits to a doctor, lawyer, or blacksmith; perhaps to get married. Roads and settlers were the cause and effect of each other.

Studying the province as a whole Simcoe was well aware of that relationship and in his few years in office worked energetically to lay down the most essential roads. In three respects the pattern of provincial highways was designed to supplement the waterways: as long portages, where no navigable lakes or rivers existed, and to carry traffic in the winter. Keeping in mind London as the future capital Simcoe began with a road from Lake Ontario toward it, using the Queen's Rangers for the tough work of cutting down and moving trees. That route was of no particular value to York, but its turn came next when the soldier-workers were transferred to the site of another road, also running inland from Lake Ontario but this time in a northerly direction. Augustus Jones, a Loyalist and deputy surveyor, was instructed at the end of 1795 to survey and open, with the aid of thirty Rangers, a cart road from York harbour to the Holland River. Construction was started northward from Eglinton Avenue.

Yonge Street, named after Sir George Yonge, secretary of state for war, fitted well into the general pattern that has been mentioned. It gave access to what was potentially a valuable agricultural area and attached it to York. Before many years had passed the shopkeepers of the town were sending shipments up this road as well as selling to those who came down to the town. The military aspect of the road had no immediate relevance to York and will be examined in the following chapter. As a portage to Lake Simcoe and Lake Huron, Yonge Street was the alternative and successor to the Humber trail of the seventeenth and eighteenth centuries. As has been suggested in the previous chapter the potentiality of the portage influenced in some degree the selection of York as the site of a town. Soon after Simcoe had taken up residence he organized an expedition northward by way of the old route as far as Penetanguishene Bay. That he went that way may prove nothing more than that it was then the only feasible route, that his primary interest was in the northern lakes, and that he was already inclined to switch to a road further to the east. Since his Indian guides lost their way on the return journey, within a few hours' walk of York, it appears that the Humber trail was disused and overgrown.

When it was decided to make a new road there was nothing mysterious about the location of Yonge Street. It was simply on a line drawn from the harbour to Holland Landing where navigation of the river could begin. What can be misleading to later generations is to think of it as the projection of a street in York. Later on it was just that, but in early years it was, for all practical purposes, a highway that began at the Village of Yorkville (Bloor Street). Teams coming down from the country were driven southeast from there, and, in Scadding's words, 'passed down in a haphazard kind of way over the sandy pineland . . . and finally entered the town by the route later known as Parliament Street.'[12] A road allowance existed south of Yorkville, but even that seems for a time to have stopped at Lot (Queen) Street, necessitating a detour by Toronto Street, a block to the east. In any case what there was of lower Yonge Street was in such bad condition as to be unusable.

These circumstances explain the meetings of citizens called to consider 'means of opening the road to Yonge-Street.' Two principal advantages in such action were advanced: to facilitate carriage of provisions to market by farmers, and to place York on the route to the northwest. The first is obvious, but the second raises the whole question of the use of the Toronto portage in its revised form as Yonge Street. From 1799 mail and passengers passed over this route between York and St Joseph's Island in the St Mary's River, and a 'winter express' went that way. Such traffic, however, was minor in volume. The value of Yonge Street as a through route depended on the use of it by the fur traders.

The citizens of York looked forward eagerly to the day when their town would be a 'depot of the exports and immense imports' of the northwest trade. In 1801 the *Upper Canada Gazette* emphasized the value of 'safe and convenient roads' and pointed to the 'certain and extensive advantages which will arise from having the rout of the North West traders transferred to this quarter.' When Lord Selkirk was in York in 1803 he noted that Yonge Street was well settled, but remarked in a matter of fact manner that 'no trade passes that way.' In 1807 the *York Gazette* (the same paper under a new name) referred to those 'who can foresee the advantages of turning the North-West communication into *this* channel.' It noted, too, a proposed visit by the lieutenant governor to St Joseph's Island and speculated that the object was 'to ascertain the practicability and advantages of diverting the North West business into this channel of communication.' The deputy postmaster general of British North America, George Heriot, wrote – still in the future tense – of the great volume of commerce passing over Yonge Street.

The North West Company was interested but cautious, exploring alternative ways of proceeding from Holland Landing to Penetanguishene, and in 1810 placed before the lieutenant governor, Francis Gore, a comprehensive memorial.[13] Reiterating their objections to the Detroit route, they expressed interest in a road they understood to be proposed from Kempenfeldt Bay to Penetanguishene. This, they thought, would provide a better route and they were prepared to give it their 'support,' which meant that they would use it. They hastily added, however, that such a change would cause them a heavy loss of capital invested in the old route. Indeed, they would expect outward and visible signs of governmental gratitude for their patronage in the form of two thousand acres of land on Kempenfeldt Bay, another two thousand on the south side of Penetanguishene Bay, and two hundred at Gwillimbury, an intended base just north of Holland Landing.

It seems evident from the memorial that if the Nor'Westers had ever used the Toronto portage at all, it was only very occasionally; and further that they had never contributed to the cost of Yonge Street in spite of a long-held belief to the contrary. What at the time was more important was that the whole project collapsed and with it some of the commercial dreams of York. Occasional loads passed that way but the procession of waggons carrying fur trade goods up Yonge Street was a figment of the imagination.

Yonge Street, then, settled down to a prosaic but essential role as a colonizing road and for the carriage of local traffic. In 1798 a highway at right angles to it, along the lake shore between Kingston and York, was started, this time under contract with an American, Asa Danforth. Already Kingston could be reached overland from Montreal, and in subsequent years the lake shore road was continued to the head of the lake. In addition to the north-south and east-west arteries was Dundas Street, officially described as open from York to the Grand River in 1799. For military reasons it was placed inland from the lake.

This was an impressive record for the first few years of a pioneer province, and as far as York was concerned the network of provincial highways left it no longer isolated. Several words of caution, however, are needed. Roads were recorded as 'open' when little more had been done than to survey a line through the forest and cut down enough trees to allow a waggon to get through. Sometimes, indeed, it meant even less, for a generous number of stumps were left in the ground. Bridges could be missing, swamps undrained, and ditching seldom if ever done. No means of surfacing existed other than laying logs across the track, in which case it was called a 'corduroy' road, presumably because of its resemblance to the cloth of that name. Hardly a reference appears to a road being 'built,' and rightly so since what was called a road was usually only a more or less continuous space between trees.

The roads of the early nineteenth century were roundly cursed by almost everyone who travelled over them. The letters and books of visitors and immigrants are full of the subject. In the spring most of the roads were impassable for wheeled vehicles and, because they went through woods and across marshes, took a long time to dry. Indeed, some low parts never became firm until they were frozen. If the snow was not too deep winter was the best time for land travel; otherwise it was best for those not burdened with heavy luggage to go on horseback. And so it long remained, not because of stupidity or lack of desire for improvement but because the population was thinly scattered, distances great, natural obstacles many, and public funds scanty. On the other hand there was a great deal of difference between being shut in by limitless forest and having roads which, however bad, could be used at times, if never without difficulty. Roads and people, people and roads, were transforming–if slowly as yet–the country around York. Soil enriched by the humus of centuries was being exploited and little villages started here and there. The head, in Russell's phrase, was to have a body.

Waggons creaked and groaned through mud or dust into the Town of York, bringing agricultural products for sale in the market or shops, struggling back with groceries, hardware, drugs, and perhaps clothes. The change from country to town was not complete. If the roads in the one were uniformly bad those in the other were hardly better. York was notorious for its mud. Many of the townsfolk were familiar with farming, whether in the park lots that formed a twilight zone between town and country, farther off on land they held in nearby concessions, or in the spacious gardens surrounding many of their houses. Vegetables and fruit were widely grown within the town.

In some other respects, however, the urban scene was distinct from the rural. Admittedly the picture that we have of York is in some respects misleading for it is based almost entirely on life as seen through the eyes of the upper classes and the prosperous, then as ever a minority in the community. The letters, diaries, and books which tell the story of those years were written by the well-to-do, whether residents or visitors. Houses described, clothes worn, food eaten, and entertainment enjoyed apply to only that part of the population. No more than glimpses are seen of the clerks, small shopkeepers, artisans, and labourers.[14] Labour is described from the point of view of employers, being scarce, expensive, efficient or inefficient. It does not follow that that class of society was miserable or bady treated, merely that it has not told its own story.

Of one class of workers a good deal is known as no subject was more common in conversation and letters than the difficulty of finding satisfactory domestic servants. Before leaving for York William Jarvis wrote from Kingston and Niagara to his father-in-law who was expecting to visit them from England: 'For God's sake try and bring out a servant or two with you, the whole country cannot produce one fit to put in "Hell's Kitchen." ' In Niagara he was paying $8 a month to a manservant who was drunk and quarrelsome and $7 to each of two girls who were good natured but inexperienced. Mrs Simcoe, who cheerfully accepted most of the conditions of a new country, found the lack of good maids the worst inconvenience she met. Some families brought servants with them but there were never enough, trained or trainable, and the gap was only in small part plugged by the slaves that immigrants had brought from the Thirteen Colonies. Some of these made satisfactory domestic or agricultural workers, some not; but when it was proposed that slavery be abolished in the province strong opposition was voiced on the plea of shortage of labour, and the act of 1793 (33 Geo. III, c. 7) was a compromise. No more slaves were to be brought in and the children of existing ones could claim freedom at age twenty-five. Slaves were never numerous, and the later negro population of Ontario is for the most part derived not from them but from slaves who escaped from the United States.

Domestic servants were important in view of the fact that the gentry of York were trying to live in a style which they considered appropriate to their station. The model they inevitably had in mind was the English town or country house, the economy of which was dependent on plentiful and well-trained servants. In letters they spoke of living in cottages, and certainly they were not comparable to the stately homes of England. On the other hand the best of the York houses had no resemblance to cottages and were sufficiently large that a comfortable existence called for a domestic staff. Labour-saving devices had not been invented. Meals were elaborate and guests frequent. Open wood-burning fires needed time and muscle, and water was carried from a cistern or a well. Out of doors lawns were to be cut and gardens tended. Riding and carriage horses needed attention. Many families kept cows (even those in poorer homes) and often chickens as well. The title 'manservant' suggests something grander than the gardener-cum-groom that he often was. It was not unknown for a butler to whitewash a hen coop.

Houses were as well or better heated than those in England although stoves came in slowly and for a time were scarce. In 1799 a merchant in Newark could not fill an order from York, reporting that none were available. The same answer came from Queenston. Lighting was by candles. Some fine furniture was imported from Britain and the United States, and increasingly local cabinetmakers were copying English designs with excellent results. Every now and then a returning army officer would sell his furniture by auction rather than pay high freight rates back to England whence it came. Some desirable pieces were acquired in this way at little cost. China, glass, and silver came from England, usually through firms in Montreal. Rough handling on the river led to considerable loss.[15]

In such a setting the gentry powdered their hair or put on their fine dresses, called on each other, wined and dined. A small place was made smaller by social distinctions laid down almost as fast as people came to live in the town. The exact boundaries are not readily comprehensible. Later on, in a wider scene, intermarriage and common tastes began to trace a pattern, but in early days such factors are not so apparent. Blue blood was very scarce and money was neither plentiful nor socially governing. Some of the officials, judges, and army officers were safely placed on the upper rungs of the social ladder, but not all were. Lawyers and merchants might be firmly fixed or hovering precariously. Quetton St George, who had been a French royalist officer and was a prominent citizen of York, was regarded by Mrs W. D. Powell as presumptuous when he wished to pay his addresses to her daughter.

In reading accounts of daily activities one wonders what could have been the hours of work. Morning calls were frequent between ladies, but men also – supposedly employed – turned up at houses at all hours. Breakfast and lunch are usually passed over in silence and dinner was the serious affair. When Peter Russell, then administrator of the province, sent out invitations to dinner in 1798 they were for four o'clock. And that was in June. Dinners were massive and prolonged. Two or three kinds of meat appeared, perhaps with fish and game as well. Whether the diners made a choice or faced the whole menu seems not to be recorded. In addition to dinner parties at private houses were those at the officers' mess where a number of civilians were (paying) guests. In house or barracks some people probably ate too much and they certainly drank too much. Great quantities of wines and brandies were assembled and consumed. It was not considered disgusting for men to be dead drunk. If challenged they could have pointed to similar excesses in the best English society.

Dinner at four or thereabouts, even if taken in a leisurely manner, left a long period before bedtime. Another meal turned up at about eight o'clock. Commonly called tea it was actually more like supper (although such an undignified word would not have been used). At that time of the evening people dropped into each other's houses for chat and often to play whist. Reading, too, passed much of an evening and in some households books were read aloud. The local shops stocked a few books and individuals supplemented them by shipments from England. They read newspapers too, and while only one was published in York others came by post.

The British Post Office, which was to operate in Canada for another fifty years, was much criticized for delays in setting up local offices and for unsatisfactory carriage of mail. The York post office was established at the turn of the century but no regular services ran to east or west, although a convention of 1792 with the United States provided for conveyance of mail overseas, and alternatively letters could go by way of the ports of British North America. By late 1800 the provincial government persuaded the Post Office to run a courier from the east on condition that they make up any deficit. Even the regular service was no more than monthly in winter. For some unexplained reason no mail was carried by lake shipping until later, except to the extent that private travellers were willing to act as unofficial couriers. Educated people wrote a great many letters, partly because that was the habit of the times and partly because many of them were immigrants. In the face of bad service and high rates they commonly asked friends who were travelling to take letters with them.

A small community largely organized its own amusements. Eating and drinking, whist and conversation, reading and writing were not the only forms. Dancing was popular and every winter subscription balls were organized. After the first few years theatrical performances of many kinds were given, sometimes by local amateurs, sometimes by visiting troupes. 'Well my dear Grand Papa,' wrote Louisa Jarvis in 1809, 'what a surprising circumstance I am about relating. Will you believe that positively there was a Play acted here last Night, and what do you think it was?' It was *The School for Scandal* on this occasion. Unhappily the gallery fell down in the improvised theatre, but an advertisement in the following year assured the public that the gallery had been 'secured under the direction of an obliging Gentleman.' A common form of programme consisted of two plays interlarded with a recitation. Outdoors men could hunt and fish without going far afield. Horse races were often organized. In the winter ladies were taken for sleigh rides, which they enjoyed even if the sleigh overturned.

Fewer opportunities, indoors or out, were available to small tradesmen, labourers, and the rank and file of the garrison. They could fish and hunt, if without the trappings that sometimes decorated the sports of the more wealthy. Indoors they had a narrower choice. Dances and elaborate dinners were out of the question and it is unlikely that they played whist. Probably

40

the humbler folk included a limited number of readers and certainly some of them were illiterate. Books, in any case, were expensive. Prices of theatre tickets varied but twenty-five cents for back seats or the gallery was about standard. To put that in perspective it will be recalled that a skilled worker might earn as much as $1.50 a day. The taverns were the clubs of the less privileged. They varied, of course, and some were undesirable – rowdy and with bad company. On the other hand the better ones offered company and games.

The only fraternal society in York during this period was the Masonic Order, and its first lodge was in the town from the very beginning. William Jarvis was provincial grand master a year before York was founded. In 1799 the Queen's Rangers' Lodge joined with the town's Harmony Lodge on the festival of Saint John in a march to the chamber of the legislative council, there being as yet no church, and there they heard an 'eloquent sermon.' Though thus early in the field the Freemasons had some difficulty in establishing lasting lodges.

After some twenty years from the time when it was founded York was still a very small place, a village as its inhabitants called it in unguarded moments. It was a curious mixture, crude in some respects and with some pomp and ceremony in others. Not having resulted in the first place from a voluntary flow of immigrants, of homemakers, its origin was in a sense artificial. In the years before the war of 1812 it had much of the appearance and many of the drawbacks of a frontier village. Set against that was its dignified and more sophisticated role as seat of the provincial government. Indeed, York was somewhat overpowered, or unbalanced, by the disproportionate place of executive, legislature, and courts. Desperately bad roads, uncertain shipping, and haphazard postal services induced isolation, and yet links to the rest of the province were forged by the presence of members of the assembly. The weakness of the transportation facilities was inconvenient in many respects and sometimes delayed for months deliveries to the shops. No acute shortages resulted, however. Slowly the society and economy were becoming more advanced and more balanced as the town and its hinterland gained the inhabitants that alone could give them life.

The dream of a capital near the mouth of the Humber had turned to reality; and near where Simcoe had held lonely court in his canvas Government House were streets and houses and shops and people. A town had been born.

# 3

## War and reconstruction

Ever since the American revolution the shadow of renewed hostilities had hung darkly over British North America. Perhaps little attention to such a threat was paid by many of those absorbed in the compelling task of establishing themselves in the pioneer province of Upper Canada; but to officials and others who followed public affairs signs of approaching collision were too evident to be ignored. It may be that international disputes over border towns and the allegiance of Indian tribes could have been resolved peacefully, but Britain's deep involvement in war with revolutionary and Napoleonic France aggravated the situation in more ways than one. While both belligerents imposed restrictions on neutral trade, the British ones were those that were felt because they could be enforced by sea power. Yet that very naval strength depended on a sufficiency of seamen, many of whom were escaping to the more attractive employment on American ships. The British government, convinced that the leak had to be plugged at all cost, caused American vessels to be stopped at sea so that deserters – or men claimed to be deserters – might be removed by force. By 1812 at least six thousand sailors had been recovered. It seems reasonable to assume, too, that Britain's preoccupation with Europe affected the issue in another way: the United States, divided in opinion and militarily weak, would have been less ready to make war on an England not handicapped by other commitments.

Be that as it may, the United States did declare war in June of 1812, albeit by a narrow margin in the Congress. In the House of Representatives the vote was 79 to 49 and in the Senate 19 to 13; and it was significant for the conduct of the war that the division was largely geographical, opposition being strong in New England and New York. The country was in other ways unready for war. The regular army had shrunk to a skeleton and recruits were elusive even when sought. The militia, with little training,

43

was in many cases lacking in enthusiasm and sometimes its employment was restricted by state regulations. The central government was as yet without adequate authority, and even when it did issue commands they were, in the early campaigns, to generals with limited competence.

On the high seas the Americans had some success in minor engagements and with privateers, but they had no fleet able to meet a large British force. Thus the maritime provinces were safe from attack and the Canadas could be supplied through the St Lawrence. In the first year of the war, too, the British held a strong position on the Great Lakes, the continuation of the St Lawrence route. The Provincial Marine had been used mainly as a transport service and did not rank high by naval standards, but its armed vessels were superior to anything the Americans possessed at the beginning; and of course it continued to be valuable for moving troops and supplies. The British weakness lay in the small number of regular regiments that could be assigned to the Canadas in view of the demands of the European theatre; and for what units could be spared the first priority was Lower Canada. If it fell Upper Canada would follow automatically.

Few as they were, the regulars in Upper Canada formed the hard core of the defensive forces. That the people of Upper Canada turned out as a man to defend their homeland is a myth that has long since been exploded. Loyalty, indeed, was a scarce commodity, and especially west of Kingston. The open-door immigration policy inaugurated by Simcoe may have brought to the province some so-called late United Empire Loyalists, but more conspicuously it allowed the entrance of those loyal only to their own interests. They came for free land, and the oath of allegiance that they took was all too often meaningless. Brighter spots showed here and there. When Brock asked in York for volunteers to serve against the invaders more men stepped forward than he could transport, and so he could accept only one hundred of those who were ready to fight. Such a response, however, was not general. In some areas individuals defected to the enemy or militia units simply refused to come out on duty. In other cases the militia was half-hearted, more concerned with the immediate harvest then defence of the land on which it grew. On the other hand some militia companies fought well, especially if stiffened by the presence of regulars.

The state of opinion in the province was bad enough but an exaggerated version of it gave rise to the American belief that no more was needed than to 'liberate' an oppressed people. The Upper Canadians, the argument ran, would welcome an opportunity to throw off British rule. With that in mind the American government was anxious to treat civilians gently, as friends rather than foes (just as the British thought it wise not to needle New England or New York into a more militant spirit). General Hull's proclamation from Sandwich was intended to implement this policy: 'Raise not your hands against your brethren. . . You will be emancipated from tyranny and oppression and restored to the dignified position of freemen.' That sort of language had been tried in 1776 without much result, but the appeal in 1812 was to those who had come from the United States not long before and the effect was considerable.

Psychological warfare, to use the modern expression, was pursued with some success but the pen could not altogether replace the sword. American military authorities were aware that their main objective should be to cut British communications as far east as possible. In his classic *Sea Power in Relation to the War of 1812* Admiral Mahan stated the issue succinctly: 'The Canadian tree was rooted in the ocean, where it was nourished by the sea power of Great Britain. To destroy it, failing the ocean navy which the United States had not, the trunk must be severed; the nearer the root the better.' That was accepted in Washington and by the generals – in principle but not in practice. Sir James Yeo, British commander of naval forces on the lakes, commented after the war that Britain owed much to 'the perverse stupidity of the enemy,' and by that he meant primarily failure to follow the strategy so obviously required. Quebec, it was true, could be strongly defended and Montreal only less so, and there was little stomach for an attack on either.

Kingston was not close to the root of Mahan's tree, but still on the trunk and American possession of it would deny British access to the lakes and thus make it virtually impossible to hold Upper Canada. With this in mind the American strategic plan for the spring of 1813 was to mount from Sackett's Harbour, the American strongpoint opposite Kingston, an attack on the latter, followed by moves against York and then Niagara. The plan was sensible but on second thoughts was turned upside down on representations to the secretary of war by the army and navy commanders, Dearborn and Chauncey. Claiming, on the basis of false intelligence, the presence of regulars in Kingston far beyond their actual strength, Dearborn asked to postpone the major task and begin with York. The object, according to his letter,[1] was to secure command of Lake Ontario by capturing or destroying the armed vessels at York; and, indeed, in the delicate balance of naval power, a vessel or two might turn the scales. In the afternoon of 26 April the American fleet was sighted from Scarborough Bluffs.

And so the war came to York, a town in almost every respect unprepared for battle. Its significance in the war was confused by compromises. It was, temporarily, the capital of the province; but the lieutenant governor remained in England throughout the war, and the administrator, as commander-in-chief, was wherever the campaigns led him. Members of the assembly seemed to be mentally incapable of comprehending the dangers to the province and any interruption of their proceedings would have involved no loss. Strongly patriotic citizens were balanced by those actually or passively disloyal.

Apart from being a source of supplies York had some other part in functions relating to the war. One was that it was on a route to the northwest which was still in the stage of planning and development when hostilities broke out. In previous months it had seemed reasonable to suppose that this way of avoiding the American border would be valuable in wartime. Early in 1812 Captain A. Gray, the acting quartermaster general, had talks with the North West and Michilimackinac companies assuring them of the interest of the governor general, Sir George Prevost, in the protection of trade. The representatives of both companies said that in the event of war they would go by York instead of Detroit. So far as is known, however, they made no use of Yonge Street during the war. Governmental authorities were also interested in the movement of troops and military supplies and in communications, and for those purposes Yonge Street did prove to be of value. The reinforcements for Michilimackinac, for example, consisting of two hundred soldiers from Kingston, proceeded up Yonge Street to Lake Simcoe in 1814.

An argument had started over the use of York as a dockyard and naval base before the town was founded and the controversy continued. In March 1812 Gray looked nervously at the concentration of naval and ordnance capacity in Kingston and inclined toward York as less vulnerable and yet having a good harbour. Unlike Kingston it was far from any of the potential bases of American strength and could be defended.

The most important consideration is the safety afforded against any Coup de Main of the Enemy. York will in all probability be held as long as we have a foot of territory in Upper Canada, as from its remote situation, and being so far retired from the frontier, it can be secured from any sudden assault; nothing therefore can affect it but operations having for their object the subjugation of the Province, and which object this Post is admirably calculated to defeat, if it were fortified in a proper manner and well garrisoned.[2]

All this had been said so often but it never seemed to penetrate. As it was York was given enough role as a shipyard and naval base to make it a target for attack but never the means of resisting. In the winter of 1813 construction began on what was to be one of the largest fighting ships on the lakes, *Sir Isaac Brock*. General Sir Roger Sheaffe, commander after the death of Brock, urged, only a month before the American landing, that York be 'put into a more respectable state of defence' in view of the likelihood that the Americans would seek to destroy a ship that could be decisive on Lake Ontario.

In April 1813 York was a sitting duck. The town, at the east end of the bay, had a simple blockhouse near the water's edge. From there a broken line of houses extended about a mile to the west. Beyond that was an open space followed by the mouth of Garrison Creek. At that point a fort had

46

been started but only the magazine finished. Close to the lake were two twelve-pounder guns behind earthworks. The Western Battery was some hundreds of yards beyond that and consisted of two eighteen-pounder guns. These were, however, of little value. They had long since been condemned and were without gudgeons, that is to say they could not be pivoted, only fired from a fixed position and for a fixed range. The troops in York were under the command of Sheaffe, who happened to be there at the time. The regulars amounted to about three hundred men, consisting of two companies of the 8th or King's Regiment; a detachment of the Royal Newfoundland Regiment, of company size; and a company of the Glengarry Light Infantry Fencibles (that is, a regular regiment raised locally). To that were added companies of the 3rd York Militia Regiment and something over fifty Indians.

The American fleet consisted of fifteen ships of various sizes, some being heavily armed. Some seventeen hundred soldiers were aboard. On the morning of 27 April the indications were that the landing would be near old Fort Rouillé. Sheaffe therefore sent toward that point the Glengarry Light Infantry and the Indians. The former somehow lost their way although there was a road of sorts. Dearborn had indeed picked on Fort Rouillé, but a strong east wind drove the boats some distance beyond that and the landing was made on a wooded shore. Contemporary accounts, being partisan, differ. Chauncey claimed that as the schooners beat into position they were 'under a very heavy fire from the enemy's batteries.' In view of the antiques with which the gunners were struggling it seems improbable that whatever fire there was did much harm. On the other hand there is more solid evidence that the grapeshot fired from the ships was a considerable aid to the landing parties.[3]

The first American unit to land, opposed by Indians, the only defenders nearby, scrambled on to the high ground. The grenadier company of the 8th Regiment hurried to the scene, tried to counterattack, but the odds were too great and they had to back toward the Western Battery. There, where other troops had assembled, a small portable magazine blew up by accident, killing and wounding several men and handicapping those who had been using it. The retirement continued to Garrison Creek and Sheaffe concluded that, against forces greatly superior in numbers and weapons, he could do nothing, and that he could save his troops only by abandoning York. He had already lost sixty-two killed and ninety-four wounded. Before withdrawing toward Kingston he ordered the destruction of the main magazine and the warship on the stocks, and left to the militia officers the negotiation of a capitulation.

The militia had barely been in the engagement but some of its officers, together with civilians, were bitterly critical of Sheaffe's handling of the engagement and particularly of the surrender of the town. Extreme things were said and written. W. D. Powell, who was away from York, first wrote a measured account including modified praise for Sheaffe, but later – probably after his return – joined in the chorus of condemnation. A strange document, preserved only in a draft in the hand of John Strachan, the new rector of York, is dated 8 May 1813. It was signed by Strachan himself, Lieutenant Colonel William Chewett, Major William Allan, and Captain Duncan Cameron, all of the 3rd Militia Regiment; also by Alexander Wood, Samuel Smith, and W. W. Baldwin. Thomas Ridout signed but on second thoughts scratched out his signature. There is an indication that the sheriff, John Beikie, refused to sign. The letter was to be sent to John Richardson, a member of the executive council of Lower Canada, with the suggestion that it be shown to Governor General Prevost and then published.

It is a foolish document, more like childish tantrums than an expression of adult opinion. None of the signatories, Strachan least of all, had any serious knowledge of military affairs and they wrote in the mood of what sports writers call a Monday morning quarterback. There was room for criticism of Sheaffe of course. Brock, whose death at Queenston Heights in October 1812 was a tragic loss, would have acted with more precision and vigour; but to claim that York could have been held is sheer nonsense. To suggest that a town defended by a few obsolete cannon and three hundred regulars, with the shaky support of an equal number of inexperienced militia, against an invading army of seventeen hundred supported by powerful guns on ships that moved at will, is absurd. It is probable that the Americans had no intention of holding York. What they could gain there would come from a short stay, and as it turned out they gained little and suffered substantial losses, mainly from the explosion of the magazine. The shower of rocks killed General Pike with thirty-eight soldiers and wounded 222 men. A last ditch stand by the little British force would have served no useful purpose, while on the other hand it was essential to preserve what few regulars there were in Upper Canada.[4]

York was left under an army of occupation. The militia officers who had been instructed to settle terms had the energetic support of Strachan, who also secured better treatment of the wounded and prisoners and protection of private property. The capitulation contained three points: that regular, militia, and naval personnel – other than surgeons – become prisoners of war; that naval and military stores be given up but private property be guaranteed to citizens; and that papers of the civil government be retained by its officials. Since the American ships were already overloaded the militia prisoners were paroled. Apart from looking after the wounded the only problem that the citizens had to face was to ensure that the promise of preserving private property was honoured. On the face of it this would seem to mean against looting by the American soldiery; and there was some of that, especially in houses abandoned by their owners, although the

American officers did what they could to stop it. The bizarre factor, however, was that not a few of the citizens were as active in looting as were the American privates, and the magistrates could do nothing to stop them. The height of absurdity was reached when the Americans hired nearby farmers to cart to the dock stores from the commissariat, paying them by a proportion of what they carried. Meanwhile the legislative buildings were set on fire, and it is consistent with what had already assumed something of the nature of a comic opera that there is still a dispute as to whether the fire was set by Americans or Canadians. The balance of evidence points toward the former but no definite proof has been found.

The Americans left as soon as they could, partly because there was no point in remaining, partly because they could not be sure that their ships were free from attack. What had they gained? Some government funds were picked up, having had no proper protection, but largely in army bills which might not be easy to cash. They collected a good deal of liquor, and took or destroyed what military supplies and food they could. Success no doubt raised the morale of their militia, though tempered by unexpectedly heavy casualties. They did eliminate the ship under construction, but the *Prince Rupert* had sailed from York shortly before they arrived, and while the *Duke of Gloucester*, at York under repair, was towed away it turned out to be unseaworthy.

The capture of York had no major effect on the course of the war other than to divert attention from Kingston, the proper target. The people of the town suffered little. Five Canadians were killed, two of them by the explosion, and five were wounded. Goods were taken from shops and some articles stolen from houses. On the other hand many of the American officers and men fraternized with the inhabitants. With unconscious irony Mrs Powell wrote to her husband that 'the Fleet so hostile to our comforts departed on Saturday morning.'

York was in a curious state of mind during and after the occupation. The militia officers complained that their force could have performed to advantage if it had been given a chance, but what part it played in the attempt to hold back the Americans gave no evidence to support that claim, and the men seemed to go on parole without regret. Behind the criticisms that have been mentioned lay the assumption that this was a British war fought (to their inconvenience) on the soil of Canadians, and indeed there is a case for such a position. It followed that the British were responsible for winning the war and defending this particular town. The corollary was that Britain should make compensation for loss of property, which to some extent it did.

The occupation left other worries. One arose out of the revelation of disloyalty and of lawlessness in the forms of theft and vandalism. Men were charged in court but in few cases would juries convict. It was also uncomfortable to realize that York, with its militia paroled and defences destroyed, could be captured at will, subject only to naval power on Lake Ontario. The sight of sails caused alarm. A second landing was in fact made at the end of July, and there are indications that renegade Canadians passed word on the location of government stores to be had for the asking. Certain it is that some Canadians helped the Americans in their search for loot, although others frustrated their efforts. Those who liked to call themselves 'the principal inhabitants' had retreated into the woods. In September ships were again seen to be bearing on York, but they sailed away.

Neither losses nor hardships throughout this disturbed summer were sufficient to put a heavy drag on the progress of the town, but a major disaster loomed as a result of the war and was narrowly averted. In 1815 the British government decided to move the capital of the province to Kingston, influenced in the main by the proven vulnerability of York. It had never, of course, been intended that York should be the permanent seat of government. Simcoe's choice of London was not reaffirmed and Kingston, which had frightened off the enemy and was still the largest town in the province, seemed to be the best bet. Loud and indignant cries came from the officials. They recalled with pride that they had heroically accepted the primitive conditions of York where they had selflessly established themselves at high personal cost; and now it was proposed that they should abandon their hard-won homes. Most unreasonable. Halfway through a memorial on the subject[5] they just remembered to refer to the overriding importance of the public interest, only to drop back into the arithmetic of what they would lose financially by another move. Why some of the junior employees might even resign! Happily for them and for the town Francis Gore, the lieutenant governor, back at his post with days of peace, was persuaded that the change would be unwise and he induced London to reverse its decision. That did not end the argument, but in fact the government stayed in York throughout the life of the Province of Upper Canada.

That York should remain the capital was regarded as important not only by the personnel of government, who were concerned with their own welfare, but also by the laymen of the town. It was an asset, but one of proportionately decreasing value as the town went through a more general development in the twenty years after Waterloo. During the period of hostilities inconveniences and shortages had existed, caused in part by the dislocation of shipping and in part by the heavy purchasing for the British forces. That very purchasing, although it might have caused some problems for civilian buyers, had brought prosperity to the town and wealth to individual merchants who were more than compensated for damages and appropriation of goods during the few days of military occupation. When the army buying stopped business slumped and prices went down, but a less transitory factor turned the economic curve upward again.

Above all the Province of Upper Canada needed people. It had, not long before, started from scratch as an unoccupied land of lakes and forests. The trickle of people into it had been stopped by the war, during which the population of York and the immediate townships declined. After Napoleon had finally been escorted to St Helena, Upper Canada's opportunity came. Peace brought to the British Isles not only its blessings but a serious economic depression which, coming on top of the enclosure movement and the dislocation that accompanied the industrial revolution, caused widespread unemployment and suffering. Emigration appeared to the victims of these circumstances to be the only expedient. A desperate one it was for many families, for they had no funds and few possessions to take to this far land of North America; and anything they may have known of the ocean crossing under the disgraceful conditions of the time would make that seem like a nightmare, as indeed it was. Yet there was a chance of a better future and little enough to lose. In addition to the poverty-stricken were substantial numbers of farmers and artisans, and of middle-class people who had some means but hoped to improve their situation in the new world.[6]

No exact statistics can be found for immigrants moving into York or the Home District as a whole, but the numbers did climb in the twenties and thirties, bringing a substantial if not spectacular flow of people. In 1816 the population of York was only slightly over prewar level but in 1818 it first edged into four figures, more than doubled in the next decade, and by 1833 was over six thousand. It seemed to some contemporaries that too many people were crowding into the town, quenching their thirst at taverns though they had no jobs, whereas they could have been usefully employed on the land. In 1830 the editor of the *York Observer* wrote:

We have been in some of the back townships, and have to regret, that the scarcity of hands will occasion very great destruction of the wheat. Hundreds of emigrants have recently arrived, and although unemployed about the town, they refuse to enter the bush! Farmers came in from the back townships and offered 3/9 a day, and board, to labourers, and they could not induce those appealed to, to proceed with them!

Immigration from the British Isles, heavy in comparison to the sparsely populated town and country to which it was attracted, changed also the political and racial complexion of Upper Canada. William Berczy's plan for large-scale settlement of Germans in the 1790s dwindled to very little, although it did result in establishing some progressive farmers in Markham County, on and near Yonge Street. The other European group, that of French royalists led by the Comte de Puisaye, faded almost to nothing on its lands near Whitby. Americans, of course, had come in large numbers and some of them became good subjects of the king. But in view of the disloyalty of others during the war further immigration from the United States was not encouraged. In any case it dwindled because of the prospects opening in the American west. The number of American negroes was not large, perhaps something over three hundred in 1830. Large-scale escapes had hardly begun.

A few families of York, such as the Robinsons, had been well established in the Thirteen Colonies while others had been there only during the revolutionary war. A strong English contingent in York included the Denisons, Jarvises, Powells, Elmsleys, Boultons, Ridouts, Chewetts, and Cawthras. The Scots were numerous too, some of the prominent ones being William Allan, John Strachan, James Macaulay, Aeneas Shaw, John McGill, Robert Hay (of furniture fame), and W. L. Mackenzie. Many more Irish came a little later, but meanwhile they were well represented by the Baldwins, Willcocks, Sullivans, John Gamble (the army surgeon), the legal Gwynnes, John Carey, and Francis Collins.

Both the Town of York and the country about it were enriched by the flow of immigrants, the one gaining more of the institutions and facilities of an urban centre and the other multiplying cleared farms and hamlets. Integration of town and country was not new; it had always been seen as essential. Now, however, it acquired more substance because of the higher scale of population and because both the rural and urban parties had more to offer. By almost any standard travel between them was difficult, for the province was in no position to make drastic improvements in roads.

In spite of handicaps, however, it is obvious that people did travel in and out of York as a matter of routine. Thomas Magrath's lovely estate, Erindale, was where Dundas Street crosses the Credit River, and he thought nothing of visiting York. 'We have frequently,' he wrote in 1832, 'occupied the morning at work in a *potato field*, and passed the evening most agreeably in the *ball* room at York!!!'[7] Mary O'Brien, who before and for a time after her marriage lived on farms between Thornhill and Richmond Hill, made frequent references in her diary[8] to visits to York by herself, her brother, her husband, and their neighbours. The drive of over fifteen miles took on the average two to two and a half hours. Occasionally trips had to be postponed because of the state of what was locally called 'the street.' Early one December Edward O'Brien had to postpone taking his oats to market until the frost returned, and in another November the road was too bad for even riding.

Ordinarily, however, the people in that area took it as a matter of course that they would go to York for any of many reasons: to see friends, shop, deliver farm products, attend meetings of the legislature, do garrison duty, or see a doctor. At one time O'Brien was going to York every day in connec-

tion with some land business. On other occasions he walked to the town, on one of these his wife remarking in a matter-of-fact way: 'Edward went to York again, and as he has walked I do not expect him to return tonight.' In general these people seemed to think no more of an expedition to York than do modern residents of northern Toronto of going to the downtown shops. How far this generalization would apply to the humbler farmers as well as to such educated, middle-class families is not clear, but there are many references to waggon loads of grain and other products finding their way to the market. Beyond the Don and Humber rivers, too, settlement was moving forward, changing the appearance of the countryside from the first stage of pioneering to something more like an established agricultural area. Roads – probably no better and no worse than Yonge Street – connected them with York, allowing what in the Upper Canadian standard of the day might be called ready access.

York grew with its hinterland – with it and because of it. The economic life of the town, however, consisted of more than local exchange of goods and services for farm products. In both buying and selling, merchants and merchandise had to cover great distances. Between the end of the war and the collapse of the Montreal fur trade in 1821 the dream of Yonge Street as an artery of the northwest trade had at last some slight reality. The evidence on the amount carried is very slight. Isaac Wilson, a settler on Yonge Street, wrote in the summer of 1815 of seeing 'waggons to carry goods through the country to the Lakes for the North West Company to trade with the Indians and bringing stores back for Government which were conveyed up at an immense expense during the war.'[9] This particular two-way traffic was by its nature ephemeral. If Wilson's description is accurate – and his letters are sensible – the Nor' Westers were not bringing down their furs by waggon, and there is little evidence that the company continued this transport on its own whenever what was presumably a cost-sharing arrangement with the government was terminated. The customs records of York for early years after the war show importations from the United States of salt and tobacco consigned to the North West Company and non-dutiable goods may also have passed by this land route. There was, then, some long-haul freight on Yonge Street but there seems to be hardly a reference to it in contemporary newspapers, letters, or diaries. This is significant in view of the publicity before the war when the traffic was only a hope.

In this period, then, Yonge Street was principally used for transport within the area between York and Lake Simcoe. The lake shore route to Kingston and Montreal, however, did carry goods over a long distance in the winter; and in the summer could be traversed the whole way or serve as supplementary to ships. In May 1831 William Weller,[10] a prominent operator of stage coaches, advertised summer arrangements:

Mail will leave York Sunday, Tuesday, and Thursday at 5 P.M., sleep at Pickering; leave there at 4 A.M.; breakfast at Darlington; dinner at Cobourg; arrive at carryplace [near Trenton] same evening in time for steamboats for Kingston and Prescott.

The steamboat, indeed, added a new dimension to travel. The *Frontenac* was the first Canadian-built steamer on the lakes. It was large (740 tons) and well equipped. Its maiden voyage was in 1817, and after an unsuccessful experiment in running to Prescott, the route was established as Kingston-York-Queenston. The fare for the first leg was £3 and for the second £1. Other steamships followed, so that in 1826 the York newspaper, *United Empire Loyalist*, could express satisfaction with the progress made:

In noticing the first trip of another Steam Boat [the *Canada* of 250 tons] we cannot help contrasting the present means of conveyance with those of ten years ago. At that time few schooners navigated the Lake, and the passage was attended with many delays and much inconvenience. Now there are Five Steam Boats, all affording excellent accommodation, and the means of expeditious travelling. The routes of each are so arranged that every day of the week the traveller may find opportunities of being conveyed from one extremity of the Lake to the other in few hours.

Sailing vessels increased steadily in numbers and carried most of the bulk freight. More attention, however, was directed to the steamships, partly because they were novel, partly because they captured a growing proportion of the passenger traffic. When Thomas Magrath and his family migrated in 1831 they went from Prescott to York by steamer, in 'first cabin,' at a cost of £20. For the benefit of his correspondent in Ireland Magrath remarked that lake travel would have been cheaper by three-quarters if they had chosen a schooner, but that their arrival would then have been dependent on the winds. Sailing vessels carried lumber as freight but steamers used quantities of wood for fuel. In 1828 D'Arcy Boulton the younger made a formal contract with Hugh Richardson of York, master of the *Canada*, to supply a thousand cords of sound dry pine to be delivered at either one of two docks. Not less than eight cords were always to be on the wharf, and if the *Canada* was held up for lack of fuel Boulton would forfeit £5 or Richardson could consider the contract void. The price was 6/3 a cord.[11]

Improvements in the harbour were overdue and now were urgently needed to accommodate more and larger ships and heavier traffic. With the facilities available little could be done to make the western gap less hazardous or to dredge the shifting silt there and elsewhere. Three wharves were constructed in 1816. The King's Wharf, close to Peter Street, was for military purposes and quite short until its enlargement in 1833 or 1834.

54

Cooper's Wharf was at the foot of Church Street, and the Merchants' Wharf, built by a syndicate, at the foot of Frederick Street. The last was 770 feet long and said to have ten feet of water at its extremity. That depth, however, must soon have become inadequate in view of the draught of even the early steamers.

The principal exports through the port were all bulky: wheat, flour, lumber, and potash. The main sales were in Britain, the grain being subject to the vicissitudes of the corn laws. Imports covered a very wide range of goods. They were drawn in the main from the British Isles and secondarily from the United States. For the latter the customs records show such goods as were dutiable. Salt and tobacco were the largest items but other imports were varied: whisky, beer, and cider; chocolates, butter, and apples; pork and hams; hats; spelling books; scythes, mill saws, gunpowder, paint, nails, and plaster; waggons and a little furniture. It is noticeable that several of the commodities were in competition with those commonly produced in the Home District. Waggons, carriages, and furniture were certainly made in York, though they may have been of limited types. Cider, hats, and probably mill saws were also made locally. Pork and hams came in from the nearby farms. No one had to go far to find the breweries of John Farr, John Severn, or the Copland Brewing Company.

Taking into account the unlisted British imports it can be said that York was importing from abroad most of the manufactured articles that it required. A few simple things were made in and near the town in addition to beer: lumber, flour, soap, leather, and some simple iron goods. But York was still preoccupied with trade, for which the growing population in the town and beyond offered greater opportunities. By the thirties some wholesalers could be identified as separate from retailers, the beginning of one of the most profitable activities for many years to come. In some cases retail shops were becoming more specialized but that trend was conspicuous a little later. Mrs O'Brien was struck by the progress of the shops, and after one of her many expeditions to York, in the autumn of 1829, wrote that 'We found the shops so much improved that it is hardly worthwhile to send for any common things from England or to bring out any stores except for the arts and sciences, which will not perhaps be well supplied for some time to come. For the rest the chances are that you may get them as well here.'

Some of the leading shopkeepers of early days dropped out, Alexander Wood in 1821 and William Allan in 1822. Quetton St George had already returned to France, but left two partners, Jules Quesnel and John Spread Baldwin, to run the business locally and send a share of the profits to him. After five years of what proved to be an unsatisfactory arrangement St George was persuaded to sell out to the other two for cash. Not long after that Quesnel returned to Montreal, leaving Baldwin in charge. In 1819

55

the firm imported goods from England to the value of £11,000 and from the United States of about £1,500. They invested in land and shipping, and Baldwin turned with particular interest to that most important innovation, banking.[12]

As business began to revive after the war and then to expand, the absence of banking facilities became more serious. Army bills, being legal tender, had served a useful purpose, but at the end of the war the whole issue was called in for redemption in cash. The need of banks was obvious, but so was the fact that whoever controlled them had powerful instruments in their hands. Montreal, the financial as well as the commercial capital of the Canadas, sought to extend its banks into Upper Canada almost as soon as they existed at home. In 1818 the Bank of Montreal appointed William Allan as its agent in York and the Bank of Canada appointed Henry Drean, a York merchant. At that stage, however, these were agencies rather than branches and appear not to have attempted a general banking business.

Meanwhile York had locked horns with Kingston, which was the most important town of Upper Canada. In 1817 a group of Kingston merchants petitioned the assembly for legislation to incorporate a bank, and a few days later a York group, headed by John Strachan, submitted a similar petition. The first only was acted on, the desired legislation being passed and duly forwarded to London for approval, as the lieutenant governor's standing instructions required. There, however, it became stuck in what Dickens called the Circumlocution Office, and in 1819 the Kingston men began banking operations as a private association.

The arrival of Sir Peregrine Maitland as lieutenant governor in 1818 allowed the oligarchy, centred at York, to use its not-very-secret weapon. Maitland's extreme conservatism brought him close to the leading York Tories and in particular to Strachan, the titular leader of the local group seeking a bank charter. After being indoctrinated Maitland dutifully reported to London that the Kingston bankers were untrustworthy and had committed the unpardonable sin of establishing American connections, that in turn suggesting to him the shadow of those impossible people, the Reformers. From the point of view of York all then went well. The Bank of Upper Canada was approved in legislation and the charter came into effect in 1821. Its business was largely in discounting promissory notes and in negotiating bills of exchange. Deposits did not constitute an important feature of banking anywhere in British North America and no interest was paid on them. The bank helped to relieve the shortage of currency by issuing bank notes, the total in circulation in 1825 being of the value of £61,000.

The Bank of Upper Canada was a remarkable organization, imbedded in the government, itself dominated by the ruling group involved in the bank. One-quarter of the stock was to be subscribed by the government,

The Bank of Upper Canada, 1821, the first building of the first bank

which was to appoint four out of fifteen directors. The others were nearly all members of the executive and legislative councils or associated in some way with the oligarchy. Authorized to do so, the bank established branches and agencies in other parts of the province and beyond. It was a neat monopoly and its stock was regarded as a gilt-edged investment. To maintain its sole rule it resisted further Montreal invaders by legislation making their position impossible. As may well be imagined the Bank of Upper Canada was popular neither with the Reformers nor with the commercial communities of other towns in the province. It made no concession to the former, but Kingston – after the collapse of its private bank (whose methods were, to say the least, peculiar) – finally reached its original objective with the incorporation of the Commercial Bank of the Midland District in 1831.[13]

Another financial institution, closely related to the Bank of Upper Canada, was the British American Fire and Life Assurance Company appropriately situated across the street. William Allan was its governor, and he was president of the bank. J. S. Baldwin was deputy, and on the board were D'Arcy Boulton and William Proudfoot – all, too, connected with the bank. Looking at these financial institutions it would perhaps be fair to conclude that here was the oligarchy at its best and at its worst. The bank and the insurance company made real contributions to the economy and the men connected with them could not be justly accused of maladministration or corruption. They could, however, be convicted of maintaining privilege and securing personal benefit.

Mary O'Brien described the York of 1829 as 'all suburb . . . the town is so scattered that I hardly know where the centre may be.' The better houses were usually in large grounds and for a long time vacant lots added to the appearance of space. She added that on the road along the lake shore were the houses of the 'principal inhabitants,' this being in general true but subject to exceptions. While port installations and some small commercial establishments had their places on the bay, the people of the town were determined to maintain the waterfront as partly residential and partly for the enjoyment of the citizens generally. For this latter purpose letters patent of 1818 vested a strip of land next to the bay 'in John Beverley Robinson, William Allan, George Crookshank, Duncan Cameron and Grant Powell . . . their heirs and assigns, forever, in trust to hold the same for the use and benefit of the inhabitants of the Town of York, as or for a public walk in front of the said Town.' Thus began the tortured history of what came to be called the Esplanade.

In a town in which commercial and residential buildings jostled each other, and indeed were often combined, it was symbolic that the road along the shore of the bay should have been divided by the public market at King and New (Jarvis) streets, Palace Street running to its east and Front Street to its west. The market was an important institution which from its origin was designed to benefit both the town and the area around it. More than anything else in York it represented the urban-rural relationship. The market in early years appears to have been entirely out of doors and no record has been found of its appearance or how it was managed. The proclamation of 1803 stated only where sales were to be made and that they were to be each Saturday. Probably the market was interrupted during the American occupation, and it is possible that fear of further invasions discouraged farmers from bringing in produce.

Some months before the end of the war, however, the legislature passed an act (54 Geo. III, c. 15) which was similar to one of 1801 that applied to Kingston. For the convenience of the inhabitants of the Home District a market was to be established, and since there had already been one this must have meant a new and more organized market. The justices of the peace were to choose a location and draw up rules for its operation. Copies of such rules were to be posted in the most public place in each township, and in York on the doors of the church and the court house. The Court of

George Crookshank's residence, northeast corner of Front and Peter streets, erected in 1824

Quarter Sessions duly issued regulations a little over a year later (in April 1815), by which time a wooden building had been erected in the old market square. Both sellers and purchasers were protected. Nowhere else might meat, poultry, fish, butter, eggs, or vegetables be sold between 6 AM and 4 PM. On the other hand tainted meat might not be offered for sale and weights must be accurate. To maintain these and other rules a clerk of the market was appointed and fines provided for violation of any regulation. In 1831 the market was further improved when the wooden building was replaced by a brick one designed by J. G. Chewett and W. W. Baldwin.

A glance at Palace Street shows that it was becoming more commercial.[14] Russell Abbey was half deserted and factories were crowding in elsewhere. Going westward on Front Street good residences began to show from about Church Street. Mr Justice L. P. Sherwood had a view of Freeland's soap factory, a lumber yard, and a ship carpenter's yard on the bay shore; but he was flanked by his son-in-law, Dr John King, and a fellow justice of the Court of King's Bench, J. B. Macaulay. Henry John Boulton, a prominent lawyer, was just east of Bay Street in what the *Directory* called 'a newly erected Gothic mansion stucco'd.' Next door was W. D. Powell. John Strachan had built himself a fine house east of York Street, and there he lived in some style. George Crookshank was at the corner of Peter Street, the western limit of the town. His sister-in-law, on a visit from the United

States, found the house pleasant and 'open to the lake.' In the garden were pears, apples, cherries, gooseberries, plums, and peaches.

Going back to the east side and inland from Palace Street the houses of several prominent citizens would have been seen. J. S. Baldwin and Alexander Wood lived on Frederick Street. Sir William Campbell, the chief justice, and T. G. Ridout, cashier of the bank, were on Duke Street. The combined properties of S. P. Jarvis, Captain McGill, and William Allan blocked the extension of Lot Street east of Yonge Street.

On the west end of the town three blocks between Graves (Simcoe) and John streets were being turned over to public purposes. From Front to Market (Wellington) Street was Simcoe Place on which were the new buildings for the legislature which had been wandering about unhappily since it was burned out in the southeast. The buildings were ready for occupancy in 1832. Designed by J. G. Chewett, they were simple but dignified and were placed on spacious grounds. In the next block north the Elmsley house had been taken over for a Government House. North of that again was Russell Square on which Upper Canada College was built. Further north again and just within the town limits was Beverley House, rebuilt by J. B. Robinson from D'Arcy Boulton's cottage. It was a large house and in even larger grounds, for they ran from John to Graves Street and from Hospital to Lot Street. The value of fire insurance on this house gives some indication of the substantial buildings of this period. The policy was for £1,500, with the contents being insured for £300 and the books for another £200.[15]

Boulton himself was one of those who chose to live outside the town, although that cannot have been for lack of space within it. The lovely house which he built about 1818, and which has happily been preserved, was called the Grange. It was on park lot 13 which he had bought in 1808 and was entered at Lot Street at the head of John Street. G. T. Denison's Bellevue, built in 1815, was another handsome house and was between the Grange and the modern College Street. North of Bloor Street and well in the country was Rosedale, built by J. E. Small in 1821 and bought by W. B. Jarvis in 1824. This pleasant house looked across the ravine to Yonge Street which was the western boundary of the property of 120 acres. The whole was considerably smaller than the area named after it. On the east it extended to a line now marked by the lower part of Glen Road; on the north to Roxborough Street; and the southern boundary was irregular, being approximately at the present Elm Avenue. The house was reached from Yonge Street by a ravine road, now Park Road.

W. W. Baldwin followed the example of Peter Russell by living part of his time in town and part in the country. Shortly before the war he built Spadina (Indian for hill) on the brow of the rise at a point just east of the present Casa Loma. The land had been left to the Baldwins by William

Moss Park, William Allan's house on Sherbourne Street, erected in 1830

Willcocks and the house cost £1,500. On the ground floor were two parlours; on the next floor four bedrooms and a study; and in the basement a kitchen, dairy, root cellar, wine cellar, and man's bedroom. As in the larger house he later built on Front Street no dining room was identified, but presumably one of the parlours served that purpose. The same is true of other old houses in York and also of houses in England of an earlier date.

Within the town it would be difficult to distinguish districts which were residential. Large and small houses, shops, small industries, offices, churches, schools, hotels, boarding houses, and taverns were intermingled. Quite often one building would serve two purposes. A doctor probably always had his office in his residence and merchants had long lived over their shops. One convenient arrangement of the day which saved steps was a 'Gentlemen's Boarding House and Liquor Store.'

Taverns were more plentiful than some of those concerned with public morals thought proper, but church buildings came slowly into the landscape. The Church of England still had the largest number of members but not to such an overwhelming degree as formerly. No exact statistics, however, exist.[16] The Anglicans were led by their vigorous archdeacon, John Strachan.[17] For long St James' remained the sole church in the town. It was enlarged in 1818 and rebuilt in stone in 1833. To finance the church the practice was to assign pews to individuals who paid for them both lump sums and annual rent. In 1820, for example, Joseph Shaw won at a public auction a pew in the gallery for which he paid £35. The formal document which embodied the terms provided that he and his heirs would continue to have possession subject to an annual rent of £2.[18] Complaints were made that little space was left for those who did not own pews.

In spite of their record of missionary work in the province the Methodists found difficulties in establishing themselves in York, and they were slow to do so although for some time preachers who were visiting there addressed *ad hoc* gatherings. In addition to the need of shifting their focus to urban communities the Methodists were accused of political disloyalty because of early American connections. It proved later that there was scarcely any ground for such charges. Furthermore they were weakened by being split two ways and sometimes more. By degrees their methods were modified and they came to enjoy the support of some of the wealthier merchants. The first small chapel was built in 1818 and by 1833 a good-sized brick church had been completed.

The Presbyterians were badly divided too, and the little congregaton set up in 1820 by a minister of the Secessionist Church who came from Ireland was regarded by some contemporaries as including too many political radicals, an impression perhaps stimulated by the occasional presence of William Lyon Mackenzie. To make matters worse the Secessionists battled with each other. So did the other main branch of Presbyterians, housed from 1830 in St Andrew's, which a year later came under the newly formed Synod of the Presbyterian Church of Canada in Connection with the Church of Scotland. The Baptists were later in the field, having no solid footing in York before 1829; and the Congregationalists not until 1834.

It seemed difficult for Christians within one church to love one another, and at moments inter-church relations looked better in comparison. Originally few Roman Catholics had lived in York, but the numbers went up with Irish immigration and in 1824 the first church was built, this being in part made possible by contributions from Protestants. The trustees of the church – James Baby, John Small, and the Reverend Alexander McDonell – welcomed this 'liberality . . . as a certain prelude to future concord among all classes of the community.' It was a nice, if an optimistic, thought; but concord was all too soon broken within the church itself. W. J. O'Grady, the Irish priest who came to York, entered too enthusiastically into politics as a radical, bringing dissension into the congregation. When ordered by Bishop McDonell to leave York he refused to go, and before he was finally forced out his supporters and opponents were completely at odds. McDonell, meanwhile, had found a new ally in John Elmsley who left the Church of England, of which he had been an active member, to join the Roman Catholics. In a small town the conversion of such a prominent citizen caused a sensation. Elmsley's own explanation of his action was that he had been convinced by a pamphlet on transubstantiation written by the Bishop of Strasbourg, and he thought highly enough of it to have five thousand copies printed and distributed throughout the province.

St Andrew's Presbyterian Church, corner of Church and Adelaide streets, erected 1830–1

It is, however, perhaps not without relevance that in 1831 Elmsley had married a Roman Catholic, the daughter of L. P. Sherwood.

One unwelcome result of immigration was the warfare between Roman Catholic and Protestant factions that broke out intermittently in York as elsewhere in Upper Canada, and in which the imported Orange Order played an active part. Previously the only fraternal society in York was that of the Freemasons and they had made only moderate progress. Simon McGillivray, their grand master for Upper Canada from 1822 to 1841, was struck by what he found when he took office, observing 'that Masonry had not been in such hands, nor conducted in such a manner as to offer any inducement to respectable men to associate with some of those whom they might be liable to meet in lodges.' His solution was to form a new lodge, St Andrew's No. 1, and it did include a number of most 'respectable men.' Membership was not exclusively Protestant. Angus McDonell was a high officer of the order in 1800. L. P. Sherwood joined in the early thirties and John King a little later.[19]

The Orange Order, on the other hand, was militantly Protestant. The first recorded march in York was in 1822 when the Orangemen went to church on 12 July and heard an 'eloquent and appropriate Discourse' by Strachan. That was a peaceful event but not much later riots occurred in Upper Canadian towns. Francis Collins, editor of the *Canadian Freeman*, a Roman Catholic paper, wrote of the danger of the 'blind folly of party spirit and religious animosity.' Presumably that shot was aimed in one direction but responsibility for starting fights was variously attributed to one side or the other. The Orange parade on 12 July 1833 ended up in a free-for-all but the magistrates were able to restore order.[20]

Religious affiliation was a thread in the social and political pattern of York. Roman Catholics and dissenters were always free to conduct services and were subject to no legal disabilities in respect of voting or holding public office. The Church of England received the lion's share of governmental funds available to the churches because it was regarded by those in authority in England and largely in Upper Canada as an integral part of the structure of a safe and sane colony. Anglicanism was strongly represented in that segment of the population of York which grew out of the little group that dominated the town in its earliest days. It was conspicuous in government, on the Bench, and on the Bar.

The preponderance of Anglicans in the community, the extent to which senior government officials belonged to that church, and the current English conception of the relations between religion and education together influenced in the 1820s and 1830s a controversy which has never flagged throughout the life of Ontario. Partly because it was the provincial capital, partly by chance, York had more than its share of the dispute over the place of the churches in education.

Schooling in Upper Canada was neither compulsory nor generally free, but neither was it in England nor in most parts of the United States. Among those who gave serious thought to the subject probably more concluded that education was for the relatively few – those who could take advantage of it – than argued that all children should attend school. Under the circumstances of the day the Common School Act of 1816, inspired by John Strachan with his Scottish belief in education, was well in the van. The act was not designed to throw all responsibility on the state but to afford financial support to common (that is, elementary) schools that already existed or might be set up by local initiative.

Such a one was started by public subscription in York, and in 1820 Thomas Appleton, a recent immigrant from Yorkshire, was appointed master. Peregrine Maitland, however, decided to introduce the Madras system under which younger children were taught by elder, and took over the Common School for that purpose. York was to have the first of what was intended to be (but never was) a series of Madras schools. One of the two branches of the Madras group, that led by Andrew Bell, was chosen and it tied the school to the Church of England. To Maitland the move would serve to offset the influence of American republican teachers (he was not the only one to be concerned about them), and he obtained public lands for the support of what came to be called the Upper Canada Central School. Charges were made that this action, including the dismissal of Appleton, was arbitrary, and objection taken to having a denominational school. In spite of these handicaps, however, the school had a healthy life. In its twenty-four years 5,514 pupils passed through it. In its first year, 1821, it enrolled ninety-five children of whom fifty-seven were boys. Of that total class only forty-three paid fees.

Since 1807 the Home District Grammar School had been located in York, the 'Blue School' as it was called from the colour of the exterior walls. In 1812 Strachan, who was the most influential educationalist in the history of Ontario, succeeded G. O. Stuart as master and held that position until 1823. The school taught everything from the classics to bookkeeping and its pupils included a long list of men later famous. It too, however, fell victim to the educational policy of a lieutenant governor.[21]

Sir John Colborne was unimpressed by the plan for King's College, another of Strachan's brain children. To him it was madness to go ahead with a university when there was 'no tolerable seminary in the Province to prepare Boys for it.' This conclusion, which may well be challenged, led him to believe that the urgent need was for an advanced secondary school which might additionally form the nucleus of a later university. The result of this train of thought was the institution with the unwieldy name of Upper Canada College and Royal Grammar School, which, as the name suggests, absorbed the District school. Indeed it occupied the old Blue

School building until the new quarters on Russell Square were ready. Upper Canada could not be neatly classified as private or public. It received funds from public lands and for many years was in one way or another under the control of government, but at no time was it a standard unit in the provincial system. Technically it was undenominational, but the principal and teaching staff, with perhaps occasional exceptions, were members of the Church of England. The first principal, J. H. Harris, was a doctor of divinity of Cambridge and the masters were chosen from graduates of Oxford. Since both English universities gave degrees only to Anglicans it followed that the teachers first chosen for Upper Canada were of that persuasion. It is relevant to recall at this point that the clergy, particularly Anglicans and Roman Catholics, had made a great contribution to education in the province, both in private and state schools.

Closing the District school was a mistake since it reduced educational facilities which were in any case hardly sufficient for the town. Moreover, parents in the eastern part of York, where the old Blue School had been, protested at the distance to be covered to Russell Square. In 1836 the school was revived and a year later it had ninety to a hundred pupils. In due course of time it blossomed into the Jarvis Collegiate Institute. Of the children who did not attend any of the institutions mentioned a number went to private schools, both primary and secondary. A considerable proportion of the children went to no school; figures are not available for this period but there is no doubt that they were quite high. For all children the school year was longer than in modern times. A fortnight at Christmas, a week at Whitsun, and six weeks in the summer were the usual holidays.

In addition to the controversy over the relation of churches and schools was that over the curricula, and it centred on Upper Canada College which had a strongly classical programme. The documents in the case[22] are far from enlightening since they confuse the secondary and university levels, and education with the training of mechanics and farmers. It may well be that the balance of subjects at Upper Canada College was too much based on that in the English public schools and in response to criticism it was modified. But the respective cases for vocational training and development of the mind were no more convincing to the unconverted than they have ever been.

In practice entrance to the skilled trades was through apprenticeship, and in the absence of universities much the same principle was applied to young men seeking admission to the professions. In 1831, however, the Law Society began specialized teaching at Osgoode Hall and the first medical school, a private one, was opened by Dr John Rolph in York in 1832. Organized theological colleges had to await the establishment of universities.

Illiteracy was declining (although figures would be no more than guesswork) but the rate of improvement was slowed by the fact that so many people kept their children from school. Some of them thought that education was useless except for the middle class; others claimed that fees and lack of clothes were obstacles. Others again were frank in saying that their children would be more usefully occupied at home.

The York Mechanics' Institute, founded in 1830, was designed for adult education. It and similar institutions in other towns were modelled on those which began in Scotland in 1823 and spread throughout industrial England. The movement in the British Isles was a child of the industrial revolution and arose specifically from the desire of skilled workmen to study science, partly from general interest, partly as an aid in their work. The institutes were successful in Britain, Francis Place noting with satisfaction that he had seen '800–900 clean respectable-looking mechanics paying most marked attention' to a lecture on chemistry. Started by leading citizens and subsidized by government the York institute had a useful life, but its clientele was limited by the fact that Upper Canada was not industrialized. As a result it was overweighted by the middle class. James Lesslie, a shopkeeper and associate of W. L. Mackenzie, had a different explanation of the small number of mechanics who attended. The institute, he wrote in his diary, was regarded with suspicion 'by some of our Gentry,' who believed that the 'lower classes' could be kept as slaves only so long as they were ignorant.

Public services other than education were showing improvement in varying degrees. A few streets were macadamized, yet Julia Lambert wrote that in the spring she was reluctant to go outdoors because of the pervading mud. Maintenance of law continued to rest shakily on the shoulders of part-time constables, but that the law was not without effect was noted by Mary O'Brien who observed that two murderers were convicted at the same assizes. The burning of the legislative buildings in 1824 demonstrated to the *Upper Canada Gazette* the necessity of having 'a properly organized company of Fire-men' instead of *ad hoc* volunteers. Two years later the York Fire Company was established and in 1831 the Hook and Ladder Company. Shortage of water, however, limited their usefulness.

Water was not only in short supply but most of it was probably contaminated. The first terrible cholera outbreak in 1832 dramatically turned public attention to the prevention and cure of disease. Under normal conditions the care of the sick was comparatively good in relation to the standards and scientific knowledge of the time. Of a number of competent doctors Christopher Widmer was perhaps the best known. An English surgeon who had served in the Peninsular War, he came to York about 1815 and there both practised and interested himself in medical education and regulations governing practice.[23] His partner, Dr Peter Diehl, had studied medicine in Montreal and Edinburgh and practised in the former.

The building of a general hospital was made possible by the transfer to that purpose of the surplus funds of the Loyal and Patriotic Society after provision had been made for those who suffered in the war of 1812. The substantial sum of £4,000 allowed for a brick building at the corner of King and John streets in 1820, but could not be stretched to pay for furniture or staff. When the building used by the legislature burned down in 1814 the vacant hospital was taken over for sessions until 1829 when the hospital could finally be opened with the additional aid of annual government grants.

As was the case for some decades competent dentists were rare. Mrs O'Brien wrote in 1829 that 'I did not describe the solemn reverence with which the apothecary at York, to whom I carried my tooth, folded his hands between every ineffectual attempt to lay hold on it, looking up with a gradual inclination of his body to Anthony [her brother] for advice and sanction for the next step.'

Little had been done to improve sanitary conditions in the town. Admittedly this was a weakness not peculiar to York. In 1832 an ex-mayor of New York described that city as 'one huge pigsty' and even a dozen years later a newspaper capped that by charging that the streets were too foul even for the hogs that rambled over them. Not all citizens of York were complacent. Even before cholera was brought to York by immigrants, and while its relentless march was being viewed with alarm, the editor of the *Canadian Freeman*, Francis Collins (who was himself to die in the epidemic), was waging a campaign to clean up the town:

All the filth of the town – dead horses, dogs, cats, manure, etc. heaped up together on the ice, to drop down, in a few days, into the water which is used by almost all the inhabitants on the Bay shore ... There is not a drop of good well-water about the Market-square and the people are obliged to use the Bay water however rotten. – Instead therefore of corrupting the present bad supply, we think the authorities ought rather adopt measures to supply the town from the pure fountain that springs from the Spadina and Davenport Hill, which could be done at a trifling expense.

In further articles Collins wrote of conditions within the town, which, he said, were enough to produce a plague. Remedial measures began. Lime was issued to householders; collection of garbage and sewage was initiated; box drains were installed at some points. All that was good for the future, but meanwhile cholera took its toll. The doctors did what they could but little was known of effective treatment. Circulars were distributed emphasizing the need of medical attention at the first symptom of the disease. In the absence of an isolation hospital the old District school was taken over at the instigation of a hastily organized Board of Health, but a vicious circle limited its value. Fatalities in it were high because individuals became patients only when the disease was too far advanced for the hospital to help, and reports of deaths deterred others from going there at the stage at which treatment might be of avail. It was a grim period, with cholera claiming (according to contemporary statistics) 205 deaths among civilians and twelve in the garrison.[24]

As a seat of government York had always been a political centre, but only after the war, when the population grew and diversified, did partisan politics play any large part. One cannot speak of party politics since parties in the modern sense did not as yet exist.

The constitution of Upper Canada was drawn up in eighteenth-century England and inevitably echoed the politico-social ideas dominant then and hardly modified before the reform bill of 1832. The monarchy, established church, and great landowners were in undisputed control. In a very real sense there was a ruling class, a fact evident in the House of Commons and throughout officialdom, the ranks of which were filled by patronage and from a very limited sector of the population. The accepted view was that those with land, education, and the tradition of public service were best qualified to carry the responsibility of government. Not all the appointees were of ancient lineage but enough were to give colour to the whole.

The British system could not be imported intact to Upper Canada, partly because the social conditions were different and partly because the latter was a colony. The head of government was not a native but a temporary visitor and one whose instructions came from overseas. In general officials were appointed by the same means and on the same principles as those in England, but with some differences. Some of them were sent from England and it proved not always possible to draw those from the cream of the crop. For local recruitment the youth of the colony and its social fabric did not present conditions comparable to those of England, but candidates did come from among a small minority of the population. An important distinction between the metropolitan power and the colony was that in the latter the elected house of the legislature was far more representative than that in Westminster.

Contemporary parallels drawn with the United States were selective and therefore misleading. In early years after the revolution Americans did not question democracy, but they did not all mean the same thing by it. Some Upper Canadians who called for a more popular control of government felt an affinity with Americans who upheld the same cause; and when that cause had a marked success with the election of Andrew Jackson in 1829 they became convinced that they had found the land of the free. The Tories – at least before that date – could have found moral support in the American ruling group who successfully maintained the principle that office holders should come from the 'responsible' class of society and keep their positions indefinitely. Strangely enough, however, the Upper Canadian Tories did not look at their powerful opposite numbers across the line but saw the American scene through the same spectacles as did the Reformers, so that republican and democrat were equated with radical, and radical with reformer.

The political argument in Upper Canada was essentially on the degree of popular control of legislation and administration. In spite of some claims that constitutional change was needed the results sought by all but the most extreme Reformers could be achieved through altered conventions and practices. In itself the constitution of the 1820s was essentially the same as that of modern Canada, in contrast with the reconstruction of the lower house that had to precede change in England. As the situation stood in the twenties and thirties, however, a small group had a stranglehold on government. This they secured by various means. They alone had the ear of the lieutenant governor whose power was very real. They held all the seats in the executive council and most of those in the legislative council, the upper house. And they had wide support among all classes of society in York and elsewhere.

They were called the 'family compact,' a phrase originally applied to an agreement on foreign policy reached between the French and Spanish Bourbons during the Seven Years' War. Though almost meaningless as applied to Upper Canada, it was a useful form of abuse since it somehow had a sinister connotation. It was, however, misleading because it glossed over the fact that the Tories who supported this group were as representative as those who backed the Reform leaders, and because the phrase conveyed the impression of a blood relationship.

In one sense the latter did exist, for in a small place, in which 'society' tended to be a closed circle, marriage tied families together to such an extent that it became dangerous to gossip. John Strachan, often regarded as the epitome of the regime, had married the widow of Andrew McGill of Montreal. His relationship to members of the oligarchy arose out of the lasting influence he had over his former pupils at the Grammar Schools in Cornwall and York. Of the orginal group in York a Heward married a Robinson, an Allan a Gamble, and a Macaulay a Crookshank. In the next generation marriages took place between a Jarvis and a Powell, a Gamble and a Boulton, an Allan and a Robinson, a Macaulay and an Elmsley, a Cartwright and a Macaulay.

These are but examples and the list could be extended indefinitely. On the other hand the small size of the group regarded as eligible offers an easier explanation of office-holding than does nepotism. Some members of the oligarchy were in business as well as government, many were large landowners. Commercially enterprising, they were politically conservative.

They were described by critics as self-seeking, inefficient, and even corrupt. They merited none of these accusations, but were vulnerable on the ground that they found an agreeable coincidence between public duty and private advantage. They had always benefited from land grants and patronage. By a convenient stretch of the imagination they associated opposition to themselves with disloyalty. Government, they argued, must be kept in the hands of loyal, educated, and capable men.

The opposition, lumped indiscriminately into the category of Reformers, had in common only the desire to dislodge the oligarchy. Unfriendly critics could accuse them of self-interest comparable to that of the Tories in that they wanted to seize the loaves and fishes. Some of the opposition had no need of pecuniary aid. Certainly the Baldwins – Dr William Baldwin and his more famous son, Robert – were in that class. Wealthy, somewhat austere, and welcome in the highest society, they were the most effective of the conservative reformers. Even Lieutenant Governor Maitland, who regarded all Reformers as far below the salt, admitted reluctantly that the Baldwins were gentlemen. Some other Reformers, who were substantial members of the community, would not have been accepted by the simple-minded Maitland: men like Joseph Cawthra, the shopkeeper; John Doel, the brewer; or Jesse Ketchum, the tanner.

The most notorious and vocal reformer in York was William Lyon Mackenzie. An immigrant from Scotland he succeeded as a shopkeeper in Dundas but abandoned that secure existence for the uncertainties of journalism. He began publication of the *Colonial Advocate* in Queenston in 1824 but later in the same year transferred it to York. Editor of a highly political paper he had no consistent political philosophy. He distrusted parties of whatever colour because he was essentially a critic and could be sure of no one who held office. His shots were aimed at the Tory oligarchy, who, he was convinced, governed in their own interest and not in that of the 'intelligent yeomanry' of York County, the farmers from whom he received his main support.

Moderation was seldom found in the newspapers of those days but the *Advocate* excelled in extremes and abuse. On a day in 1826 Mackenzie made in his paper violent personal attacks on several of the official families. It was journalism of the gutter, wholly indefensible and unrelated to public questions. Some of the young men whose relations were maligned marched to the newspaper office, did as much damage as they could, and threw the type into the bay. It was a stupid act as Robert Stanton, a Tory journalist, was quick to point out in a letter to his friend, John Macaulay:

Entre nous I fear the zeal of some of our friends has been rather intemperately expressed in the destruction of some of Mackenzie's printing apparatus ... The measure was too strong I fear and may be the means of affording the blackguard a sort of triumph at the expense of respectability – he had gone and we heard of him from persons who saw him at Youngstown, and I have no doubt we should have been entirely rid of him and very soon of his paper too ... the fellow will now I think return to prosecute the parties.[25]

He did indeed, and was awarded substantial damages which enabled him to resuscitate a dying paper. That is one interest of the episode, but it also illustrates the persistence of the oligarchy and their friends in putting themselves in the wrong. Magistrates were, with good reason, accused of being partisans in that they did not quell a disturbance. The stupidity of the young was excelled only by that of their elders in ostentatiously collecting money to recompense law breakers who might have learned sense if their pockets had been emptied. All good grist for Mackenzie's mill – a martyr now, and richer.

As is usually the case only a limited number of people – probably a minority – took an active part in politics or perhaps were even consistently concerned. From that point of view the local press may have been un-representative but probably no more so than in modern times. The papers of the day, however, were in most cases more violently partisan than were later ones. Mackenzie plumbed the lowest depths but nearly all York editors went to extremes. On the Tory side the *Upper Canada Gazette* was an official paper, published by the King's Printer, Robert Stanton. In 1821 it was broken into two parts, that under the old name carrying government announcements and the other (successively called *York Weekly Post, Weekly Register*, and *U. E. Loyalist*) contained the news and editorials. The *Courier of Upper Canada*, which began in 1829, was also a Tory paper. The editor, George Gurnett, was later mayor of Toronto. The *Patriot*, later in the field, was Thomas Dalton's paper; an ex-brewer and ex-radical he had moved far to the right.

In addition to the *Colonial Advocate* the papers consistently in opposition were the *Canadian Freeman* edited by Francis Collins, and the *Canadian Correspondent*. James O'Grady, the radical Roman Catholic priest who quarrelled with the bishop, was editor of the second.[26]

On balance York was Tory. From the war of 1812 until 1834 it elected, with one exception of a few months' duration, government supporters to the assembly. Some of the majorities, however, were narrow. All those connected with the government voted Tory but there was not otherwise a simple split between the prosperous and influential on the one hand and the more obscure on the other. The open ballot left no mysteries. The generally Tory character attributed to Toronto by Charles Dickens and many others was more evident after the shock of the rebellion of 1837, an event which could be construed to mean that only Toryism was safe.

72

Some impressions of the Town of York and of how it changed over fifteen years may be gleaned from the writings of contemporary residents and visitors. John Duncan, an educated Scot who was in York briefly in 1818, found that an hour's walk showed him everything except the garrison. 'This town,' he wrote, 'consists of one street lying parallel to the lake, and the beginnings of two or three more at right angles to it . . . ' The harbour might be a good one if only a well-sheltered bay were necessary to form it, but the entrance was narrow and difficult, and in time of war the harbour was completely defenceless.

Julia Lambert, on a visit from the United States and staying with her sister Mrs George Crookshank, in 1821 reported that 'The houses are a good deal scattered. The town would make much more of an appearance if it were more compact, but probably the dwellings would not be as pleasant . . . There appears to be considerable style kept up, tho' I cannot see the necessity for it, in so small a place, but, I suppose, it is owing to its being the seat of Government and most of the Government Officers being here.' The country in the immediate vicinity of York she found to be uncleared, being held for sale at higher prices. Few roads out of town were good enough for carriages so the ladies rode into the countryside on horseback.[27]

Frances Stewart, an intelligent pioneer in the Kawartha Lakes area, was not attracted by what she saw of York in 1822.

The town or village of York looked pretty from the lake as we sailed up in a schooner [from Kingston], but on our landing we found it not a pleasant place, as it is sunk down in a little amphitheatre cut out of the great bleak forest. The lake in front is full of rushes which have been caught and left to decay in the shallow water, causing it to be very unhealthy. It is not a healthy town (fever and ague are common), and it is said to be much fallen off within the last two years; a deadness hangs over everything. Kingston is much preferred as a place of residence.[28]

John Elmsley, of a leading York family, returning after serving in the Royal Navy, wrote enthusiastically in 1827 of the changes he saw. 'Six magnificent Balls in the space of little more than a fortnight.' A dinner for twenty-two guests was given by Archdeacon Strachan in a house built on ground once considered to be of almost no value. The president of the council, he said, drove in a four-in-hand with outriders when once he would have been glad of an ox cart. Steamboats were plentiful, mail came twice a week, and people were happy and contented.

After she had ridden in 1830 to York, which she frequently visited and knew well, Mary O'Brien entered comments in her diary: 'We marvelled much at the rapid improvements surely but quietly going on in York. The style of these bespeak them to be the effect of increasing prosperity rather than speculation. This makes a very marked distinction between it and the recent towns of the United States, where everything bespeaks hurry and anticipation.'

George Henry, author of one of the innumerable guides for immigrants, looked at York in 1831 and saw much that pleased him: pretty villas, a bridge over the Don, a substantial Roman Catholic church, and elegant stores. York, he wrote, had an extensive trade with the settled townships, and in the winter wheat was brought in for storage and forwarding in the spring. York, too, was the supplier of a wide area of the province. In the harbour steamships regularly landed cargoes and sailing ships were numerous. York was making 'inconceivable progress' with fine new buildings and 'elegant private residences.' Workers were well paid.

Francis Jackson, who had evidently migrated several years earlier from Yorkshire, was a tailor in York, and from his rather different viewpoint he was optimistic too. 'Thirty years ago,' he wrote in 1831, 'it [York] was a forest and 7 years since it was only a small village; it is now a flourishing place, and laid out for a large town.' Well-stocked shops were placed on wide streets, and buildings, of stone or wood, were of good quality.[29]

After an absence of some years Julia Lambert came back to live in York, and in 1833 was struck by the rate at which the value of property was appreciating, as fast as anywhere she knew in the United States. People of small property, she observed, were coming in numbers from the British Isles and investing their money in Upper Canada.

And on that cheerful note the curtain falls on the Town of York.

# 4

# *Government and governed*

In York, as in other Upper Canadian towns, views of the people on the methods by which their local affairs were administered grew increasingly critical in direct ratio to the rise of population and the complexity of the problems. Some minor officials were appointed or elected for duty in the town but it could not be said that there was any local government. In language that reads almost like an afterthought, a statute of 1792 had assigned to the magistrates in quarter sessions responsibility for making orders in any town or village with as many as forty houses.

When he was administrator of the province Peter Russell asked the chief justice to draft a 'police bill' to obviate the difficulties which he had been quick to see in the plans for governing towns. Quite why he used the phrase that has been quoted is puzzling. In England, whence the language and forms of government were largely derived, it was rare and even suspect as foreign. It did not, of course, refer to officers who enforced the law. These were constables. It meant the regulation, discipline, and control of a community; and as such has been used ever since. Russell's argument was that the existing arrangement was simply not sufficient to take care of the great variety of matters which needed attention in a town. The Court of Quarter Sessions, with its responsibility for a District as a whole, could not give enough time to towns and in any case it met only at intervals. He advocated the appointment of full-time superintendents of police who, assisted by two or more local magistrates, would frame such regulations as were deemed to be necessary.[1]

No such bill was drafted, or if drafted was not presented; but similar ideas found their way into later legislation. The justices of the peace were as conscious as anyone of the unsatisfactory character of the régime. They were well aware that they could not give adequate and consistent attention to the towns, and those in the Home District favoured a salaried official as had been proposed by Russell. The first moves, however, did not reach that point. A number of statutes, including one of 1817 that applied to York among other places, created 'police' towns. Such measures contained a more comprehensive list of subjects calling for administration. The Courts of Quarter Session, however, continued to be responsible, gaining only authority for additional taxation of the people in a town.

The next stage in legislation is not always recognized for what it was, the beginning of the system of municipal government more fully worked out in the 1840s. The new plan, applied first to Brockville in 1832, provided for an incorporated police board of five members of whom the four elected in wards would name a fifth. Some support for that method of government, which evidently had been discussed for some time before it was put into effect, was found in York, but majority opinion there was in favour of incorporation as a city.

For six years drafts were drawn up, debated, and amended,[2] until, in 1834, the provincial legislature passed an act (4 William IV, c. 23) which made York the first city of Upper Canada. 'From the rapid increase of the population, commerce and wealth of the Town of York,' the standard preamble read, 'a more efficient system of police and municipal government than that now established has become obviously necessary.' The name was to be changed back to the original Toronto as individuals had from time to time suggested, but nominally on the ground that 'the name of York is common to so many towns and places.' Impressed by this pursuit of tidiness the legislature authorized the lieutenant governor to change the name of any other place called Toronto if such were found.

In thinking of boundaries for the city the draftsmen were faced with a problem, for the community of York was larger than the town. Some of the park lots had seasonal or regular homes and others had been in part subdivided. This produced no difficulty so long as local administration was in the hands of the District, but if Toronto was to have a separate existence its boundaries assumed a new importance. The city itself was not to be much larger than York. On the west it was extended to Bathurst Street and on the north four hundred yards to Crookshank Street. Beyond the city proper was a ring of 'liberties,' – an old English word meaning territory within the jurisdiction of a city rather than a county. The liberties in this case were the park lots to the north, beyond Bathurst Street in the west, roughly from Parliament Street to the Don in the east, and in the south from the water's edge to the far side of the peninsula. The southern liberty became the Port of Toronto, and the remainder were 'attached' to wards (whatever that meant). Whenever the population justified such a change a liberty could be integrated into an existing ward or made into an additional one. If this exercise in geography seems complicated now it may be consoling to recall that the first city council protested that it had no record or plans of the city, the harbour, or the liberties.

From the terms of the statute the purpose of liberties appears to have been to facilitate orderly expansion of the city as the growth of population made that logical, while allowing for uniform administration in the preparatory period. Inhabitants of the liberties were members of the body corporate and subject to the same laws and court as were those of the city. They had, however, no votes and their taxes were on a lower scale. Cartographers showed the city and liberties without distinction between the one and the other, and perhaps that was the way in with they were commonly thought of by contemporaries. Toronto was not an isolated case, for liberties were attached to both Kingston and Hamilton when they became cities. The municipal act of 1858, however, abolished the system with no more ado than the curt sentence: 'There shall be no liberties in outer Wards of the Cities.'

Under the new act the authority of the District and township over the local affairs of Toronto disappeared, the justices of the peace losing both their judicial and administrative jurisdictions. Aldermen and councilmen were to be elected in each of the five wards; but the mayor was not to be elected directly by the citizens as intended in some of the early drafts but chosen from among the aldermen by a majority vote of aldermen and councillors. This was the procedure in force in the police towns that had elections and it had the effect of severely limiting the field of choice. Mayor, aldermen, and councillors together made up the common council of the city, in which was vested legislative authority as defined by the act. A new Court of Record, or Mayor's Court, replaced within the city the Court of Quarter Sessions. The mayor was to preside, but under an amendment of 1846 he was replaced by a recorder who was to be a barrister of five years' standing.

The administrative responsibilities of the municipal government were similar to those in police towns. Roads were to be built, maintained, and kept free of wandering 'cattle, horses, sheep, goats, swine and other animals, geese or other poultry' and of encumbering wheelbarrows, carts, carriages, lumber, stone, and other materials. Horses were not to be driven immoderately on the roads and neither they nor cattle on sidewalks. Regulations were to be made with a view to reducing the hazard of fire; one or more fire companies were to be established; and cisterns for water provided. 'Good and wholesome water' for domestic use was to be found (as if that was easy). Some control was to be exercised over retail trade in respect of price, weight, and size. A share of the moral code was passed to the city fathers: 'the due observance of the Sabbath,' suppression of 'tippling houses,' and the regulation or suppression of all billiard tables. The need was recognized 'to regulate and prevent the firing of guns, pistols, and other fire-arms.'

Payment of civic officials took different forms. The mayor was to receive between £100 and £500 a year, a wide range indeed. The chamberlain (treasurer) was to retain such percentage of moneys paid to him as might be determined by the common council. Other officials were to be allowed salaries or perquisites of office. Constables, assessors, collectors, and other 'inferior officers' might be employed at rates set by the council.

To meet the salary bill and all other expenses of government the city was to have limited resources. Except to pay off the debt on the market building it could borrow money only to the amount of five years' prospective revenue. Residents of the city and liberties continued to be subject to District taxes until an amendment of 1837 made them exempt under an arrangement by which the city paid a lump sum of £400 to the District each year. Their Toronto taxes, before and after that year, were on real and personal property but with a ceiling of four pence in the pound of assessed value within the city and two pence in the liberties. Assessed value was set not according to time, place, and circumstances but found in a provincial list of fixed values of land, buildings, and other possessions. Any town lot, for example, was valued at £50; a house at from £20 to £60 according to type of construction and number of fireplaces; a horse of three years or more at £8; a four-wheeled closed carriage kept for pleasure at £100; and so on. Some further income came to the city from commutation of labour on roads. On the whole the prospects were for revenue insufficient to meet the demands of routine expenditure and needed public works, but the pressure in favour of low taxes was strong. Money, it seemed, was to be as short as in the days of rule by the Court of Quarter Sessions.

In the course of long debates on civic administration before 1834 the virtues of self-government had been extolled, but its effective practice did not come automatically. The only opportunity previously afforded to the citizens was in provincial elections and it is perhaps not surprising that they did not at once lower their sights when called upon to vote for aldermen and councillors. Both Tory and Reform groups swung into action through their respective newspapers and at public meetings. As it turned out the vote (which was open) was not entirely on party lines, but in general it was. Views on how the city should be governed and what programmes should be followed by the council received little attention. W. L. Mackenzie pressed the argument that the statute of incorporation, which he had criticized, provided powers which could be abused; and that evil results could be avoided only by putting the Reformers into office. The election campaign, in short, threw little light on the problems of the city and how they might be solved.

The Reformers won the election as they did the provincial one a few months later. The first council for Toronto consisted of twelve Reformers of various persuasions and eight Tories; and if there had been any doubt about party lines during the campaign there was none after the council took office. The first item on the agenda was the election of a mayor. Mackenzie was now, thanks in part to blocks in the Tory mind, at the height of his influence in Upper Canada and he was named mayor on a straight party vote in the council. From any point of view it would be difficult to imagine a worse choice. To the Tory minority he could do no right, and if he had set out to justify such an opinion he could not have done better. His interest was not in the administration of a city but in provincial politics. By nature he was a controversialist, a critic, a fighter against everything of which he disapproved (and that was a long list). He gave less time and attention to the duties of his office than were needed, and always he was looking over his shoulder at the provincial scene. The practical day-to-day affairs of the city interested him little. As a self-appointed crusader he spurned compromise and moderation.[3]

Given this situation the first year of the city was almost wholly devoid of accomplishment. Disputes, bickering, and party advantage took the place of efforts to build solid foundations for a new order. The Tory members were not without guilt and probably would have been unreasonable about any Reform mayor; but one who gave a lead would have suffered less obstruction. Even Mackenzie's own followers began to show a lack of confidence. A little was done on roads and sewers, and financial chaos was staved off when Truscott, Green and Company lent money to the city when no other bankers would. By the autumn of 1834 the city administration was virtually at a standstill and the voters had had enough. In the next annual election only five Reform candidates were elected as against fifteen Tories. The fact that in 1836 the party positions were again reversed indicates that the vote after the first year was specifically a reaction against Mackenzie and his friends. Meanwhile the second mayor, R. B. Sullivan, did something to set the council on the right path, to face the needs of Toronto rather than to use the municipal forum for provincial debates. After all, the whole point of the act incorporating Toronto was to provide local government that was by as well as for the citizens, and not something incidental to the District or the province.

One of the specific criticisms of Mackenzie was that he failed to deal effectively with the second cholera outbreak in 1834. Robert Stanton, editor of the *Upper Canada Gazette*, was not without political bias, but his letters to John Macaulay reflect an opinion shared in some degree by a large number of citizens.[4] Throughout August 1834 he gave news of the epidemic. As a member of the Board of Health he emphasized the necessity of immediate treatment and of taking personal precautions. Cases, he said, were numerous and severe, and most were fatal. The arrangements made by the city authorities he found neither consistent nor effective. How scandalous it was, he protested, for the mayor at such a time to be irritating the public mind with his political meetings and his *Advocate*. Hot weather brought more cases and the Board of Health was breaking up, interfered with and thwarted by the mayor. In the middle of August Stanton reported at least twenty-five deaths but the situation improved after that. Not all was well after the change of administration in 1835. In May of that year the Board of Health (which had apparently been in touch with the Medical Board of the province) concluded that 'the city is at present in a most deplorable state of filth and uncleanliness – so much so that the Board of Health cannot dwell upon the prospect of the ensuing summer without the most serious apprehensions.'

The second cholera outbreak had not been as bad as the first and the fear of a third in the summer of 1835 proved to be unfounded. Complaint of the dirty state of the city and the consequent danger to health was a hardy perennial and before long the citizens had something else to worry about. In 1836 an economic depression spread from England to the United States where it had devastating results, particularly on the banks; and it moved on to Upper Canada. In the Home District, as elsewhere, the word that 618 banks had failed in the United States inevitably raised the spectre of similar events locally, with losses to depositors and shareholders. W. L. Mackenzie, whose understanding of finance was clouded by political prejudice, did his best to make matters worse by encouraging withdrawals from the Bank of Upper Canada and attempting to organize a run on it and so secure its collapse. He seemed to be incapable of comprehending that his methods could lead only to suffering on the part of those who would be caught if the bank did fail. It was crippled but it survived. Financial stringency handicapped the city administration as it did business. In 1837 the council was not able to raise any loan and as an alternative issued its own bonds bearing interest and payable in six months. These proved to be popular and helped to relieve the shortage of cash.

Before the economic depression had run its course the people of Toronto were faced with an armed rebellion in the province, with Mackenzie returning in another role to plague them. In the security of a century or more later those who have looked back on the events of 1837–8 have been prone to think in abstract terms, to forget that to contemporaries the immediate prospect was of fire and blood and not constitutional debate. Many of those who lived in Toronto knew what war meant for they had been through it in 1812, and not a few had lost relatives or friends in the fighting at that time. Rumours spread faster than accurate information. In the city it was known that a rebel force was building up in York County, uncomfortably close; but how large or effective it was could only be guessed, It was a reasonable assumption that it would march on Toronto as the seat of government. Little is known about how the citizens as a whole viewed the rebellion. Not long before Mackenzie had been something of a hero, and the names of a few men in Toronto who concurred in his plans for violence are known. The indications, however, are that, while there was discontent with the existing government, only small numbers in Toronto were prepared to solve that problem by shooting their fellow subjects. If force of arms had always been considered the appropriate response to imperfect government the years of peace in Canada could have been quickly counted.

It is difficult to decide whether governmental or rebel leaders showed greater incompetence. To the confused mind of the lieutenant governor, Francis Bond Head, rebellion was bad form and should not happen at least while he was in office: therefore it would not happen. Most of his principal advisers reached no higher intellectual level. At first they insisted that the stories of men arming were poppycock, and when convinced that something was going on panicked into belief in a great force of five thousand men instead of sending scouts to find the scale of mobilization. If York had been vulnerable in 1813 Toronto was far more so in 1837. Head had foolishly sent all the regular units to Lower Canada instead of retaining a small nucleus to which militia could be attached. More than that, he frustrated all efforts to put militia regiments into a state of readiness. Most of the members of the oligarchy seem to have concurred in the stubborn refusal to take precautions; and the fact that they shouldered muskets in a gentlemanly way at the last moment arose only out of their failure to act at the proper time. The amateur strategists who had been so quick to condemn Sheaffe in 1813 fumbled badly when the ball was thrown to them.

The rebel cause suffered even more from ineffective leadership. It soon became evident that Mackenzie's lack of success as mayor was not an isolated incident. He had little capacity for administration and none for keeping his head in a crisis. Just how many potential recruits for a rebel army were in York County and beyond will never be known, but not a large force was needed to catch Toronto unawares. On the other hand the men had to be organized, fed, and armed. Virtually all contemporary accounts agree that none of these conditions were met. It is difficult to understand why men, however heroically, were setting forth to battle armed with pikes and pitchforks. In Toronto six thousand arms stood unguarded to be taken in a quick raid, and throughout the country shotguns must have been plentiful. Even the latter would have been quite formidable against inexperienced defenders.

Toronto, in its then boundaries, was at no point entered by rebels. Amidst alarums and excursions two military engagements can be distin-

Death of Colonel Moodie at Montgomery's Tavern in 1837

guished. Early in December a group of Mackenzie's supporters marched down Yonge Street as far as the modern Carlton Street where they encountered a picket of some thirty men under the command of Sheriff Jarvis, stationed there contrary to Head's orders. In the twilight the defenders fired at close range, and although they apparently hit no one the shock drove the attackers helter-skelter up Yonge Street. The members of the picket equally lost their nerve and made for the south, unconscious of the fact that their one effort had made it impossible for Mackenzie to get his men back on what was now an undefended road. By this time the issue was resolved, but that was not evident and a substantial force of militia could now be put together. Under the command of Colonel James Fitzgibbon, a soldier of some experience, it set out in numbers of more than a thousand toward the rebel centre at Montgomery's Tavern. Meanwhile Mackenzie had secured the help of Colonel Anthony Van Egmond, a Hollander with long military service, as commander but he could get no reinforcements and his own wild antics cancelled out Van Egmond's ability. He took to robbing stage coaches and found other ways of wasting time or causing confusion. His little army was in any case not large enough, or well enough equipped or trained to resist a determined attack. Fitzgibbon had no difficulty in dispersing the hapless rebels. After a skirmish north of Toronto – and it was no more than that – the disillusioned rebel soldiers went back to their farms and Mackenzie escaped to the United States.[5]

There he and other renegade Canadians did all they could to exploit sympathy with the rebel cause. Some of the Americans who were prepared to take up arms and march into Upper Canada were simply adventurers, but the motives of others recall the thinking of 1812. The poor benighted Canadians, so it seemed, still groaned under British rule. On principle they must be rescued from this grim fate, but with the agreeable by-product of cheap or free land as recompense for the idealists. Perhaps among the Americans who marched into Canada were some who had no thought of annexation, but many more were encouraged by the hints in Mackenzie's writing and talking that Upper Canada would become part of the United States. As in the purely Canadian stage of the rebellion no one could be sure how serious the threat was, but this time proper precautions were taken. British regulars were stationed at Toronto as elsewhere in Upper Canada and the militia was called into active service in large numbers. Some of the plans for attack included the capture of Toronto; and although such incursions as were made were repulsed without difficulty uncertainty and apprehension were inevitable.

To judge by the formal record the city council had no comment to make on the events of December 1837 but in 1838 they were much concerned about the threats from across the border. Discussing a warning from the lieutenant governor of the danger of an attack on the city their first idea was to appoint ten extra constables, whose method of meeting an advancing army was not explained. On second thoughts they concluded that defence of Toronto against what were variously described as foreign blackguards, rebels and pirates, and lawless banditti could best be organized by enrolling volunteers to supplement the existing military units. A committee was appointed for each ward to visit all adult males and invite them to enlist.[6]

The fact that the rebels were assisted by groups of Americans made them all the more unpopular. Responsible Reformers had been in no way connected with the rebellion and wholly disapproved of it, but by many officials and members of the public their innocence was not believed. Sir George Arthur, the lieutenant governor in succession to Bond Head, received many alarming reports and for a time tended to exaggerate the strength of disloyalty; but even so he was worried by 'the alacrity of those who had been too ready to testify their Utter Loyalty or to gratify bad passions by giving information against persons *suspected* of treasonable practices.'[7] The evolutionary Reformers in Toronto were for the time being under a cloud as the city, which for some years had been a meeting place for left and right, now lurched heavily to starboard.

The conservative trend in Toronto that followed the rebellion embraced a wide range of people and ideas – some moderate, some extreme – but essentially it rested on two factors. The immediate one was horror at armed rebellion. The other was revulsion against the purposes of the rebellion, or what seemed to be the purposes. With few exceptions the people of Toronto did not want to be republicans or Americans. By pulling the reform movement to the extreme left the rebellion automatically distorted the opposition to reform. It is idle to expect shooting to be answered by detached logic.

Had it not been for changes in the political framework the rebellion might have produced in Toronto no more than damage to the Reformers and advantage to the Tories. As it was the oligarchy centred in Toronto lost the stage on which it had long performed, sometimes wisely, sometimes not. The Province of Upper Canada, in which Toronto was struggling toward a position of leadership, was merged into a greater whole. The rebellion in Upper Canada, together with the much more serious one led by Louis-Joseph Papineau in Lower Canada, induced the Earl of Durham to reconsider his refusal to investigate the causes of discontent in British North America. He spent only a few days in Upper Canada and it was claimed, with some reason, that his description of the province was inaccurate. Certainly he made minor errors of fact, but it is doubtful that that had any bearing on his general conclusion that a new régime was needed for the Canadas. When the union of the provinces, which was one of his main recommendations, came into force the old Upper Canada was no more.

Toronto was not even to be the capital of the new Province of Canada, for on Kingston, the old rival which commercially had been outpaced, was bestowed that honour and advantage. Gloomy forecasts were made of the evil results, of depreciation of property and decline of business. The city council voted £100 to send one or more delegates to England, and the mayor wrote to the mayor of Quebec City suggesting a common front in support of a plan for the legislature to meet alternately in the two cities. Jarvis moved for an address to the Queen on 'the great loss the citizens of Toronto have sustained in the depreciation of their property by the removal of the seat of government from this city.' Her Majesty was to be encouraged to intervene because of the great possibilities for British emigrants in the Toronto area; and she was to be impressed by the argument that Toronto would become the centre of population of the united province and thus be the logical capital. Such protests were bound to be made, but much water had flowed over the dam since the similar threat in 1815. Certainly to lose the status of capital was a blow, but in the intervening thirty-six years Toronto had developed stronger foundations for its economic life.

As it turned out, moreover, the loss was only partial. The seat of government was transferred to Montreal in 1844, but after the riots and destruction of the parliament building in 1849 an awkward arrangement was made – that which has been mentioned as an earlier proposal – under which the capital moved periodically between Quebec and Toronto.

The union of 1841 brought together not only two areas but two societies, different in important respects. Durham, with the best intentions but a singular lack of judgment, anticipated that union would result in the peaceful absorption of the French by the English; whereas the real question proved to be how two diverse groups could, to use Durham's own phrase, exist within the bosom of a single state. In Upper Canada most of the small minority of French origin were close to the Ottawa River and in Toronto no word of French was heard. A substantial number of Roman Catholics – ones determined to protect their rights – were in Toronto, but they were Irish and had little sense of affinity with the Roman Catholics of Lower Canada. Two subjects on which there might have been severe controversy were eased by the device of legislation applying to only one of the component parts of the province. Civil law was separated in that way and so were the school systems.

The second main proposal made by Durham cut across opinion within the old Upper Canada (and which was usually still called that, even officially). He was insistent that British North America should have responsible government, that is, the cabinet system under which the administration is under such control as the legislature may care to exercise. This political flower had been nurtured in a Toronto garden, planted and cultivated by the Baldwins, father and son, and offered by the latter to Durham. Bond Head had shied away as if it had been poison ivy and the British government first regarded it as quite the wrong species for a colony. Yet its admirers increased, and as they became a political force battle raged between supporters and opponents in the province. To Toronto Tories the practice of responsible government would mean the end of the framework of government that they had known and valued; and certainly it would mean the end of the oligarchy.

Opinions were publicly expressed, mainly in the press, by candidates for the Toronto seats in the legislature, or by persons resident in Toronto but running in other constituencies. The number of Toronto seats varied between two and three and those who held them fell into no simple party pattern. To the first parliament of the united province Toronto elected two moderate Reformers, J. H. Dunn and Isaac Buchanan, with the Tory mayor, Henry Sherwood, as the third member. From the election of 1844, at which responsible government was turned down, Conservatives were generally successful, a striking exception being the election of George Brown who held a Toronto seat from 1858 to 1861. In the new arena some old names appear, such as Boulton, Ridout, and Robinson. Some of the most influential Toronto politicians, Francis Hincks and Robert Baldwin among them, never held Toronto seats.[8]

The newspapers published in Toronto offered fare for the politically minded of most shades. The *Patriot*, under changing owners and editors, continued to uphold the Tory cause. In 1854 it was merged with the *Leader* which, published from 1852 by James Beaty, was first a moderate Reform and then a moderate Conservative paper. The *British Colonist* was a Conservative paper which began publication in 1838 and, after various vicissitudes, was sold to James Beaty in 1860. Of the principal Reform newspapers Francis Hincks' *Examiner* began in 1838 as the first Reform paper after the rebellion. It merged in 1855 with the *Globe* which was founded in 1844 by George Brown at the request of a group of Reformers and with some financial assistance from them. Its outlook was provincial and its circulation was geographically wide.

The menacing outbreak of cholera in 1834 and the subsequent economic depression were overshadowed at the time – and have been in this history – by the political and military crisis of 1837-8. The rebellion had two incidental effects on those problems. Young men found temporary employment in the militia during the prolonged period of invasion or threatened invasion, and Dr John Rolph's connection with the uprising forced him to abandon his medical school and seek sanctuary in the United States. Otherwise the problems of health and welfare, sidelined for the time, awaited solution.

Hospitals were considered to be almost entirely for the poor, for those who could not be adequately cared for at home. The new General Hospital, opened on Gerrard Street in 1855, was, with its large wards, intended to meet this need. Two dispensaries of the sixties were similarly for the poor. The Toronto Eye and Ear Dispensary was a public charity financed by private subscriptions. It was open from nine until four, six days a week. The Toronto Dispensary was supported by the Church of England. Open for two hours in the middle of each day, it had six attending physicians. A hospital for the mentally ill had long been delayed and only temporary quarters were available until 1850 when the large Provincial Lunatic Asylum, designed by J. G. Howard, was opened on Queen Street West. Somewhat curiously it was announced that 'idiots and persons afflicted with paralysis, are inadmissable.' Joseph Workman, considered to be the pioneer of psychiatry in Canada, became superintendent in 1854. He found that the asylum was in bad condition physically since the drains in the building were unconnected with any sewer. That remedied, he turned his attention to methods of treatment of patients. His ideas were criticized at the time but they were humane and imaginative.[9]

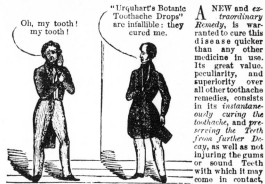

## TOOTHACHE CURED IN A MINUTE!

Oh, my tooth! my tooth!

"Urquhart's Botanic Toothache Drops" are infallible: they cured me.

A NEW and *extraordinary Remedy*, is warranted to cure this disease quicker than any other medicine in use. Its great value, peculiarity, and superiority over all other toothache remedies, consists in its *instantaneously curing the toothache*, and *preserving the Teeth from further Decay*, as well as not injuring the gums or sound Teeth with which it may come in contact, which is more than can be said of any other remedy in existence. It is also rather pleasant than otherwise to some people.

For Sale by S. F. URQUHART, Wholesale and Retail Agent in Canada, Temperance Buildings, Yonge Street.

Dangerous or useless patent medicines were still widely sold and quack doctors not wholly eliminated, but the progress of schools of medicine and surgery ensured a continuing supply of trained doctors. Back from exile in 1843 Rolph reopened his school which was enlarged under the name of the Toronto School of Medicine. In 1844 a faculty of medicine was attached to King's College, and in 1850 two doctors, E. M. Hodder and James Bovell, organized the Upper Canada School of Medicine. The Toronto *Directory* for 1868–9 listed seventy-two physicians and surgeons. One of these was described as 'eclectic' but a 'clairvoyant physician' was in a category of his own. At that time there were apparently only nine dentists.

Hospital and medical resources were severely tested in the late forties when Toronto, in common with other parts of the Canadas, was almost overwhelmed by the tragic immigration of Irish, who brought with them disease and want. In 1847 John Strachan wrote that nearly six hundred people were in temporary hospitals. Two physicians died as did laymen who attempted to help the stricken newcomers. 'This town,' said Strachan at the end of 1847, 'has during the whole season resembled a lazar house.' He found, too, that among the Irish were old people and children who could not work and able-bodied men who refused to do so.[10]

Provision was with difficulty made for aid to the poor, the unemployed, and the disabled. During the depression of the late thirties the provincial legislature voted £350 for the poor and distressed of Toronto. In 1836 a meeting on behalf of the poor was called in the town hall, and of those who attended one was surprised and disappointed to hear no mention of a workhouse, which in his opinion would have ended begging. The city council, too, was worried not only by the suffering it saw but by the practice of begging. Early in 1837 it authorized the expenditure of £40 to fit up the old court house on Richmond Street as an almshouse, and a few months later voted another £40 for relief. In July it thought of tapping another source by asking that a collection for the poor be taken at St James', the money to be distributed by the mayor. In November members of council viewed 'with great satisfaction the laudable and praiseworthy exertions of the principal Inhabitants of this city in their determination to suppress the degrading practice of street begging and the provision made for the support of the destitute in the city convinced as they are of the expediency of assisting the Inhabitants in that measure they deem it expedient that the sum of £100 be appropriated toward the support of the House of Industry.'

The depression of the late fifties again caused widespread suffering. The municipal authorities still had but slim resources to apply to welfare but they did accept a degree of responsibility. In 1859 the mayor expressed in council his deep concern about the distress of mechanics, labourers, and clerks, half of whom, he said, were out of work. Some were destitute and one had committed suicide because he had no food for the family. Industrious and deserving people, the mayor went on, were in misery. He proposed that the city should, so far as its funds allowed, initiate public works. Examining the city's authority in the field of social welfare he noted that by-laws could be passed for public relief, or to provide almshouses, a house of correction, a house of industry, a workhouse, or a house of refuge. The last would soon be ready for use and the mayor suggested that the municipality should feel free to send to it the idle, the lewd, dissolute, or vagrant. It is noticeable that through all such discussion a distinction was drawn between the deserving and the undeserving poor.

Private charity carried much of the burden, both in the form of contributions of money and in welfare organizations. Six ladies of Toronto wrote to the mayor on the problem of youthful vagrancy. They proposed the establishment of a boys' lodging house similar to those in London, Manchester, and New York. The house, which was to have that luxury a bathroom, would be supported by public subscription. Each boy in it would be given a slice of bread morning and night and would deposit two pence a day against clothing. The Boys' Home, which appears soon after this and had prominent citizens on the board of management, may well have been the result of this initiative. The Girls' Home was for 'the rescue from vice of young girls, and the bestowal of careful attention on their religious, moral, and temporal welfare.' It was also for the maintenance of children under seven years of age. At the end of the sixties it was preparing to take over a new building on land given by William Cawthra and which would have accommodation for a hundred children. A statute of 1862 incorporated the Toronto Female Industrial School 'designed for the education, maintenance, and protection of young females, who would otherwise be exposed to evil influences, and to promote and encourage habits of honest industry.' In the fifties and sixties the Toronto House of Industry, the Orphans' Home and Female Aid Society, and the House of Providence and Orphan Asylum were all active. Most of these and similar organizations were supported in whole or in part by private funds and guided by committees of citizens.

Were there, then, many people who suffered from extreme poverty? The number certainly varied from time to time, depending on the extent of unemployment and the peaks of immigration of those with no funds and few skills. Reliable statistics of unemployment, of wage rates, and of the standard of living are not available for the forties and fifties. One long-time resident of Toronto who worked his way up from the ranks looked back at the forties when he was first employed and was satisfied that the purchasing power of salaries and wages was then as high as it was in 1914. In his youth $500 a year was considered to be a very good salary for a family that could rent an adequate house for $100 to $125 a year. Beef or pork, he said, were 5 to 7 cents a pound, chickens 25 cents a pair, and eggs 10 cents a dozen. Bricklayers were paid about $1.25 to $1.50 a day, carpenters $1, and labourers 75 cents.'[11]

Toronto was a fairly typical small city, commercial like the others, and with the free enterprise economy of the day. As the scale of business increased so did the number of wealthy or comparatively wealthy men. Few of them had names famous in early York. More room was made for a white collar class employed in large wholesale firms and financial establishments. That made for a slice of the middle class that was neither rich nor poor but had for the most part security and could live in modest comfort. It was for such people that lines of respectable houses reached out in one street after another.

The population of Toronto was predominantly British and Christian. When Sigmund Samuel's parents came to Toronto in 1855 they looked about for fellow Jews and found only a handful. Marcus and Samuel Rossin, who had come from Germany in 1842, were jewellers and the builders of the hotel that bore their name. Abraham and Samuel Nordheimer were also Germans. The former was a teacher of music to Sir Charles Bagot's family in Kingston, and in 1844 moved to Toronto. By 1851 only fifty-one Jews were known to be living in Toronto, but five years later they are said to have had control of eleven clothing stores, ten jewellery stores, and four or five tobacco shops.[12]

The number of American negroes in Toronto has been worked out from directories but the results are contradictory and uncertain. A detailed list by families, drawn up in 1840 by an unknown hand, gives a total of close to five hundred of all ages and sexes. Occupation and religious affiliation were also given. In addition to labourers all skilled trades were well represented, and there were odd shopkeepers and an innkeeper. A few women were hairdressers. As would be expected the Baptist Church came first but a considerable number of families were Methodist, with the Church of England coming a poor third and only two families shown as Presbyterians.[13]

The American Fugitive Slave Law of 1850, permitting the recapture of slaves who had escaped to free states, greatly accelerated the exodus to Canada and the efforts of Canadians in the underground railway and settlement in the province. In 1851 Toronto was chosen for the North American Convention of Coloured Freemen, the sponsors apparently believing that the population would be sympathetic, and many of them undoubtedly were. The Elgin Association, which organized large-scale settlement of negro immigrants in Kent County, was actively supported by Peter Brown, his son George, and other Toronto men.

Another cause that the *Globe* supported was sabbatarianism, opposing, for example, the carriage of mail on Sunday. Provincial legislation represented, of course, much more than Toronto opinion but was consistent with it. A statute of 1845 (8 Vict., c. xlv) set up wide defences against profanation of the Lord's Day. The only allowable business was in conveying travellers, selling drugs, or performing works of charity. No public meetings were to be held; no games or sports; no public bathing in any city. A law of 1856 (19 Vict., c. xlix) made lotteries illegal at any time. Probably the greatest effort made in improving public morals was directed toward temperance. At a time when Toronto had a tavern in almost every block and whisky was twenty-five cents a gallon, excessive drinking was creating many problems. Several organizations were established by citizens, many of them connected with or inspired by temperance groups in the United States. Regular meetings were held at which individuals were encouraged to sign pledges to abstain from drinking, and pressure was exerted to secure legislation to limit or prohibit the sale of liquor.

In varying degrees the churches were involved in such causes as have been mentioned and in other aspects of public and private morals. The Baptists were particularly concerned with slavery and the well-being of those who escaped. The Methodist Church was strongly prohibitionist, even if three of the principal brewers of Toronto were members of its congregations. The Roman Catholic and Anglican churches were less convinced of the desirability of prohibition or of full-scale sabbatarianism; but in general it was accepted that the churches were necessarily and properly involved in morals.

In general the churches kept pace with a growing population. In 1837 John Macaulay wrote that he had never seen so many communicants in St James'. At that date it was still the only Anglican church but others followed before long. The first St Paul's, a wooden building designed by

St Stephen's Anglican Church, opened in 1858

J. G. Howard, was opened on Bloor Street (outside the city proper) in 1842. In 1861 it was moved on rollers to the Potters' Field west of Yonge Street and replaced by a stone church designed by E. Radford. Trinity Church on King Street, St George's on John Street, and Holy Trinity, the gift of an Englishwoman, belong to the forties. St James' itself was rebuilt after the fire of 1849 to the design of F. W. Cumberland and Thomas Ridout, although the building in its present form was not completed until the seventies.

The Roman Catholic cathedral of St Michael's, no less fine, was erected in 1845 not far away, designed in the main by William Thomas and in part by Henry Langley. The third in the Gothic group in this same area, the Methodist Metropolitan Church, came later, in 1870. By 1846 the *Directory* showed that the total of churches in Toronto, the liberties, and Yorkville was twenty-two. In addition to those mentioned the list embraced three branches of Presbyterianism, three of Methodism, Congregational-ists, Unitarians, Baptists, a Christian Meeting House, a Disciples Meeting House, an African Baptist church, and an African Methodist church. Although figures of membership are untrustworthy the order of size was Church of England, Roman Catholic, and then Presbyterian and Methodist approximately equal.

The path toward an agreed pattern of higher education was long, winding, and thorny. A paper start had been made in 1827 in the charter for King's College. John Strachan, the designer and moving spirit, intended it to be a Church of England college but without the restrictions which, in Oxford and Cambridge, excluded students on religious grounds. He claimed that it had caused him a great deal of trouble to have both teachers and students freed from religious tests and was prepared to make further concessions. From the first, however, King's College was bitterly attacked, not so much from a belief that education should be separated from denominational religion (although that view was held by some contemporaries) or even because it was to be in Toronto, but rather because in the field of higher education it gave to one church a monopoly of funds long since set aside in the form of public lands.

King's College and its successors were battered by controversy led by men to whom controversy was second nature, among them Strachan, Egerton Ryerson, and George Brown. Strachan was, and is, usually cast for the role of villain. As a Tory and firm believer in the British connection he might at least have been expected to be in tune with governors, but in fact he as often disputed with them as he agreed. George Arthur, writing to John Colborne in 1839, described in words floating in a sea of exclamation marks, how a committee of the executive council had delved into the curious affairs of the still inactive college: 'The sum of nearly £7,000 has been expended in enclosing, embellishing and keeping in order the avenues and grounds of King's College! Another sum of about £5,000 has been expended in payment of salaries, office incidents etc! The land purchased for the site of the college cost £4,400 thus between 16 and 1700£ have been expended before a stone of the university has been laid.'

Advances had annually been made to Upper Canada College, and it seemed to Arthur that both institutions could not go on. He therefore proposed to delay King's College as Colborne had earlier done. Strachan expressed willingness to explain finances that indeed seem strange, but the offer was not accepted. Meanwhile the Presbyterians and Methodists had set up their own colleges, Queen's at Kingston and Victoria at Cobourg. Still only gardening in the King's College grounds. The second governor general of the united province, Sir Charles Bagot, was more interested in getting something done than investigating the past of King's College. He insisted that the 'scandal' of twelve years' inactivity be ended and in April laid the cornerstone of the college. Designed by Thomas Young in classical style it was placed where the main parliament building now stands, for at that time the later Queen's Park was included in the college grounds. A move forward at last, but Bagot also urged that teaching begin at once, there being 'plenty of public buildings in Toronto now lying useless.' The parliament buildings on Front Street, vacated when the legislature moved to Kingston, were chosen as a temporary abode and there instruction began in the autumn of 1843. When the legislature returned in 1849 the college was ejected and tried, unsuccessfully, to squeeze itself into the one completed wing of its own building in Queen's Park, which had been used as a college residence.

But more was involved than a physical move for in 1849 King's College was legislated out of existence by Robert Baldwin's act. This, one of several attempts to reconstruct the university scheme in Canada West, created the University of Toronto which was to take over the endowment and be a wholly secular institution under government control. Now the shoe was on the other foot and the major churches protested against a godless university. The Presbyterians and Methodists had their colleges and the irrepressible Strachan started all over again at the point he had reached in 1827. The lineal descendant of the deceased King's was the University of Trinity College, and for it Kivas Tully designed an interesting building on Queen Street West. The resources of teaching organizations and the number of students were now spread too thinly, but the governor general, Lord Elgin, who might have acted as mediator, was too opinionated to be useful. The only assets left to the stranded University of Toronto were a small teaching staff and the endowment, and it could be sure of keeping neither.

Dissatisfaction with the act of 1849 induced the passing of another in 1853 under which the university became only an examining body with University College as the teaching unit, and with provision for any other college to be affiliated. Here was the germ of the later federation; but for the moment the perceptible interest among other colleges was in sharing the famous endowment which, under the new act, was to spread beyond the University of Toronto only when there was a surplus. Universities do not have surpluses.

Once again the university was turned out of a building when the provincial government took over the Queen's Park building, sending the university back to Front Street, only to reverse that when the legislature came back to Toronto once more. In this maddening game of musical chairs the old King's College building was taken over as a lunatic asylum in 1856 and the unhappy university held its lectures in a little building formerly used for the medical school only. The university could have named some candidates for the lunatic asylum.

After that last blow a successful effort was made to secure governmental authority for a new building and a start was made at once on University College at the location it now occupies. One incidental but not unimportant objective was to protect the endowment by putting some of it into the immovable form of bricks and mortar. The remainder was still vulnerable. In 1859 the Wesleyan Methodists started a campaign for the division of the funds. Egerton Ryerson sharpened his pen and the Methodist Conference sent to the assembly a memorial that was referred to a select committee. Representatives of Victoria, Trinity, and Queen's brought before it charges of waste, inefficiency, and improper monopoly of funds. The committee never reported because it reached no agreement, Ryerson being balanced by George Brown with his firm belief in non-sectarian education. The Ryerson group then secured the replacement of John Langton as chancellor by James Patton, who was in accord with their views. At the same time they obtained the appointment of a royal commission of which the membership was heavily weighted against the University of Toronto. Its report recommended giving control of policy and a share of the endowment to affiliated colleges. At that point two young graduates of the university and members of the senate, Adam Crooks (later minister of education) and Edward Blake (to be a leading lawyer) called a public meeting which condemned the commission's report, and they then persuaded the senate to record the same conclusion. The University of Toronto, in Sir Daniel Wilson's words, had 'escaped extinction.'

While the smoke of battle still hung over the university scene the modern pattern of primary and secondary education was being evolved. In a series of statutes between 1841 and 1871 the plan of common and grammar schools (that is, of public and high schools) was radically revised. Instead of the unsure procedure under which common schools depended on local initiative there were to be throughout each county schools financed by a combination of provincial grants and local taxation. Provision was made for 'separate' common schools when these were desired by communities, ones that would be specifically Roman Catholic or Protestant. The remainder – the great majority – would have non-denominational religious instruction, which sounded more feasible than it proved to be.

A scheme which looked tidy enough in the statutes was not implemented in Toronto without a series of misadventures, with the result that little if any progress was made for some years. The difficulties were financial. The 'school fund,' the total of provincial and municipal contributions, was earmarked for salaries of teachers, and the implied assumption that the city would provide buildings proved not to be sound. In 1843 and part of 1844 nothing was accomplished. From the middle of 1844 to the end of 1847 education was kept alive by adding to the school fund rates imposed on parents. Worse was to come. The act of 1847 allowed for standardization through a single board of school trustees in a city; but as it did not authorize charges on parents the new board in Toronto found itself with no evident alternative to free schools, whether or not that had been the intention of those who framed the act. With the government grant schools could be operated for half the year, but the city council refused to provide money for the remainder. Consequently the schools were closed from the middle of 1848 until the middle of 1849.

The board then decided that the lesser evil was to return to the rate system, even if that had no legal sanction, and it was reintroduced in 1850. Attendance fell badly and the board (which from 1850 was elective) was much concerned. The number of children of school age in the city was 6,149 but those attending either public or private schools totalled only 2,746. This was simply not good enough and the only answer was free schools. So still another switch was made in 1851, but not without protest. A group of citizens, some eminent and some not, demanded a public meeting to discuss the subject and one was held in 1852 in St Lawrence Hall with four hundred people present. After a spirited debate the free school supporters triumphed.

At last the common schools got under way. The curriculum was drawn separately for the 'male' and the 'female' departments. For both the day opened with prayers and reading from the bible and followed with the same basic subjects: reading, writing, arithmetic, grammar, geography, and history. While the girls were then instructed in sewing and singing the boys were plunged into algebra and geometry. School hours were from nine until four. Average daily attendance in relation to total population did not go up as steeply as had been hoped. In 1844 (city population 18,500) it was 1,194 and in 1858 (population 47,500) it was 1,987. Although it was now possible for all children to go to school attendance was not made compulsory until 1871. A study made in 1863 showed that of 9,508 children of school age 1,632, or more than 17 per cent, were not in attendance. Some reasons were given: 453 were employed, 263 'wanted at home,' and 216 lacked clothes. Enthusiasm for education was slow to grow.[14]

Once the concept of education for the masses had gained acceptance public attention was rightly directed to the development and improvement of the provincial system of common and grammar schools; but so great was the concentration on that problem that, while private schools were taken for granted, the scantiest records of them were kept. In rural areas there were probably none at this time, but for the cities and towns a misleading picture has been allowed to stand. It is, of course, legitimate to disapprove of private schools but not to ignore the facts that they were the pioneers, have existed ever since, and have been preferred by a minority of parents.

No one can tell how many children in Toronto went to private schools in the forties and fifties. The names of a number of schools are known from advertisements and other unofficial sources but no complete list can be made and only in the case of a few is there a record of the number of pupils. The city *Directory* for 1850–1 mentioned what they regarded as the principal private academies. Of the four for boys three were directed by clergymen. For 'young ladies' eight schools are named, and of those one is of particular interest as offering for girls a school comparable to Upper Canada College. In 1850 Monsieur and Madame Deslandes (about whom nothing is known) rented 'Pinehurst,' a house at the head of John Street, that is, at Grange Road, built by Clarke Gamble and designed by J. G. Howard (appropriately the drawing master at Upper Canada). The school was under the patronage of the hierarchy of the Church of England and the Bench: the bishop, the rector of the cathedral, chief justice, and puisne justices. In 1853 the Deslandes disappeared as mysteriously as they had come, and the school was taken over by a lady whose name led printers into variant spellings but was evidently Mrs Forster, widow of a British army officer. She was a successful headmistress but her health broke down in 1866. In the following year a new school named after Bishop Strachan took over Pinehurst house and inherited the same kind of patronage.

The provision in all the school acts of the forties and fifties for separate schools had at first little application to Toronto. The *Directory* for 1846 records fifteen common and only one separate school. It appears that at no time was there a Protestant separate school in Toronto. This general situation may in part be explained by the existence of private schools related in some way to churches. In the fifties, however, active – even bitter – controversy developed on the place of separate schools, Toronto newspapers devoting a good deal of space to partisan arguments.

Education outside the classroom overlapped with enjoyment and the pursuit of personal interests. The City of Toronto Ethical and Literary Society was formed in September 1836. It excluded political and religious questions in a programme of debates on such subjects 'as accord with the name of the Society.' The Commercial News Room was in fact a library to be used by subscribers. The Toronto Atheneum was incorporated in 1848 but had existed before that with Henry Scadding as president. It had a library and museum and arranged lectures in 'various branches of knowledge.' In 1855 it amalgamated with the Royal Canadian Institute which originated in 1849 and had much the same purposes although it emphasized the sciences. In 1858 the membership of the combined bodies, under the name of the second, stood at five hundred and included many prominent persons in the professions and business. The Toronto Literary Debating Society was active in the fifties.[15]

A great many people were able to enjoy music either as participants or as listeners. Choral music had the advantages of involving many men and women, being inexpensive, and drawing on the skill of choir masters in the larger churches. A whole series of choral societies gave concerts of good music, particularly oratorios. Regular concerts were given in the St Lawrence Hall from 1851 beginning with the incomparable Swedish singer, Jenny Lind, who responded to the wild enthusiasm of Toronto by stretching her concerts from one to two and then to three.[16] Painting did not reach great heights but many amateurs, professionals, and semi-professionals did creditable work. The Society of Artists and Amateurs of Toronto (a name invidious probably without intention) was formed in 1834, two of the leaders in it being J. G. Howard, architect and drawing master, and Captain Richard Bonnycastle who would have been taught to draw as an officer of the Royal Engineers. James Hamilton, a landscape painter, was one of the principal exhibitors.[17]

Plays were performed from the early days of York but it was not until the mid-forties that the first proper theatre, the Royal Lyceum, rang up its curtain. In 1852 the management was taken over by John Nickerson who in the following years brought many famous actors to Toronto. When he returned to the United States his daughter, Charlotte Morrison, succeeded him and she too had long success as a manager. The theatre itself was renamed Prince of Wales in 1860.[18] Many of the plays performed in early Toronto have long since been forgotten, but one would like to know more of the new and beautiful drama, *Love's Frailties, or passion and repentance*. The mixture on one bill of *Othello* with *Family Jars, or the mistaken father* seems a little strange as was the combination of *The Merchant of Venice* with a farce. *Hamlet*, one is relieved to find, was played alone.

Outdoor sports and games of all kinds were plentiful. Horse racing had begun as informal and wholly amateur but by the early forties more organized meetings were held. The bay provided excellent facilities for boating. The sailors organized the (Royal) Canadian Yacht Club in 1852 and the oarsmen the Toronto Rowing Club. The first formal races seem to have been for keel boats and single sculls in 1848. Lacrosse was the most popular land game although cricket appealed to a devoted minority, some of them in the Toronto Cricket Club. Baseball was a new game played in Toronto from about the early fifties. Ice hockey was much later, but skating and curling had many followers. If the Toronto Chess Club be added, card games played at home, and meetings of fraternal societies, entertainment was found for almost everyone.

'Toronto,' wrote Sir George Arthur in the summer of 1840, 'is just now quite a scene of gaiety – the resort of the fashionable world.' Glimpses of high society run through the diary of Larratt Smith, a law student of eighteen years of age articled to W. H. Draper.[19] Not all was luxury. His lodgings were on one occasion flooded to a depth of three feet and he seemed not to think it out of the way when he wrote: 'hardly slept all last night – killed seven fleas & 1 bug – fleas on the whole pretty plentiful.' He entertained men friends in his lodgings with whist, vingt et un, chess, or backgammon. He played the violin and piano, sang in church, listened to concerts, and attended the theatre. He went to dinners and evening parties at which he danced the waltz, galop, and Sir Roger de Coverley. And he could play 'Racket Ball' in the court in John Macaulay's house.

Invited to a dance at Government House young Smith made due preparations. He was measured for a 'pr. of best black trowsers £2–10 – & satin waistcoat £1–12–6.' Suitably garbed he set out for the ball where he found six hundred people, 'a regular crush.' The band of the 32nd Regiment played overtures in the foreground while in the ball room the band of the 93rd played quadrilles. Smith had a 'capital supper,' danced with various girls, and at half-past three walked home with one of his partners. Young ladies of the Toronto of the mid-nineteenth century were evidently allowed more freedom than is commonly supposed.

# 5 ∎∎

## *Urban supremacy*

Few observers in the early nineteenth century would have wagered that York, tucked obscurely in the bush, would outstrip its elders and – they would not have hesitated to say – its betters. Cities do not grow and prosper by chance, neither can their courses be predetermined by immutable laws drawn into formulas of attractive simplicity. In finding the reasons for success account must be taken of a whole set of factors of which the favourable outbalance the unfavourable. Any one advantage may be possessed in no greater degree than by other cities but it is the total sum that counts. Luck may play some part, as will certainly the enterprise of the inhabitants. One consideration of basic importance is geographical location.

Toronto was fortunate in its immediate environment, being placed at the edge of a potentially rich agricultural area. Farmers and villagers exchanged with townsmen their respective goods and services. Hamilton, too, had fine land at its door, although access to it was somewhat hindered by the escarpment. Kingston, on the other hand, looked back on rocky stretches.

The commercial life of all three had been nurtured by harbours, largely formed by nature; and indeed several other towns on Lake Ontario had ports on which they depended for their trade. The question arises, then, whether Toronto was in this respect better off than other towns. Comparison by the volume of shipping or cargoes would be misleading since the character of the harbour would be only one explanation. Fortunately the commodore of the Royal Canadian Yacht Club, Dr E. M. Hodder, published a detailed study that he had made of all the ports on Lake Ontario.[1] He rated that of Toronto as 'without doubt the best natural harbour on Lake Ontario,' with that of Kingston next. He added, however, that the entrance to the latter was intricate and consequently dangerous.

The harbour at Hamilton in some respects resembled that of Toronto in that Burlington Bay was made by a ridge of sand and gravel. Entrance was by way of a canal about half a mile long, but he understood that it was next to impossible for a sailing vessel to enter during a gale from the east or southeast without hitting the pier. Of harbours in the smaller towns he gave high marks to Whitby where a breakwater enclosed a 'capacious basin.' In several other ports – Port Hope, Cobourg, and Oakville among them – he found serious weaknesses of one kind or another. Hodder was in the main writing for the skippers of sailing vessels and to some extent his judgment would be modified as applying to steamers, for example in the case of the Hamilton entrance.

The Bay of Toronto was formed by a long, low-lying peninsula which ran from the marshy area at the mouths of the River Don in a sweeping curve until its narrow tip pointed toward Bathurst Street.[2] There a wide opening was left. Along the mainland was a series of wharves from Gooderham's on the east to the Queen's Wharf on the west. The number changed from year to year. Because of their length and the depth of water some of the wharves could be used by the larger steamers; others were for more limited purposes. In the newspapers of the day frequent references were made to new wharves, to old ones being repaired, others that should be, requirements for dredging beside them, and their lighting. Although grain had long been stored over the winter the first elevator appears to have been that built by John Sheddon for the Grand Trunk Railway at the foot of Brock Street. Completed in 1863 it had a storage capacity of 200,000 bushels and could elevate four thousand bushels of grain in an hour. Unfortunately it was burned a year later. The second elevator, finished in 1865, was at the foot of Jarvis Street. It had storage space for 175,000 bushels and some two thousand barrels. Two more were built in 1869–70. One of them, owned by the Northern Railway, was in use until it was destroyed by fire in 1908.

Seen from the waterfront the bay appeared as a large body of protected water on which ships might move about at will or pass as they wished through the wide opening. Actually, however, a shoal of hard sand ran around the western end of the peninsula forcing ships into a narrow channel some three hundred feet in width and on the side of the mainland. Even in the stretch normally navigable shifting sand was a danger. The same difficulty existed near the wharves and in both places dredging could barely keep up with the silting. The western gap was, indeed, so unsatisfactory that suggestions were made that it be abandoned. Furthermore, it was from some points of view at the wrong end of the bay. As had been observed from the first days of York sailing ships had to beat out through a confined passage against the prevailing wind; and for both them and steamers it was a long way around if on the way to the St Lawrence, as most of them were. It has been stated[3] that schooners sailed through Ashbridge's Bay and Marsh to the harbour, but if so that must have been slow and difficult even for small vessels.

In view of such circumstances the idea of cutting through the peninsula at a narrow point on the eastern end occurred to a number of interested persons. The project was examined by a commission set up in 1833 to report on improvement and preservation of the harbour. One of the commissioners, R. H. Bonnycastle, gave the written opinion that the harbour could be ruined by such an eastern gap if ill-advisedly constructed, and twenty years later W. H. Merritt, promoter of the Welland Canal, warned of the same danger: that sand forced through the gap could fill up the whole harbour. One answer at the time of a public meeting held in 1833 by friends of a cut across the peninsula was to have a gate that could be opened or shut. That was a touch fanciful, but the arguments in favour of the opening were substantial: saving of time (one hour was the estimate for steamers); releasing windbound schooners; and bringing in pure water. The harbour commissioners, however, were not in favour of an eastern gap and no conclusion was reached.

The decision was made not by man but by towering seas roaring before easterly gales. In the early 1850s waves two or three times opened and closed a channel, but finally a storm in 1858 cut a great swatch across the peninsula through which sailing and steam vessels passed in nine feet of water. Buoys were set and the passage continued to be used although not without some risk at times, for the sand did not stop moving in from the east (it was thought from erosion of the Scarborough Bluffs) and deposits were dropped by the Don. The depth varied in an alarming fashion and various plans were discussed for protecting the new gap. It was, however, to be many years before either it or the western gap was free from trouble.

Meanwhile the fickle lake did not confine its attention to that part of the peninsula where demolition was useful but, time after time, caused apprehension that the whole stretch which made the harbour would go back to the depths from which geologists assumed it had come. If so there would be no harbour. In spite of a breakwater Quinn's Hotel at the eastern end was washed away in April 1858. One section or another suffered flooding and erosion. 'What,' asked the *Leader* in 1862, 'is to be done to prevent the utter destruction with which the harbour is threatened? . . . One thing is certain, it will not do to delay taking active means to arrest the destruction of the Island. We only hope it is not already too late.' A select committee in the same year pointed a finger at the eastern gap which showed signs of widening and thus exposing the wharves to heavy seas and slowly destroying the port. In 1865 an optimist claimed that the danger was over, that natural processes had re-formed the island; but in fact it was a subject for worry for years to come.

The island (for so it had become) was a place for recreation but more important as making the harbour. At all costs the port must be preserved for transportation, around which substantial investment had grown up on shipping lines, and in the construction, maintenance, and supplying of ships. Through the greater part of each year the local papers carried advertisements and news stories relating to shipping, and from them can be seen both the importance attached to that form of transport and much of its character. Local traffic had a place, but major stress was on long-distance freight: through the St Lawrence, on the upper lakes, and in connection with American transport. In the 1840s voyages were relatively short and exchanges were made where necessary. In every spring the newspapers watched for the opening of navigation and listed the steamship services offered. In 1843, for example, the *Examiner* noted that three ships of the Daily Mail Line would pick up at Coteau du Lac light goods sent up from Montreal and transfer them at Kingston to ships bound for Toronto. Travel time from Montreal would be three and a half days. The editor welcomed competition between British and American lines as likely to improve service and prices. Vessels left Toronto for Rochester three times a week. The *Admiral* went to Oswego twice a week and the *Eclipse* to Hamilton daily.

After 1850, with the St Lawrence canals open, voyages were longer. Three lines of freight steamers ran between Toronto and Montreal. Occasionally greater distances were covered. In 1850 the steamship *Western Miller* took a cargo of flour from Toronto to Halifax; and in each of the years 1853 to 1855 a sailing vessel carried lumber to Liverpool.

Steamships became more numerous, larger, and better; one particular advance being the introduction of propellors in place of paddle wheels. So much was written about them that the erroneous impression might be gained that they had taken the place of sailing vessels. In the end they did, but not for many years. Sailboats were out of the passenger business by the middle of the century but still carried a considerable portion of the bulk freight. They were slower and subject to delay by weather but their tariff was lower. In 1860 a newspaper published the anticipated freight rates, showing the differential:

|  | Steamers | Sailing vessels |
|---|---|---|
| Toronto to Kingston. | Wheat 4 cents, flour 20 cents | Wheat $3\frac{1}{2}$ cents, flour $12\frac{1}{2}$ cents |
| Toronto to Montreal. | Wheat 9 cents, flour 30 cents | Wheat 8 cents, flour 20 cents |

The larger number and smaller size of sailing ships are indicated by the statistics of ships and cargoes entering Toronto in 1864:

| | |
|---|---|
| Total number of steamers | 850 |
| Aggregate tonnage | 176,518 |
| Total number of sailing vessels | 946 |
| Aggregate tonnage | 121,281 |

At the time when steamships were slowly squeezing out sailing ships they themselves appeared to be threatened by that new form of transportation, the railway. Contemporaries, however, correctly judged that this was not a comparable situation, that water and rail travel should be complementary. Two limitations stood in the way of the free movement of ships. One was frost, even if the harbour of Toronto was open for a surprisingly long time. The average length of the season for the period after 1868 (when figures become available) was 264 days. The earliest arrival in the harbour was on 27 February in 1882 and the latest on 28 April in 1884. The date of the last incoming ship ranged from 2 December in 1873 to 31 December in 1885.

Subject to variations from one year to another the seasonal barrier to water travel was absolute, but the other barrier – absence of navigable waterways – was not; for to some extent it could be and was overcome by canals. The residual requirement for land transport could not be met by roads. The inadequacy of existing ones was reflected by a remark in a Toronto newspaper of 1844 that communication with the seat of government (Montreal) would be slow until the sleighing was good. No radical improvement could be expected when population was scattered, provincial funds small, terrain difficult, and mechanization absent. Once its practicability was proven the railway seemed to be the only answer.

Railways were functionally suitable for local traffic but too expensive to be strewn around in place of concession roads. Attempts, therefore, were always made to fit them into large strategic plans in expectation of a large volume of long-haul freight. British North America was not industrialized but was an exporter of staple products. To these, it was hoped, could be added the goods of the American middle west – the whole being exported by way of the St Lawrence which was, according to all those in central Canada, the logical route. The Toronto reading of commercial geography was that the city was placed directly on the most direct line between the west and the sea. To go by way of Detroit added hundreds of miles to the journey.

As applied to the fur trade this argument had failed, but then waggons on muddy Yonge Street left a good deal to be desired. When Toronto businessmen wanted to get a railway started in the 1830s they looked northward in conformity with tradition. The surveyor they employed, Thomas Roy, expressed the thinking:

The excellent harbour formed by York Bay is decidedly the greatest natural advantage which the City of Toronto possesses. – it has no navigable river stretching into the interior of the country to enrich it with its commerce, nor does its position on Lake Ontario give it very decided advantages, over the Towns which possess Harbours less spacious and commodious – neither does it command by its situation the commerce of the interior on the East or on the West – but as the country has become settled, it has obtained an ascendancy in the *North* – from these circumstances it must be obvious that the commerce of the City of Toronto must increase as these northern counties are settled, if she opens up and maintains her lines of communication ...[4]

Like many other railway projects of that decade the Toronto one was long delayed; but in the autumn of 1851 Lady Elgin, wife of the governor general, turned the first sod for the Northern Railway on Front Street, in the presence of a distinguished company gathered there after a parade and planning to celebrate the event by a ball in the evening. The line was opened for traffic as far as Bradford in 1853 and Collingwood in 1855. Extensions were later built to Orillia and Gravenhurst and to Penetanguishene. The Northern had its ups and downs financially and it was local freight that proved to be its most profitable business.[5] It played a part, too, in relating York County to Toronto. The first train had barely arrived at Aurora when a Toronto newspaper carried an advertisement of the sale of land around what was to be known as the Village of Maple. The city, the advertiser claimed, could be reached in half an hour by any one of several trains; and those living in Maple would have lower taxes, cheaper firewood, and churches within a short walk. And this suburban prospect was opening up only some twenty years after men living near Richmond Hill had been in the habit of walking to Toronto when the roads were too bad for carriages.

The Northern chartered ships on Lake Huron as part of what an American newspaper described as 'a pathway to the west, over Canadian territory, avoiding the tedious route around the lakes.' The Northern's limited success in this connection, as a portage railway, did not discourage those who were convinced of the logic of their geographical concept. If the *Leader* represented commercial thinking in Toronto – and certainly it did to some extent – opinion was against 'the suicidal policy of competition between the lake and land means of transportation.' The other means of diverting traffic through Toronto would be a canal between Lake Huron and Lake Ontario, and that was explored before the Northern was built and continued to be pursued long after the railway was in operation.

Kivas Tully, a civil engineer as well as an excellent architect, surveyed lines north from Toronto in 1846, 1851, and 1855 and concluded that a 'ship canal with an ample supply of water, only eighty miles in length,

Davenport station, on the Northern Railway, about 1857

*can* be constructed to connect the waters of Lakes Huron and Ontario.'
Placed by the Board of Trade before it, this information led a convention
including representatives of Chicago, Milwaukee, Oswego, Barrie, and
Orillia to the same view.[6] In 1857 a statute incorporated the Toronto and
Georgian Bay Canal Company. The canal, to be built at an estimated cost
of $22 million, had grown to a hundred miles. It was to begin at the
Humber River with a branch to the Don and an eastern entrance at
Ashbridge's Bay. It would follow the Holland River, Lake Simcoe, and
the Nottawassaga River to Georgian Bay. Ships going from Chicago to
Liverpool would, it was claimed, save 857 miles over the existing route by
Buffalo and New York.[7]

Through the 1860s exploration of routes and controversies about them
were frequent. The County of Ontario employed T. C. Keefer to make a
preliminary survey. He reported that of several possible routes all would
be through Lake Simcoe, but south of that point alternative courses were
anywhere from the Humber to the Bay of Quinte.[8] The Trent Valley
Canal, on which a little work was done in 1833, was to follow one of the
routes described, but it was not revived until the twentieth century and

was never completed. Select committees made reports on the proposed canal. In 1864 approval was expressed in principle but without a choice of routes. In 1869 F. C. Capreol appeared before a committee on behalf of the canal company and reported offers by American capitalists to undertake half the construction in return for half the stock and ten million acres of land. He and other witnesses protested that a canal utilizing the Ottawa River would be for barges only.[9] Shortly after confederation a royal commission on all canals, actual and proposed, regarded the Georgian Bay scheme as only a remote possibility.[10]

The Northern was Toronto's own railway, but not because the city had a unique geographical advantage. Rails could be run to Georgian Bay from other ports on Lake Ontario. This was evident to the businessmen of Hamilton who built in the seventies the Hamilton and North Western Railway to Collingwood. It competed so successfully that the Northern found it necessary to make a partial amalgamation of the two. Meanwhile, however, groups in Hamilton and London had given priority to a plan designed to take advantage of their geographical situations as distinct from that of Toronto. The Great Western Railway was expected to find profitable traffic in the immediate, well-settled country, but its larger purpose was to carry American freight on a short cut across Canadian soil from the border at Sarnia to the Port of Hamilton.

The extension to Toronto was an afterthought but had the effect of putting Toronto on an all-rail route from the St Lawrence ports to the American middle west as created by the amalgamated Great Western and Grand Trunk. Toronto, in this and other ways, was a beneficiary of both railways but had little part in the origination or direction of either.[11]

Nearer home the growing network of railway lines brought dozens of small towns within easy reach of Toronto, but it did not follow that Toronto was automatically turned into a magnet. The pull in the other direction was strong too. A number of cities and towns which, like Toronto, had harbours and were served by railways, seemed to have all that was needed to increase their own shares of commerce and industry. If goods and services could be sent outward from Toronto could they not equally be sent inward? Ships and trains ran in both directions.

The business community of Toronto, which had shown enterprise in exploiting a favourable environment, was made up of three main elements: trade, finance, and manufacturing. They overlapped in personnel and to some extent each group was dependent on the others, but they had distinct functions and different relationships to the needs of an urban centre. In any particular town or city trade might form a greater or lesser proportion of the total economic effort, but it could not be absent and could not fall below a certain minimum. Like trade, finance was essential, both for the city itself and for the surrounding area for which it provided services. Manufacturing was in a somewhat different category. Any city was bound to have some industry and Toronto did in some degree, but Hamilton was better known in this respect. The amount of manufacturing was not a sure test of the strength of a city since it tended to move to the surrounding area as the value and availability of land within the city created problems.

Being the capital had brought more than prestige to early York, for the presence of government pumped money into the town and led to a demand for goods and services which would not otherwise have existed. As York grew into Toronto the scale of commercial operations made it necessary and possible to separate wholesale from retail trade, and for a long time it was the men in the former who led in the commercial scene. They dominated the executive of the Toronto Board of Trade, which was founded in 1844 and incorporated by statute in 1845; and they had their fingers well into other commercial and financial pies.[12] To assist dealings in commodities the Toronto Exchange was incorporated in 1854, its purpose being 'to afford facilities for the transaction of the mercantile business of the said city and of the surrounding country.' On the Exchange building and the property on Wellington and Berczy streets the merchants spent close to £15,000. In addition to private offices and committee rooms was the Exchange itself, measuring fifty by thirty feet and some forty feet high. It was quite a handsome building with a classical touch.

The statute incorporating the Exchange referred to the business of the city and surrounding country. It has earlier been seen that from the first the shopkeepers of York cast their net as widely as circumstances permitted; but when wholesaling became a separate function and transportation improved, the area of possible exploitation was multiplied many times. Not content with southern Ontario the Toronto merchants, through the Board of Trade, added their voices to the *Globe*'s campaign for the release of the northwest from the grip of the fur traders. Their channel of communication with what they hoped to see as a new market would be the rail-and-water route of which the first stage was the Northern Railway. In this way they would defeat not only the Hudson's Bay Company but Montreal as well.

Their reach, as it proved, far exceeded their grasp, but the volume of trade centred in Toronto was nevertheless considerable. In figures no measure can be found except of imports and exports.[13] The former were usually several times larger than the latter and included almost every kind of commodity that can be imagined. Staples produced in York and other nearby counties went out of the province at a number of points, leaving Toronto with a respectable but not overwhelming share. Wheat, other grains, and flour were the most consistent items of export, with lumber

distinctly less and varying from year to year. The early fifties were prosperous but the depression of 1857–9 caused bankruptcies and slowed up
business generally. Recovery came after that and was enhanced by the
American civil war.

As trade grew so did both the need for banks and the financial resources
on which they could rest. Two early and ephemeral institutions were
connected with the Reformers rather than with the Tory political and
commercial group. George Truscott and J. C. Green, retired English army
officers, tried their hand at banking in 1834. Their Agricultural Bank
antagonized older rivals by paying interest on deposits and by, it was
said, adopting risky policies. Its political flavour would not have added to
its popularity in Tory ranks. The two men won suits for slander and were
given a clean bill of health by the grievance committee of the house of
assembly (of which W. L. Mackenzie was chairman), but the other banks
forced collapse of the Agricultural Bank by gathering in its notes and
pressing for their redemption, so depriving them of specie. It failed in
1837 with considerable loss to depositors and holders of notes.

In 1835 a group of Reformers formed the Bank of the People. James
Lesslie wrote that it 'was established to counteract the political influence
of the two Chartered Banks then in existence the Bank of Upper Canada
and the Commercial Bank, both of which, especially the former which
were controlled by the oligarchy then in power, employed their influence
throughout the province against the advocates of civil and religious freedom.'
Dr John Rolph was the first president and Lesslie the second; Marshall
Bidwell and J. H. Price the solicitors; and Francis Hincks succeeded
Lesslie as cashier. It did not fail but it ran into problems. The bank's
capital was too small and each shareholder was in the uncomfortable
position of being responsible for its debts to the whole amount of his
estate. In about 1840 it was decided to pay off the shareholders and sell
out to the Bank of Montreal.[14]

Some years later new banks with no distinct political flavour began to
set up house. In this financial field, as in trade, consciousness of the city
as the focal point of an area was marked. The Bank of Toronto, which
began business in 1856, was first incorporated under the suggestive name
of the Millers' Association of Canada West. The millers concerned were
in a series of towns both literally and financially within reach of Toronto,
in Thornhill, Weston, Lambton, Milton, Streetsville, Guelph, Waterdown,
and Oshawa. J. G. Chewett, of an original York family, left the Bank of
Upper Canada to become president. William Gamble, a miller among
other things, was vice-president. George Michie, a retailer, and H. J.
Boulton, a lawyer, were on the board. The cashier was Angus Cameron
who had been in the Bank of Montreal. In conformity with its regional

origin the bank opened its first out-of-town branch within a few weeks of its own birth.[15]

Banks, like individuals and firms, gained when the confused currency was unified in the decimal system in 1858; but, like the others, they were badly hit by the depression of 1857. The Bank of Upper Canada, so much a part of the old régime of York, remained outwardly powerful but actually was running deeper and deeper into the red. During the boom days of the early fifties it had, like other banks, plunged heavily into land, railways, and inflated milling enterprises. It was then caught with bad debts when times were hard and the provincial government, whose account it held, arranged in 1861 that the cashier, Thomas Ridout, be replaced by Robert Cassels, a Scot who had been in the service of the Bank of British North America for twenty-four years. Cassels was aware that the bank was in difficulties but understood from the minister of finance, who asked him to accept the appointment, that the government would stand behind him.

Improvement in business brought a respite, but instead of helping the government transferred its account to the Bank of Montreal in 1864. In terms of money this meant little since the Bank of Upper Canada was in debt to the government for nearly $1.5 million (most of which was never recovered). Such desertion, however, was with some reason taken to signify a lack of confidence, a final blow which forced the bank to close its doors two years later. Cassels, who under the circumstances had attempted an impossible rescue operation, turned to other fields. With his brother, Walter Gibson Cassels, who had also been in the Bank of British North America and came to Toronto as its manager in 1845, Robert Cassels founded a distinguished financial and legal family of Toronto.

It was in the shadow cast by the failure of the Bank of Upper Canada and the knowledge that its old rival, the Commercial Bank of Kingston, was near the same fate, that a group of Toronto men established the Canadian Bank of Commerce. The prime mover and first president was William McMaster, an Irishman who had come to York in 1833 and started a successful drygoods firm. He was a pillar of the Baptist Church and the benefactor of McMaster University. The vice-president was H. S. Howland, a miller and one of the four brothers who had migrated from New York State. When he left the Commerce eight years later to become president of the Imperial Bank he unwittingly forecast the merger of nearly a century later. Among the other directors of the Bank of Commerce were John Macdonald, a Scot and head of a wholesale drygoods company; John Taylor, who had a paper mill in the Don Valley; William Elliott, another wholesaler; William Alexander, a stockbroker; and T. S. Stayner, son of the former postmaster general and a financier. The Bank of Commerce was ready for business in Toronto in the spring of 1867 and saw its stock oversubscribed. Perhaps that was a sign of improving conditions since the Bank of Toronto had had to scramble to sell its issue. The Commerce grew rapidly, thrusting out branches across southern Ontario.[16]

Other types of financial institutions were keeping pace with the banks. The Home District Mutual Fire Insurance Company was started by a group of Reformers as a rival to the older British American Fire and Life Assurance Company in much the same way as the People's Bank had been intended to offset the Bank of Upper Canada. W. W. Baldwin was president of the new company and Francis Hincks the secretary. James Lesslie, J. H. Price, and W. J. O'Grady were among the organizers. The Western Assurance Company, which by the twentieth century had representatives in every part of the world, dates from 1851. Isaac C. Gilmour, a wholesale drygoods merchant, was the first president, and all but one of the other directors were in wholesale or retail trade. The company suffered heavy losses in 1862–5 but recovered its strength.[17]

The Toronto Building Society (1846) and the Farmers and Mechanics Building Society (1847) were, as had been the custom, terminating bodies; that is, they would be disbanded when all the members had received their allotments. It was intended that both should come to an end in 1854, but a bookkeeper in the second, J. Herbert Mason, proposed a merger of the two on a permanent basis. From this suggestion the Canada Permanent Building and Savings Society emerged. The chairman was J. G. Chewett; the president J. D. Ridout, hardware merchant; and the vice-president Peter Peterson, general merchant. Mason, the originator, was secretary treasurer. The Canada Permanent extended throughout Ontario, and later well beyond it.[18]

Transfer of stocks and other securities was first effected either by advertisements in newspapers or by auction. As business developed the inadequacy of these methods led to proposals for the establishment of a stock exchange, and at a meeting in 1852 of those concerned that step was taken. It was argued in the resolutions that greater importance than formerly was attached to Canadian securities because the low rates of interest in the London market were leading capitalists to turn to Canada, and that Toronto was 'the most central point of attraction to capitalists seeking investments in Canada.' Finally it was resolved that those present were 'discharging an important duty in taking the lead in Canada by the establishment of an Association' and this was to be known as the Toronto Stock Exchange. Until 1861, however, when regular meetings of the board began, the members transacted business by going to each other's offices.[19]

Trade and finance were acquiring strength and stability, bringing wealth and power to Toronto. Manufacturing, third member of the triumvirate, looked in comparison less impressive. A great many things were made but on a scale small in relation to the total economic effort of the city. The response to new demands, however, showed some enterprise. The Toronto

# CHEAP BOOT AND SHOE STORE.

## (LATE P. R. LAMB'S,)

# No. 93 YONGE STREET,

## Corner of Temperance Street,

# TORONTO.

# G. W. MORGAN,

PRESENTS his thanks to the Inhabitants of Toronto, and the Public in general, for the handsome support he has received since purchasing the above business from Mr. P. R. LAMB, and respectfully assures his customers and friends, that in excellence of material, solidity of workmanship, and moderation in price, he cannot be surpassed by any House in the Trade.

All Goods sold by G. W. M. will be made in Toronto, by first class Workmen, from the best Leather, and warranted to be as good as can be produced.

Repairing attended to.

## N. B. No. 93 Yonge Street, Corner of Temperance Street.

### C. & J. MITCHELL,
# LOVEJOY HOUSE,
#### KING STREET, TORONTO.
### LIVERY STABLE AND BOWLING SALOON.

Dry Dock Company was cheerfully prepared to make almost anything: ships, engines, boilers, and other machinery. In 1855 Hayes Brothers built the *City of Toronto*, of 1,070 tons, entirely of white oak and ready for overseas trade. Repairs and supplies for ships and construction of docks occupied a number of firms on the waterfront.

Railways offered opportunities for manufacturers as they did for engineers and other employees. The second locomotive for the Northern Railway was built by James Good at his foundry at the corner of Queen and Yonge streets and in 1853 run over temporary rails for delivery at the foot of York Street. Good also made threshing machines, steam engines, boilers, castings, and so on. In the same year as the locomotive made this remarkable journey through the city the Toronto Locomotive Manufacturing Company, of which James Beaty was president and C. S. Gzowski a director, offered stock for sale. Somewhat later the Toronto Car Wheels Works, branch of a Buffalo firm, was manufacturing for the Grand Trunk and Great Western railways.

Another new demand was for mass production of nails, arising out of adoption of the 'balloon frame' type of building construction, that is, the light framework that replaced the heavy bearing walls. The Toronto Rolling Mills, under the management of D. L. Macpherson and C. S. Gzowski, had in 1866 an output of twenty thousand tons of nails.

One demand that was not new was for spirituous liquors, and that it did not diminish is suggested by the fact that in 1860 the two distilleries in Toronto together headed the list of value of annual produce.[20] Breweries, too, were numerous. Other traditional industries continued and most of them expanded. The factory of Jacques and Hay, near the waterfront, produced furniture for houses, schools, and offices. It also did upholstering and something close to interior decorating. In 1866 it was said to be employing four hundred hands, and ten years earlier had established its own sawmill near New Lowell. Four firms made soap and candles, with a combined annual value second only to the distilleries.

It is not possible to fix with any accuracy the proportion of the working population employed in manufacturing. In 1851 it would appear that some three hundred persons, or approximately 4 per cent of the work force, were on the pay roll of all the factories. Fifteen years later the numbers were materially higher but the information available is not sufficient to allow even a rough estimate.

In an advertisement of 1844 the Toronto Axe Factory appealed to the public to 'keep your money at home and encourage home enterprise,' thus touching off protests against protective tariffs. The Board of Trade held the view that, while domestic manufacturing should be encouraged, the tariff was not the proper means. The *Globe* printed a statement, with which it agreed, issued by a committee of the board:

In a country thus prematurely attempting the establishment of manufactures, by Legislative protection or prohibitions, the capital of the inhabitants is forced into unnatural channels, to the serious detriment of the branches of industry more appropriate to its circumstances and capability. Those branches of manufactures in which Canada may embark with the surest prospects of success, will be rendered more obvious by leaving them uncovered by those heavy duties falsely designated *protection*. The quantity of woollen cloth made in western Canada is actually undergoing a rapid increase. This is a branch of industry adapted to our rural population.

Agricultural interests, the committee concluded, were paramount and must not be damaged by high tariffs. The powerful merchants, then and for some decades after, consistently argued against restrictions on trade, opposing protective tariffs and inclining toward free trade. As manufacturing grew in the fifties and sixties, however, the balance was somewhat modified as between trade and industry, the leaders in the latter deciding that they too must organize. Their difficulties in the depression led them to call a meeting in St Lawrence Hall in April 1858 at which two decisions were reached. The first was to urge on the government a policy of fiscal protection, and the second was to set up a standing body, the Association for the Protection of Canadian Industry. When Alexander Galt raised the tariff in 1859 the association was dissolved, perhaps in the belief that its purpose had been accomplished.[21]

The growing strength of the economy and rise in population went hand in hand; and from the combination of the two came changes in the boundaries of the city, the buildings in it, and the public services supplied. This physical development of the city is another measure of its progress.

Until the 1880s the territorial extension of Toronto is explained not by annexations but by consolidation of the city and liberties and encroachment on the Military Reserve. The liberties, it will be recalled, might be assimilated into wards whenever their population justified such action. That process was carried out in two stages. By a statute of 1846 (9 Vict., c. 70) St James Ward and St David's Ward were extended to Bloor Street, the northern limit of the liberties. By the same act the university lands were incorporated in the liberties. A royal proclamation of 3 December 1852 ordered St John's Ward extended to Bloor Street, while St Patrick's Ward was to be similarly enlarged to the north, and also westward to Dufferin Street, the limit of the liberties.

Thus when the liberties in all Canadian cities (Kingston and Hamilton were the others) were abolished by the statute of 1858 (22 Vict., c. 99) Toronto appears to have had none left except for the panhandle running along the shore of Ashbridge's Bay and Marsh. No record can be found of

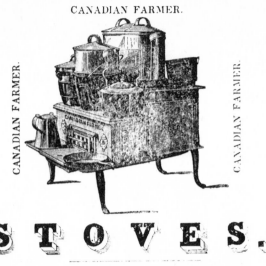

# STOVES.

## J. R. ARMSTRONG & Co.

*City Foundry,* 116 *Yonge Street, and 2nd door east of St. James's Cathedral, King Street, Toronto, C. W.*

MANUFACTURER OF

## CANADIAN FARMER COOKING STOVES,

### Nos. 6 & 7, (SEE THE CUT).

| *Burr Cooking Stoves.* | *Box Stoves* 6 *sizes.* |
|---|---|
| *Premium do.* 5 *sizes.* | *Air Tight do.* 6 " |
| *Bang-up do.* 5 " | *Parlor do.* 7 " |

*Dairymaid Stove and Cauldron, 3 sizes.*

The Canadian Farmer was patented by J. R. A. in June, 1850, and took the second Premium at the Provincial Fair this year, when the competition was very keen. It is the best stove in use for the county. because,

1st. It takes larger and longer wood than any other—from 2½ to 3 ft.

2ndly. It has more holes on the top to boil—No. 7, seven holes. No. 6, six holes.

3rdly. The plates are thicker, being from ⅜ to ½ inch thick.

4thly. It bakes beautifully, and holds 9 large loaves of bread.

The celebrated BANG UP is better adapted for the town, where saving of fuel is an object—the oven being large and high. And for roasting and broiling it cannot be surpassed. The Dairymaid Stove and Cauldron, for steaming feed for cattle, boiling water, and for dairy purposes, should be used by every good farmer. It took the first Premium at the late Fair at Niagara.

POT ASH KETTLES cast with the mouth up, two sizes weighing 800 and 1100 lbs

POT ASH COOLERS.

SUGAR KETTLES, three sizes, and a variety of castings.

COAL GRATES of the latest and most chaste styles from New York

N.B.—Old Iron taken in exchange.

Troops defiling past the grandstand during a military review, 8 October 1863

the means by which this strip was added to the city, but so it was, as subsequent maps show.

As originally laid out when York was founded the Military Reserve contained about a thousand acres, running from the lake shore to Queen Street and from Peter to Dufferin Street. Grants to individuals were made from it, but the first large portion to be detached was as the result of a suggestion by the lieutenant governor, Sir John Colborne. With a view to extension of the town toward the 'salubrious' west (the east being blanketed by 'effluvia' from the Don marshes) his first idea was to rent lots in the reserve. On second thoughts he proposed instead that the 240 acres east of Garrison Creek be sold to the public. This would have several advantages, he said: it would provide for the desired expansion, raise money for roads into the town, employ immigrants who were temporarily in York, and create a fund for construction of new barracks near the old Western Battery. Authorized to act on this, Colborne sold eighteen lots in 1833 to test the market and selling continued until the whole eastern part was taken up by 1836.

The British government, however, was reluctant to build new barracks or military installations. The inspector general of fortifications was in the tradition when he pointed out in 1833 that York was 'wholly without Defence against a land attack,' that 'its situation is in no way connected with the Military Defence of the Province,' and all that had ever been intended was to protect the entrance to the harbour. In spite of that he agreed that some provision had to be made for the garrison and advised an estimate of the cost.[22] The estimate was so high that it was turned down out of hand. Bond Head protested against the deplorable state of the old barracks, and in 1837 the imperial government attempted unsuccessfully to make a bargain with the provincial legislature one part of which was that the military reserve would be surrendered if the assembly would vote £10,000 toward the erection of new barracks, the total cost of which had been estimated at £59,205. Some temporary accommodation was provided but it was not until 1841 that the new buildings were ready. Originally it had been intended to have a fort, and plans had been drawn for stone fortifications in the conventional form of a star; but such works were not even started and the later name of Stanley Barracks was more appropriate than fort.[23]

Successive imperial regiments were housed there until the Crimean war when other demands had priority. After an interval renewed attention was given to the defence of Canada as British-American relations deteriorated during the American civil war. After a visit of imperial officers in 1861 the *Globe* reported that 'The defences of Toronto are now being rapidly strengthened . . . Yesterday afternoon the work was commenced of erecting a new battery of ten guns on the south side of the barracks, overlooking the extensive warehouses of the Grand Trunk Railway, the Queen's Wharf and the Channel.' Reading on in the story the fortifications grew larger and larger.

Meanwhile the city had been angling for at least some of the broad acres remaining in the reserve. As the *Globe* remarked in the middle of a negotiation toward that end: 'We require parks very much, when the west end of the City becomes a manufacturing district, which it is likely to be, the open common will be invaluable. We are only sorry that to the north there is not such open space which can be retained for that part of the City corporate.' In 1848 a lease for 999 years of 287 acres in the reserve – what had then come to be known as Ordnance Land – was granted to Toronto at an annual rent of one penny sterling. The land was to be laid out as a park 'for the purposes of pleasure, recreation and amusement to the inhabitants of the City of Toronto, and with a view to the ornament and salubrity of the City.' The city was to make roads and bridges and fence the whole. All development was subject to the approval of the British military authorities. The final condition of the lease was that all or any part of the land could be recovered at any time, with or without notice.

Horticultural Pavilion, Allan Gardens, destroyed by fire in 1902

Some but not all of the agreed works were carried out, but the city was shaken when, only two years after the lease began, the War Office expressed the desire to take back the whole property. They wanted to settle on it discharged soldiers who were to have – while the land lasted – two acres each and be available for military service in Canada if need arose. What annoyed the *Leader* was the comment that Toronto was a very small place for which a park of 250 acres was altogether too much. Various suggestions were made of how to save even a small area for the citizens. Toronto was unhappy but it had no bargaining power. However, an unexpected change came in 1856 when the unsold ordnance lands, totalling a little over five hundred acres, were turned over to the province as part of a widespread transfer, and thus the city had to deal with the provincial government. By a compromise agreement the city surrendered the lease of the 287 acres and received instead two parcels of land. The first, of twenty-two and a half acres, was to be a public park; and of the second thirty-two and a half acres twenty were to be used for the Exhibition.

It was just in time. The Provincial Agricultural Association and Board of Agriculture for Canada West was founded in 1846 and decided that annual fairs should be held at different centres, the first to be in Toronto on the grounds of Government House. It was a small concern by catered to various tastes with judging of cattle, exhibition of carriages, carts and farm machinery, display of needlework, paintings, and wax flowers. In 1852 it was Toronto's turn again and this time a more elaborate fair, lasting

A ball in St Lawrence Hall, 1862, in honour of the
governor general, Lord Monck, and Lady Monck

four days, was held to the west of University Avenue. The third in Toronto,
in 1858, was in the part of the Military Reserve that had been designated
for that purpose, located south of the Provincial Lunatic Asylum. The
triumph of that year was the Crystal Palace, inspired by the London Crystal
Palace of 1851. The Toronto version, designed by two engineers, Sandford
Fleming and Collingwood Schreiber, was built of iron and glass in the form
of a cross, and measured 256 by 96 feet. Its beauty may have been ques-
tionable but under its alternative name of Palace of Industry it housed
many exhibits.[24]

Some open space had been found on land not previously under the
authority of the city, but the council suddenly awoke to the fact that it
had done almost nothing to preserve ground for parks in the area which it
did control. In 1859 it sent a memorial to the governor general pointing
out that of the five hundred acres once in the possession of the government
only four small parcels remained: the nine acres of Simcoe Place on which
stood the parliament buildings; the hospital block of six acres, site of the

executive council; nine acres of Russell Square, held by Upper Canada College; and six acres between Simcoe Place and Russell Square, the grounds of Government House. Since, the council wrote, the government was to leave Toronto they asked that the first and last of these lots be vested in the city so that a public park might be made with entrance gates on Wellington Street.

One park had been given to the city two years earlier. Allan Gardens exist because of the generosity of G. W. Allan, long the president of the Horticultural Society of Toronto. It consisted of five acres at the corner of Sherbourne and Carlton streets. In 1862 Allan offered to sell a further five acres of Moss Park at a low price provided that the land was used in ways approved by the Horticultural Society. A number of leading citizens urged the city to take advantage of the offer:

Your Memorialists need scarcely remind your Worshipful Body that at present the City of Toronto is without a single Park or Square, and that nearly all the available lands within a reasonable distance of the centre of the city, are so divided and sub-divided with small building lots that if you omit to take advantage of the present opportunity for securing so desirable an object, you will never have it again in your power to obtain so advantageous a site for the purpose.

The purchase was made and the gardens have for a century afforded great pleasure to the people of Toronto, but it is noteworthy that it was fortune rather than management that gave to Toronto that park. The same is true of Queen's Park, which was saved from subdivision into building lots only because it had been the property of King's College. After the charter was granted in 1827 the college authorities looked about for suitable land and, after considering various sites, concluded that their best course was to buy portions of park lots. In 1828–9 they purchased the northern halves of lots 11, 12, and 13, the whole bounded by the present College Street, Bloor Street, Surrey Place on the east, and a line short of St George Street on the west. The total was 150 acres plus road allowances.

In 1842 the cornerstone of the college building was laid where the main parliament building now stands, but neither the building, the property, nor the college itself was to survive. In 1853 when the succeeding University of Toronto was reorganized the provincial government appropriated all the university land lying within the oval formed by the road which circles the present Queen's Park. This action was under authority of a statute by which the government was empowered to take as a site for public buildings such portion of what was incorrectly described as the university endowment as was 'not required for collegiate purposes, as may be found requisite.' Since the university was not consulted and since it had built on the ground taken over, the episode reflects only the weakness of the university's position at that time.

Queen's Park itself arose out of a statute of 1854 which authorized the university to lease to the city for 999 years up to fifty acres of land. A lease was effected in 1859, with the arrangement that the land would be kept in order by the city which would also pay rent to the university.

The land which had from early days been designated as free for the pleasure of the public was that which produced the most complicated problems. When three railways came to Toronto at about the same time they all made like homing pigeons for the waterfront, where they would connect with lake vessels as well as pick up the business of a city that was mainly along the lake shore. How to reconcile commercial interests with public recreation then became a puzzle. 'Most of our readers,' wrote the *Globe* in August 1853, 'know that for a great number of years it has been intended that an esplanade should be constructed along the front of the City, but we venture to say that very few of them had very clear notions where the Esplanade was to go, or how it was to be made. They had, doubtless, an idea of a narrow strip of land, covered with trees, but they were misty and indistinct.' The course of events did little to simplify the issue in the public mind. The strip of land which in 1818 had been vested in a group of citizens had remained in an undeveloped and apparently nebulous state until the arrival of the railways forced some kind of decision.[25]

Various solutions were offered. The city surveyor, J. G. Howard, proposed a broad walk between Front Street and the edge of the bank. From there he would fill in the bay for a considerable distance. F. C. Cumberland, chief engineer of the Northern Railway, produced a more elaborate and more expensive scheme. It called for the widening of Front Street and its continuation to the Don (instead of the existing line to the northeast); having an esplanade sixty-six feet wide to the south of that; and making land to the height of the existing wharves. The city called for tenders for the construction of an esplanade and received twelve. The one accepted, although a latecomer, was from Gzowski and Company, that company being in this case indistinguishable from the Grand Trunk Railway which was to receive a forty-foot right of way for the length of the esplanade.

Then the storm broke. The owners and lessees of water lots (and they were influential people), while agreeing that they were obligated to contribute to the filling needed, complained that the terms on which their obligation rested had been changed. Two newspapers, the *Colonist* and the *United Empire*, supported them. In 1855, with work under way, charges of corruption in connection with the contract were made and the council appointed a commission of inquiry under Adam Wilson, later mayor and still later chief justice. The commission held that owners and lessees of water lots had not failed in their duty, their claim that the proper conditions had not been met being accepted. The commission then commented that

Gzowski residence, Bathurst Street, 1860

the Gzowski bid had been late and higher than the others and ostensibly was accepted because the Grand Trunk threatened that otherwise it would go north of the city and not through it. This, they thought, was nonsense and alleged that on the part of the city there had been not only dereliction of duty but also dishonesty and fraud. The contract in their opinion was a bad one and should be cancelled.

It was cancelled, but a good deal of work on the esplanade had already been done and Gzowski and Company claimed compensation. Then came a passage of arms between the city and the Grand Trunk, the latter at one time warning that they would run their line on Queen Street all across the city. Prodded by the provincial government both sides agreed that the Grand Trunk should take over negotiations from Gzowski and Company and the claims against the city go to a board of arbitration. It was further agreed that the Grand Trunk was to have a forty-foot right of way south of Front Street and would assist in constructing or contracting for the esplanade. The railway then put in a claim for £45,725-1-1 and was awarded £40,973-1-6. A statute of 1857 (20 Vict., c. lxxx) in effect replaced the trustees of 1818 with the municipal government. By 1859 the basic work on the esplanade was finished and in 1865 more water lots were filled in and some macadamizing was done. That was the tortured story of the esplanade.

If handsome avenues and ranging parks were conspicuously lacking the appearance of the city was enhanced by buildings of distinction.[26] When the market of 1831 was burned in the fire of 1849 it was replaced by the St Lawrence Market, with which was combined a hall for entertainments and other gatherings. The architect, William Thomas, designed well both in and out. For University College F. W. Cumberland was appointed architect. The goodwill of the governor general, Sir Edmund Head, was unfortunately accompanied with amateurish proposals for alterations in Cumberland's original Gothic plan. While Head was blessedly out of town 'we polished away,' wrote John Langton, the vice-chancellor, 'almost all traces of Byzantine and got a hybrid with some features of Norman, of Early English, etc., with faint traces of Byzantine and Italian palazzo, but altogether a not unsightly building.' That was an over-modest description of a building placed by necessity to the west of Queen's Park where it stands as largely reconstructed after the fire of 1890.

To the decade of the fifties belongs the credit for the alteration and completion of Osgoode Hall. The east wing, dating from 1829, is the oldest part, but it is not known whether it was then in the classical form of today or was modified in 1844 when the central and western sections were added with something like the present appearance. No certainty exists as to which of several architects were employed up to that point, but undoubtedly the major reconstructon of 1857 was directed by the firm of Cumberland and Storm. To them are due not only the handsome exterior but much of the beauty of the interior, including the Great Library.

The new gaol on Gerrard Street, designed by William Thomas, large and quite attractive, was in pleasant surroundings. A fire delayed the opening until 1865. The Rossin House was, at the end of the fifties, the largest of the hotels. It was opened in 1857 at the corner of King and York streets. It had 252 rooms, all lighted by gas and the principal ones heated by steam. The Queen's, which had existed under another name, began a famous career in 1862 on Front Street as a centre for Torontonians and visitors alike. Betz's Hotel was from 1861 on the esplanade at the foot of Simcoe Street until it was swept away in 1872 to make room for the new union station.

The census of 1851–2 shows 4,558 families and 4,621 houses (of which 103 were vacant). The great majority of the houses – 3,630 – were frame, 938 were of brick, only twenty-four of stone, nineteen were log, and ten were 'shanties.' Ten years later stone houses were still rare but the proportion of brick had increased. That change was at least in part the result of

University College, before the fire

restrictions imposed after the fire of 1849, wooden buildings being no longer allowed in the central area.

Most of the houses were quite small but fine ones remained from earlier days and the new so-called 'mansions' reflected the growth of a wealthy class. The downtown district being still residential, William Cawthra (who owned property there) set his new house on Bay Street at the corner of King in 1852. It was large and designed in classical style by Joseph Sheard. The rambling Sleepy Hollow, built in 1849 for J. B. Robinson, son of the chief justice, on what is now College Street just west of University Avenue, was pretty much in the country and had a trout stream running through large wooded grounds. By the sixties some prosperous businessmen were moving far beyond the city limits. Senator John Macdonald, a wholesale drygoods merchant, chose a kind of Victorian architecture for his Oaklands on the east side of Avenue Road hill. James Austin, a wholesale grocer, built another large house in 1866 on the site of Spadina, the Baldwins' country house.

As the size, population, and wealth of the city grew so did both the demand for better public services and the financial resources to support them. In addition to taxation based on principles of assessment that were modified many times, the city was authorized by a statute of 1846 to issue the equivalent of bank notes. By 1851 the value of outstanding notes was £19,632. After that year it seems that reliance was placed instead on the sale of debentures. The facilities provided were not extended equally over the city and liberties (or the city after 1858), being fuller in the built-up areas.

Water was, as always, the prime need. In 1836 a committee appointed to study means of securing an adequate supply reported alternative sources, the headwaters of Garrison Creek or the bay, and after some delay the latter was chosen. In 1841 three men who had had experience in Montreal obtained, under the name of City of Toronto Gas-Light and Water Company, a franchise for fifty years. Using wooden pipes they pumped water from an intake at the foot of John Street into a reservoir placed on Huron Street just north of St Patrick Street. After fifteen years only one-ninth of the houses were attached to mains, but the principal need for water was in extinguishing fires. The company ran further wooden pipes into twenty outlets throughout the city but the flow was not good enough and the city was highly critical. For its part the company claimed that the city had not lived up to promises.

A test of both water supply and fire fighting equipment came with the so-called great fire of 1849. A by-law of 1845 had drawn together into a single code scattered regulations. The clauses that dealt with prevention forbade smoking in stables or carpenter shops, placed restrictions on the conditions of stoves and chimneys, required ladders leading to chimneys, directed disposal of hot ashes and the circumstances under which bonfires were permissible, and curtailed the discharge of firearms or fire crackers. For fighting fires once started, the by-law placed the fire companies under the control of the chief engineer although they might choose their own officers. By 1846 four fire engine companies and two hook and ladder companies, all made up of volunteers, stood ready. Lack of confidence in the water supply was indicated by continuation of the requirement that all carters were to bring water, being rewarded in the order of their appearance. The fire of 1849 broke out at one-thirty in the morning in the centre of the city and spread rapidly. The flow from the fire plugs was insufficient and some of the engines did not perform well; yet neither can have been as bad as represented, since, in a highly vulnerable city built mainly of wood, the blaze was put out by firemen and assisting troops before six o'clock in the morning.

A journalist writing a little later, in 1858, still condemned the water supply, claiming that it was inadequate in quantity and impure. For a hundred miles of streets, he said, only fifteen to twenty miles of pipe were laid. Private wells were still numerous.[27] For those who lacked water public baths on King Street offered a family season ticket for £4, a single hot bath for 1/10½, and a cold one for 1/3.

The same company as provided water was also to supply gas. In this respect too it was much criticized. The price was said to be too high and the quality low. Indignation mounted to the point at which a public meeting resolved to incorporate a new company, and so the Consumers' Gas Company was born. It bought out the rights of the old company in 1848.

The cloister at University College

Instead of meters the company used means of controlling the volume used, the contract reading in such a way as to suggest that the company was reluctant to sell gas:

Lights must not commence on any day until the sun has set, and all lights must be extinguished each night within ten minutes after the hour contracted for. If otherwise, they will be held as used for an additional hour each night ... In like manner, if the flame is allowed to burn higher than stipulated a corresponding price will be charged, and if on occasion more burners or jets are used than contracted for, the additional number will not only be charged but the offender will besides subject himself to a penalty provided for by the statute.

It sounds rather like the rules in a boarding school, but without the resident staff to enforce them. Coal oil lamps were not on the market for another ten years and even then were too expensive for general use.[28] Perhaps candles enabled those afflicted with insomnia to read in bed without fear of reprisals by the gas company. Some of the streets were lighted by gas, but how many householders availed themselves of the opportunity to install gas in their houses is not recorded.

The city struggled with streets. Crossings for pedestrians were laid with stones and a few flagstone sidewalks were added. Plank sidewalks were more common and were a boon except when the nails came loose and boards sprang up to hit the pedestrian from behind or rotting wood made holes to trap the unwary. In 1859 Ellen Gibson petitioned the city council 'for compensation on account of injuries occasioned to her daughter through falling into a hole in the sidewalk on Spadina Avenue.' More stretches of road were macadamized and others gravelled, but that travel was not without hazards is illustrated by the adventures of John Moor in 1859.

Driving in his buggy he noticed a hole ahead and tried to avoid it 'when the earth fell in, and the crust of the road was undermined for some distance, the result was, that your petitioner and the buggy found the bottom very quickly.' At first the Board of Works refused to pay for damage to the buggy on the ground that Moor should have got out and inspected the hole. Later they relented and paid him $25. Perhaps the city was doing all it could. In 1860 it spent $1,109.37 on macadamizing and $31,304.58 on repairs. When dust took the place of mud substantial sums were spent on watering the streets. The bill for that in 1857 was $7,073.

Apart from carriages for hire public transport began in 1849 with Williams' Bus Line on which you could travel from the St Lawrence Market to the Village of Yorkville for sixpence, and in a few years on additional routes. The success of street railways in American cities encouraged the creation of the Toronto Street Railway Company in 1861. By agreement with the city the horse-drawn cars were not to exceed a speed of six miles an hour. The fare was five cents and no transfers were given. The company began with six miles of track and eleven cars on which were carried two thousand passengers a day.

Development of the police force was broadly parallel to that in much larger American cities: from amateur to semi-professional and then to wholly professional. It was 1844 before New York reached the final stage and another dozen years before its police force ceased to be politically controlled. The skeleton of a professional force in Toronto dates from 1835 when five men were appointed as full-time police constables and fourteen others were put on call. An important change came as the result of a provincial statute of 1859. A Board of Commissioners of Police, made up of the mayor, the recorder or a county judge, and the police magistrate, was constituted. The force was still small (thirty-four in all ranks) but it nearly doubled in ten years and after that increased rapidly. A mounted section was added.[29] The force had plenty to do. A table showing 'offenders apprehended or summoned by city police' in the year 1859 gives a total of 4,593 offences. Much the largest category was drunk and disorderly conduct with a count of 1,188 males, 961 females, and 117 boys. The next largest – about half the first – was larceny, and the third was assault. Other items were small. Traffic offences were rare, eight arrests being made for 'furious driving.'[30]

The need for sewers was a constant refrain at council meetings and in the press. Some had been laid and householders could run pipes into them for a financial consideration. The method of charging seems odd now, as if calculated to discourage their use; and one can only deduce that it was not considered equitable to place the whole cost on those, the majority, who had not taken advantage of the sewers. The city granted individual licences to householders permitting them to use the sewers. To the embarrassment of

128

the council, however, they discovered that this practice was illegal. Clinging to the belief 'that to allow parties to enter the sewers [*sic?*] without giving any remuneration therefor, to be unjust and impolitic,' they secured an amendment to the Municipal Act authorizing the city to impose rent.

Although no accurate figures exist, the evidence suggests that few houses had all the facilities which later were regarded as standard: piped water, indoor plumbing, gas lighting, and central heating. All these were available, at least in parts of the city. Central heating came slowly and houses could be made comfortable with stoves, but the *Directory* for 1856 contained an advertisement by one company for warm air furnaces and another for 'hot air stoves.' Water from the city system was less prized when it was impure. Only some of the well-to-do had most or all of these comforts and most of the families in the lowest income brackets had none of them.

Carriage of mail was not a municipal responsibility but was, from the point of view of the inhabitants, an important public service. In 1837 letters were dispatched to many points on six days of the week, made possible by the more frequent and faster stage coaches. They went daily to Holland Landing in six hours and to Hamilton in ten. Service to the Bay of Quinte was also on six days of the week. Letters for Europe could be sent by Quebec in the season of navigation or by Halifax or New York at any time of year. The last was much the quickest, averaging five weeks. In 1847 the staff of the Toronto Post Office consisted of the postmaster, three clerks, and one letter carrier. Office hours were from seven in the morning until seven at night, with (unpaid) overtime frequent. On Sundays the post office was open for an hour in the morning and an hour in the afternoon.[31] The movement of mail was of course accelerated by railways. Before the middle of the century Toronto was connected with American telegraph systems. In 1866 a cable from Newfoundland was completed.

In the mid-1860s the people of Toronto, a city then of close to sixty thousand souls, were discussing the project for the union of the provinces of British North America. Upper Canada – or Canada West by its official but little used name – was generally in favour. As the largest political unit it had no fear of being absorbed and saw positive advantages in the proposed scheme. Here and there were pockets of opposition but in the end only eight out of sixty-five Upper Canadian members of the legislative assembly voted against the Quebec resolutions for confederation. One criticism was that no opportunity was given for an expression of popular opinion. In the absence of such no numerical estimate of Toronto views is possible, but the indications are that the proportion of pro and con was about the same as in Upper Canada as a whole.

The united Province of Canada had turned out to be a mixed blessing. One of its advantages, the St Lawrence entrance, would be retained in a

Key to a picture of Toronto, 1854, made by Mr Whitefield in 1853–4. He was an American artist and made views of all the principal Canadian cities

| | | | |
|---|---|---|---|
| 1 | City Hall | 18 | Weigh House |
| 2 | Lunatic Asylum | 19 | Coffin Block |
| 3 | Trinity College | 20 | Wellington Hotel |
| 4 | Osgoode Hall | 21 | St Lawrence Market |
| 5 | St Lawrence Hall | 22 | Canada Company |
| 6 | St James' Cathedral | 23 | The Fair Green |
| 7 | Congregational Church | 24 | Gas Company's Wharf |
| 8 | St Andrew's Church | 25 | Taylor's Wharf |
| 9 | United Presbyterian Church | 26 | Leak's Wharf |
| 10 | St George's Church | 27 | Beard's Wharf |
| 11 | Knox Church | 28 | Maitland's Wharf (Church Street) |
| 12 | Mechanics' Institute | 29 | Brown's Wharf |
| 13 | Holy Trinity | 30 | Yonge Street Wharf |
| 14 | St Michael's Cathedral | 31 | Tinning's Wharf |
| 15 | Normal School | 32 | Queen's Wharf |
| 16 | Unitarian Church | 33 | Asylum Water Works |
| 17 | Dr Widmer's House | | |

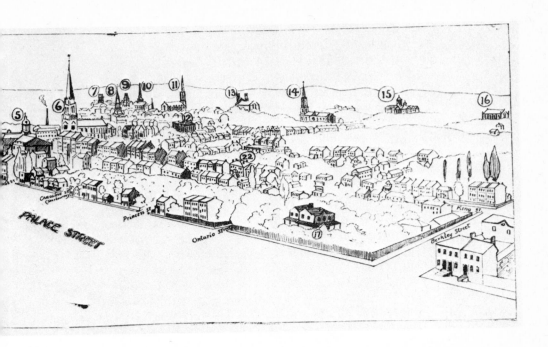

general union, but the uncongenial marriage of English and French cultures would be annulled. As a commercial city Toronto was attracted by the economic arguments in favour of confederation, railways across the continent and an impetus to internal and external trade.

Of the Toronto newspapers the *Globe* was a vigorous advocate of union. The *Leader*, the most important Conservative paper, was at first critical of the confederation proposals but in the end backed them. Any aid that came from Irish papers was tepid indeed. The *Canadian Freeman* was apprehensive that federalism would endanger the Roman Catholic minority in a province that would be largely Protestant. The *Irish Canadian* was sure that some change in the constitution was needed but not prepared to say that confederation was the right answer.

After the conference in Quebec in 1864, at which the lines of union were agreed, the delegates set off by train to popularize their resolutions. In Toronto they were greeted by a large crowd, by cheers, bands, and fireworks. The carriages could barely make their way to the Queen's Hotel through a Front Street lit with torches. Not too much should be deduced from a demonstration of this kind except that there was an absence of hostility. Probably most of the crowd had no idea what the Quebec resolutions were.

The positions taken by Toronto representatives in the legislature should afford a more measurable judgment of opinion. Of the two nominated legislative councillors resident in Toronto James Gordon was silent in the council. John Ross spoke at length in defence of confederaton but mainly in verbose references to historical parallels or in refutation of J. G. Currie of Niagara. G. W. Allan, the elected councillor, supported the resolutions, claiming that they would solve the differences between Upper and Lower Canada, bring commercial advantages, and constitute acceptance of proper responsibility for military defence.

The two members of the assembly spoke on opposite sides. John Macdonald expressed himself as in favour of union in principle but dissatisfied with certain details of the scheme before the House. Upper Canada would be called upon to pay an undue share of the general expenses. Alexander Smith made a patient, routine defence of confederation. He had not, he said, originally been in favour of it, but the abrogation of reciprocity put it in a different light. He spoke on behalf of 'the first commercial city of Upper Canada' which must have opportunities for trade, and in this connection the Intercolonial Railway was necessary. He went on to describe a public meeting in Toronto the results of which, he suggested, cast doubt on whether Macdonald reflected the views of his constituents.

I attended a large and influential meeting of the citizens of the City of Toronto before the meeting of this House, and a gentleman then proposed that the scheme should not be carried into effect until it was referred to the people, but he could not even get a seconder to his resolution. For myself, I feel justified by the results of that meeting in supporting the scheme throughout. The meeting was extensively advertised – all had the opportunity to attend, and both sides of the question were ably argued.

Two of the three members for York County said nothing in the House. The third was W. P. Howland, postmaster general. If, he said cryptically, he had been a delegate at Quebec he would have opposed certain sections but now it was necessary to accept or reject the whole. Not much inspiration so far, but little evidence of opposition. To find the resident of Toronto who exerted great influence one has to go beyond York County to Oxford South, represented in the House by George Brown. This politician-journalist was one of the principal fathers of confederation. An early and forceful advocate of union he spoke for Ontario as George-Etienne Cartier did for Quebec. Even to outline his arguments and recount his actions would be to tell much of the story of the confederation movement.

In its issue of 1 July 1867 Brown's *Globe* hailed the 'dawn of this gladsome summer morn.' Already at midnight the bells of St James' Cathedral had announced the union of the provinces, and at four in the morning the Union Jack had been hoisted on a new flagstaff and greeted with a salute of twenty-one guns. At six o'clock began the roasting of a whole ox, to be distributed later among the poor. At nine-thirty a gathering in the Mechanics' Institute invoked divine blessing on the Dominion. Next came a military parade and a *feu de joie*, and in the afternoon a picnic or trips around the island in a vessel hired for the occasion. In the evening a concert and dancing were arranged for the pleasure of the public. Finally a band played among the trees of Queen's Park and fireworks lit up the sky. It had been a long day with nothing missed to mark what the *Leader* described as 'the most important day for the Provinces of British North America.'

**JOSEPH LYONS, TOBACCONIST,**

**WHOLESALE & RETAIL,**

## 39 KING STREET, TORONTO,

OPPOSITE MESSRS. JACQUES AND HAY,

IMPORTER OF

# PRINCIPE & HAVANA CIGARS

Cavendish Tobaccos, Cut do.; Meerschaum Pipes, Fancy Clay do.;
Snuff Boxes, Cigar Cases, Pipe Tubes, &c. &c.

### SNUFFS OF ALL KINDS.

A large and well assorted stock of the above articles always on hand,
and will be sold at the lowest possible rates.

# 6

# *Provincial capital*

Toronto was a capital again. Territorially Ontario was a revival of Upper Canada, not only in the extent of its boundaries but also in that the population, though multiplied many times, had still barely touched on the wide ranges of the Canadian Shield. In many respects change had been rapid. The new government settled in on a location hardly recognizable as that to which Simcoe and his little band had come seventy-five years earlier. The harbour into which a lone fur trader had guided the lieutenant governor's little ship was now alive with steam vessels. Trains puffed over the area where the canvas Government House had once stood. Streets and solid buildings stretched back from the bay as far as the eye could see.

According to those who designed the federal constitution of 1867 a province was to play a very minor role. The revolt of the provinces, led by Ontario, against that concept is germane to the story of Toronto only to the extent that its success meant that the legislature which had its home in the city developed in function, and therefore in size, to a degree never dreamt of by the fathers of confederation. To be the capital of Ontario was of much greater significance than could have been expected.

In the century-long battle over federal and provincial powers responsibility for municipal institutions was one of the few subjects not in dispute. That it should be assigned without question wholly to the provinces was consistent with the principle that provincial governments were to be restricted to local affairs and to be, as some politicians said, themselves scarcely more than large municipal councils. If any other argument had been needed it would have been that in the maritime provinces municipal institutions had hardly been separated from provincial ones.

Toronto was in much the same relationship to the government of the new province as it had been to that of the old. The authority of the city continued to be no more than what was permitted by the province. Sauce for the provincial goose was not sauce for the municipal gander, since the province, while successfully resisting the extreme federalists, not only maintained but enlarged its control over cities in the nineteenth and twentieth centuries.

Within itself the government of Toronto experienced little constitutional change. The first act of the Province of Ontario relating to municipal institutions (30 and 31 Vict., c. xxx) was passed in 1868. It was brief and made no substantive amendments to the lengthy statutes of the Province of Canada on the same subject. The mode of election of the council continued to be periodically altered. The choice of a mayor, from 1859 by vote of the citizens, reverted in 1867 to the council, only to return to popular vote in 1874. From time to time provincial statutes amended the methods of raising revenue, whether by authorizing debentures to a specified limit or permitting rates for local improvements. The following assessment statistics show taxes and property value.

| Year | Value of real and personal property | Rate in mills | Total city and school tax | Local improvement rates | Total of city taxes |
|---|---|---|---|---|---|
| 1879 | $49,757,562.00 | 17½ | $870,763.52 | $43,239.13 | $922,109.46 |
| 1881 | 53,540,910.99 | 16½ | 883,425.03 | 46,255.12 | 936,116.40 |
| 1883 | 61,954,635.00 | 15½ | 960,296.84 | 131,381.64 | 1,091,620.44 |
| 1885 | 68,988,567.00 | 17 | 1,172,805.02 | 139,488.45 | 1,304,717.86 |
| 1887 | 83,259,533.00 | 15¾ | 1,311,337.64 | 170,112.09 | 1,482,555.68 |

One attempt in the 1880s to re-examine the municipal institutions of the province and of other countries, to see if improvements could be made at home in the light of experience elsewhere, was a failure. The three commissioners – T. W. Anglin, E. F. B. Johnston, and William Houston – reported that they had little information and seemed to have little idea of how to go about their task. Some factual material included in the report, such as the figures of assessment quoted above, was useful, but no suggestions for change were made.[1]

Contemporary judgments of the wisdom and effectiveness of local government in Toronto varied, but more is recorded of criticism than of praise. The *Evening Telegram*, self-appointed monitor, claimed in the seventies to find instances of inefficiency, extravagance, and corruption. It dismissed any comment by the *Globe*, which, it said, should never be listened to on municipal affairs since it persistently glossed over the sins of Reformers on the council. No doubt there were weaknesses and would have been more without the press as watch-dog. Looking at the personalities involved it is evident that the families of early York were dropping out of local government, but among their successors were men of ability and probity.[2]

The empire over which they reigned remained for several years constant in size until the first series of annexations began. Yorkville came first, in 1883, a move desired by city and village alike. Renamed St Paul's Ward, the former village's boundaries ran from about Sherbourne Street to Bedford Road, and from Bloor Street to Walker Avenue. It should be noted, however, that while in this and other cases street names give approximate limits they are not necessarily exact. In 1884 two further and large areas were added. The new St Mark's Ward included High Park and the former village of Brockton. St Matthew's Ward, between the Kingston and Danforth roads, was the first major advance to the east of the Don River. In 1887 St Paul's Ward was extended to the Don and on the west to Kendal Avenue. The latter area, between Bloor and Dupont streets, came to be known as the Annex. In 1888 another large area north of Bloor and west of Bathurst Street was added – with Sunnyside in the same year and the Town of Parkdale in the next. That completed the major annexations of the nineteenth century. From 1883 until 1893 the additions, large and small, amounted to 5,231.8 acres, or a little more than half of the original size of the city and liberties combined.[3]

In this larger city it was becoming less common for men to live cheek-by-jowl with their offices, shops, or factories. There was no legal zoning. Voluntary segregation of the commercial and the residential, of large and small houses, was slow but beginning to show. Exceptions can be found to every generalization that can be made as to the pattern that Toronto was gradually assuming in the seventies and eighties. Some old houses in the lower part of the town were still lived in by the same families and others were converted into boarding houses or business establishments; but on the whole it could be said that a section was asserting itself as primarily for trade or finance. Landing at one of the wharves the first crossroad encountered was Esplanade Street, reached after clambering over railway tracks and around warehouses and sheds. Its only similarity to the sylvan retreat once envisaged was that it was close to the bay, which could be seen if no train or building were in the way. Such small houses as were on its extremities were those of persons employed nearby.

Front Street belied its name for the bay shore had withdrawn from it. It was not without distinction for on it were some of the best hotels. At the corner of Simcoe Street, too, the legislature of Ontario had moved into the old government buildings after they had undergone major repair. Beyond them Clarence Square was a pleasant residential oasis, though only partly built up. The central parts of King and Queen streets were being taken over by one form of business or another, although on the eastern and western reaches some houses were mixed in with commerce. Duke and Duchess streets were losing caste as residential districts. The north-and-south streets were going through much the same change in their southern blocks.

It would be generally true to say that south of a line cut across at about Gerrard Street the predominant character was coming to be commercial, interspersed with poorer houses. Thus Beverley, Church, or Jarvis streets were no longer 'good addresses' in their lower blocks but higher up were choice places in which to live. Good houses were going up along Carleton Street (to give it the original and proper spelling), around Queen's Park on the university lots, and on Simcoe and Wellesley streets. St George Street was one of the few that had never had a double life. It was opened late in the day with substantial houses being built on it.

Some of the minor streets south of Bloor were filling in slowly. Harbord Street, for example, had hardly any houses in 1878 and Willcocks had only two. Except in its middle section Bloor Street was largely residential. On the west it ran into open fields beyond Bathurst Street, having already lost quality as it went. On the east it was spottily taken up to near the Don Valley. North of Bloor Street lots in Rosedale were for sale but being bought slowly, perhaps because of their distance from the centre. Further west the less pretentious suburbs of Seaton Village and Dovercourt were fairly well inhabited. Beyond that again West Toronto Junction was building up. All expansion was mainly to the north and west, with the lands beyond the Don coming into the picture only later.

The growth of a district given over primarily to business was a sign of economic progress. That advance in the main continued along the same lines as in the sixties, with the modification that manufacturing was taking a somewhat larger though still secondary place. The firm of Christie, Brown and Company, which from 1868 made biscuits, was using twenty thousand barrels of flour in a year. Transfer to Toronto of the Massey Manufacturing Company in 1879 and of John Abell's factory a little later was an indication of a trend away from the smaller towns, many of which had had small factories making agricultural implements. But the list in 1885 was still not long. The brewers and distilleries continued to flourish. Robert Hay and Company, successor in 1872 to Jacques and Hay, employed about 575 men. The St Lawrence Foundry had 150 employees; P. W. Ellis and Company, manufacturing jewellers, had 100; Latham and Lowe, who made clothing, had 100 hands; Theodore Heintzman, 150; Taylor Brothers (paper), 100; Cobban Manufacturing Company, 125.

Another Toronto bank, the Dominion, was added in 1871. The president was James Austin, who had left the board of the Bank of Commerce after a difference over policy with his fellow Irishman, William McMaster. Once a printer, he had done well as a wholesale grocer, switched to management of the Consumers' Gas Company, and built the fine house that has been mentioned. The vice-president was one of the Howland brothers, Peleg. Frank Smith, also Irish, also a grocer, was one of the directors. He was one of the most influential Roman Catholics in Toronto.

McCall Stock & Anderson's Oil Works, Adelaide Street East,
dealers in lubricating and lamp oils

Don Brewery, T. Davies & Bro., maltsters, brewers, and bottlers, about 1877

Wholesalers were at the top of their form and some changes were showing in retail trade. Later speciality shops were to the fore, nearly all of them on a short stretch of King Street. The W. A. Murray Company carried drygoods, millinery, and clothes. John Kay had drygoods too but was turning to concentration on carpets. John Catto was the arbiter of linen. A different approach was followed by two newcomers, Timothy Eaton and Robert Simpson. The first was an Irishman who had, with his brothers, operated a drygoods store in St Mary's, near Stratford. Simpson, thirty-eight years old when he came to Toronto, had migrated from Scotland eighteen years earlier and worked in a shop in Newmarket. Both started drygoods shops on the unfashionable Yonge Street, Eaton in 1869 and Simpson in 1872, and both converted them into department stores.

The success of the two new shops in Toronto and beyond was due to no particular innovation and no single cause. Department store was no more than a longer name for general store, and that was the oldest form of shop in Toronto. Fixed prices instead of bargaining and cash in place of credit had been introduced in many towns of Ontario more than a generation earlier, and it is probable that both Eaton and Simpson had become familiar with these practices before they came to Toronto. Importing was as old as Toronto and some of the early shopkeepers had gone abroad to do their own buying. Bargain sales were traditional. The mail order business had been handicapped by inadequate postal services but had been common for fifty years. From the early thirties Toronto shops had been enterprising in promoting business in York and Simcoe counties, going to their customers as well as waiting for them.

It was a wise blending of known techniques, together with skilled management, that enabled Eaton's and Simpson's to outdistance other shops. In Toronto they became in time institutions, and beyond it extended their reach as no other shops had previously succeeded in doing. Another example of the widespread operation of Toronto as a trading centre is in an advertisement in the *Leader* in May 1871: five sailing vessels were to go to the lower provinces with grain, three of them to Halifax, one to Pictou, and one to St John's, Newfoundland; the main return cargo was to be coal.

Economic progress, however, was slowed by the depression of the seventies. A letter to the *Telegram* in September 1877, though perhaps overdrawn, is a reminder that failure ran parallel with success.

During the last two years we have all felt more or less the depression in trade, and the class of business people who have suffered most are jewellers, booksellers, and dealers in fancy goods, for all those articles are luxuries and things people can really do without. The large number of vacant stores in the city tell a melancholy tale. The hundreds of families who but a few years ago occupied them, and thrived and were happy, where are they now? A few of them have left the city to seek a living elsewhere, but the majority of them, not being able to pay house rent, have huddled themselves together, two or three families now living in one house. There are not less than a hundred vacant stores on Queen Street alone at the present time, and many business people, who just manage to stand the pressure now by dragging out a miserable existence, hoping for better times, which come not, will fall like leaves in autumn.

Better times did come shortly after that was written, but it would be interesting to know how substantial was the exodus mentioned by this anonymous writer. The United States government, at least, thought it worthwhile to maintain in Toronto a United States Land Agency with a resident agent whose business it was to encourage people to leave. He advertised 'the sale of improved and unimproved land and city property in the western and southern states, for cash or long credit.' Those buying such lands would be given free railway tickets to reach them.

Unemployment affected all classes of people, not least the wage-earners, but it was in the years just before the depression that there occurred in Toronto a head-on collision between employers and organized labour. Trade unions had been slow to develop in Canada and some of those which did start lasted for only a short time; but little is certain about the history of most of them. The Toronto *Directory* for 1868 lists only five, those of the carpenters, moulders, shoemakers, bakers, and printers. There may have been others. Certainly there had been before, and were to be after, more unions than those. In 1871 the Toronto Trades Assembly was formed.

The trade union movement, which had limped along, was approaching the point at which it might become a major force, as had already happened in England. From there had come influences on both employees and employers. Immigrants had brought with them belief and experience in unions and hence a desire to promote them in Canada. Capitalists and employers for their part were inclined to accept the English doctrine of laissez faire and to frown on unions of any kind. The social conditions of Canada, however, were in some respects very different to those of England. Canada had no great landowning class or peasantry, no extensive inherited wealth, had been little affected by the conservative reaction after the French revolution, had been through no industrial revolution, and was not an industrial state. When Canadian employers urged the free operation of the law of supply and demand and represented the opportunities that lay before each individual they were wrong in degree but not in kind. It was possible for a penniless immigrant, with no outside help, to rise to a position of wealth and power. William Davies, for example, started with little to create his empire of meat packing. Timothy Eaton was a poor Irishman. Alexander Mackenzie came as a stonemason and ended as prime minister.

George Brown, who was at the centre of the controversy in 1872, was another success story. He and his father had earlier brushed with the Typographical Union and he had never left any doubt of his opposition to unions. In a long article on 11 May 1867 the *Globe* remarked that 'Both Europe and America [that is, the United States] appear to be suffering from an epidemic of strikes among labourers of almost all sorts . . . We have had, even in Toronto, a touch of the same troubles, though Canada is, and has been, fortunately, very little affected by these movements.' The *Globe* thought it hopeful that 'labourers' were trying to improve their position and added that 'the co-operative principle is a sound one if judiciously applied.' It was unfortunately the case that capitalists and labourers were in opposition to each other. Was there any common ground? Surely it was that 'competition comes in to hold the balance between employer and employee.' In rare instances wages were unreasonably forced down, and then 'combinations' to raise them could do good service. The article went on to rehearse the usual charges against unions: loss of time from strikes, opposition to labour-saving devices, deprivation of liberty of action by the employee. Co-operative groups rather than unions were needed.

Most of the employers of the day would have agreed that unions were undesirable, even if they had not sat down to think out a philosophy on the relation of labour and capital. They would keep unions out of their plants if they could – one conclusion which they shared with that self-appointed friend of 'the people,' William Lyon Mackenzie. The strike which broke out in 1872 was not by factory workers but by the relatively venerable Typographical Union. Its demand for the nine-hour day, however, was an objective pursued in England and the United States, and recently by the newly formed Toronto Trades Assembly. The printers demanded both shorter hours and higher wages. The Master Printers (that is, the employers) resisted: or rather most of them did, for a minority, and notably the Conservative *Leader*, backed the strikers.[4]

The master printers then made a bad tactical error in laying charges against the strikers, leading to the arrest of fourteen of the leaders. The methods of the magistrate were brusque in the extreme but he was on sound legal ground in holding that a labour union was an unlawful combination in restraint of trade. Incredibly, neither the unions nor anyone else seem previously to have grasped the significance of leaving the unions in that position, or perhaps even appreciated that such was the case. The hard fact, however, was that the Canadian parliament had done nothing to change the position as defined by common law. The Conservatives now saw very clearly the delicious opportunity opened by the popularity of James Beaty, publisher of the *Leader* and member of parliament, as a result of his support of the union's cause. The prime minister, John A. Macdonald, who had been watching his party's support slip away, was quick to appreciate that he could kill two birds with one stone: pick up, without effort or commitment, such labour votes as there were, and score in the senseless vendetta that he and Brown had long conducted.

It was important, however, not to kill the wrong birds; for it would be suicidal to sacrifice middle-class votes while gaining labour ones. Presumably for that reason the government went no further than to adopt the defective British legislation of 1871. That on the one hand had strengthened the act of 1824 (to which there was no Canadian parallel) under which unions had been made legal, but at the same time had amended the criminal law in such a way as to make any strikes dangerous for those taking part in them. The Canadian parliament passed two acts, virtually copies of the British ones, with hardly a question. The immediate results were the collapse of the case against the Toronto strikers, compromise settlement of the labour dispute, laurels for Macdonald, and two Conservative seats in Toronto.

Yet even while applauding, the trade unionists had reservations about a legislative package which seemed to take away with one hand what it gave with the other; and the new labour organ, the *Ontario Workman*, did not hesitate to denounce the criminal clauses as 'iniquitous and degrading.' But it was not until 1875 that remedial legislation was secured. Meanwhile the labour movement was slipping backward under the effects of the depression. The Canadian Labour Union, which held its first convention in Toronto in 1873, was hardly accurately named as it was representative of Ontario only. Of the fifteen unions that sent delegations twelve had branches in Toronto. From then the union went downhill until at the third meeting in 1875 a bare quorum was present.

With declining incomes and rising unemployment the wage-earners of the city suffered, and with the weakening of their position came a slowdown of unionization, which in any case had not gone far. By the eighties, however, industry throughout Canada had grown sufficiently for it to became necessary to examine the situation of those employed in it. In 1882 two commissioners appointed by the federal government to inquire into 'the working of Mills and Factories, and the labor employed therein' made their report.[5] It was factual, succinct, and grimly revealing. The commissioners visited five provinces, finishing their travels in Toronto. The factories that they examined were not identified, but since all the important conclusions were based on multiple cases it can be assumed that they applied in general to Toronto.

The commissioners found that a number of firms were far from helpful, and indeed they were refused admittance to several, especially those of which they had information 'that a not very creditable state of affairs existed.' They were concerned with the extent of child labour, of children of fourteen and even less than ten years of age – and all too often employed because of the cupidity of parents. Hours of work varied, a general opinion being that they should be ten for adults and less for children. Accidents from unprotected machinery were numerous. Steam engines and boilers were entrusted to youngsters who were quite untrained in their operation. In most of the mills fire escapes were inadequate. Ventilation had been given little attention and overcrowding was common. Washrooms were sometimes primitive. Such were the weaknesses of many factories and mills; others were well conducted.

Two years later the Ontario legislature passed the Ontario Factories Act (47 Vict., c. 39) which outlined standards to be observed and provided for inspectors to be sure that they were. Precautions were to be taken against accidents and fire, and children might be employed only if there were no danger to their health. In itself a good act, practice showed that it was ineffective because it was not enforced. In 1886 the federal government tried again through the appointment of a royal commission with sweeping instructions to inquire into the whole field of labour.[6] Unlike its predecessor the royal commission was verbose, opinionated, partisan, and naïve. Too much weight cannot, therefore, be placed on its findings. On the other hand the evidence put before it shows all too clearly that in some factories outrageous conditions and procedures existed. The wages quoted in the report seem to have been unreasonably low, but as insufficient attention was paid to the cost of living the real income of employees cannot be calculated from the information supplied.

Considering on the one hand the growth of industry in Toronto and on the other a composite picture of factories as they were at the time suggests a number of causes which could appropriately be espoused by the trade unions. The two which always received first attention were wages and hours of work. In the absence of agreed norms there could not be on these other than subjective views. On measures designed to avoid accidents, to improve ventilation, sanitary conditions, and the like it was possible to lay down rules with more confidence. This is just what the Ontario legislature sought, unsuccessfully, to do in its legislation of 1884, and what the Canadian parliament consistently failed to do because of the uncertainty of the jurisdiction of federal and provincial authorities.

The unions, depressed as was the economy, revived with it at the end of the seventies. The Toronto *Directory* for 1878 has a long list of unions which held meetings in the Trades' Assembly Hall on Adelaide Street. When the International Typographical Union convened its annual convention in Toronto in 1881 the opportunity was seized to call a public meeting to organize what became an important factor in the labour movement, the Toronto Trades and Labor Council. Two years later the latter body went a step further by inviting all Canadian trade unions to a gathering in Toronto, and on that occasion the Canadian Labor Congress was established.

The economic-social order in which the trade unions were promoting through collective action the interests of their members was based on the doctrine and practice of free enterprise. The unions, which as yet represented only a segment of the labour force, might at times be inclined to brand as hard and selfish the owners and managers of factories, but in not a few cases it was those same men who contributed money and time to the least fortunate citizens – the poor, the sick, and the unemployed. To them tough rules in business and charity to the distressed were not contradictory. To criticism they could answer that while it was true that some of them – those who succeeded – made substantial profits while paying low wages and demanding long hours of work, that was of the essence of the competitive system.

George Brown, on whom had been heaped the odium for the actions of the master printers in 1872, was depicted by some opponents as a ruthless exploiter of labour; and yet he believed as strongly in social justice as he did in the unfettered authority of employers. He had been a leader in assisting escaped slaves and in battling for prison reform. Reporters from the *Globe* were sent to explore and publicize the most sordid districts in Toronto, and the accounts of what they saw revealed ghastly conditions. On Christmas Eve of 1868 one such reporter found a half-frozen, six-year-old girl afraid to go home until she had sold all her papers. Having bought the remaining stock the man followed to her house where he saw a callous mother and a drunken brute of a father who was preparing to beat the child for an alleged shortage of two pence. Proceeding through slums he entered one dilapidated house after another in which, amid poverty and dirt, were drunken women of all ages, some old hags, some prostitutes. The last word was not one that could be printed in a newspaper, but lest it be thought that the Victorian eye was blind, it should be noted that the writer made quite clear what he meant.

Evidence of the evils arising out of excessive drinking in Toronto had in generation after generation been too strong to be refuted, but in each age the problem faced contemporaries. The wisdom or practicability of legal prohibition was disputed but no sane person questioned widespread drunkenness. Toronto was the centre of a crusade for what was still called temperance, although the distinction between wine and hard liquor had long since been dropped. The supporters of temperance had come to put less hope in pledges of abstinence and turned to measures for stopping the sale of spirituous liquors. Propaganda, however, continued to be directed toward both ends by a number of organizations in the city. The Temperance Reformation Society held a 'public religious temperance meeting' every Sunday afternoon in its hall on Temperance Street. The Sons of Temperance had meetings every Monday and Wednesday evening. The Independent Order of Good Templars had four temples in Toronto, each of which met weekly. The Christian Total Abstinence Society gathered fortnightly in the Methodist church on Berkeley Street. The Order of British Templars had three lodges in Toronto, each with a weekly meeting. Innocent entertainment without speeches was provided by the Toronto Coffee Association, founded in 1881, with C. S. Gzowski as president.[7]

Overlapping with the efforts of such bodies and influenced by them was legislation enabling urban or rural areas to prohibit the sale of liquor. The Dunkin Act of 1864 was superseded by the Canada Temperance Act (the Scott Act) of 1878. Both had strong advocates in Toronto but neither was accepted by the city as a whole. When the issue was being discussed in 1877 the *Telegram* and the *Globe* were cautiously in favour of local option but the *Leader* and the *Mail* were opposed. Attention later turned to the control of liquor outlets. In 1885, in spite of four hundred licences, 370 cases of illegal sale came before the police court. The Municipal Reform Association supported W. H. Howland's candidacy for mayor and in 1886 he was elected by acclamation. During his régime the number of licences was reduced, the system of licensing overhauled, and illegal sales cut to a low figure.

The municipal government, the churches, and individuals struggled, according to their various lights, against immorality, poverty, dirt, and disease. No one could seriously question the existence of social deficiencies that were evident on every day of the week. Slums were not new, but as the city grew so did they. In one year eighteen tenement houses were condemned as unfit for habitation, and the *Globe*, after another of its explorations, described a particularly obnoxious set of buildings on King Street known as Elliot's Row. It found both the houses and their inhabitants to be highly undesirable. King Street was all things to all men. In some sections it had the worst dives in Toronto and in others fashionable citizens paraded on Saturday afternoons.

Even for those who clung to the escapist doctrine that the poor preferred squalor the danger to health from unsanitary conditions, magnified in slum districts, could not be dismissed. Since 1834 the city had had a board of health, the constitution and duties of which were frequently amended. Under a comprehensive by-law of 1869 council's authority in matters of health was delegated to the Board of Works which was given sweeping powers in respect of 'all nuisances, sources of filth, and causes of sickness within the said City, or in any vessel within the harbour.' In a detailed list of matters for attention were dirty buildings or streets, infectious diseases, impure food, slaughter houses, drains, and privies. An elected health inspector was to take steps for the removal of dirt or decaying matter from streets; analyse the water in any well and if necessary forbid

Doing King Street, 1879, by H. deT. Glazebrook

its use; check sewers and other public works; make regular visits to
butcher shops and slaughter houses; and board any ship in harbour
suspected of being dirty or having sick personnel. Council was also to
appoint medical health officers as needed, either full or part time. The
obvious weakness of the structure was that no one health officer could
carry out all the duties assigned to him. This was remedied in a further
by-law of 1890 under which the city was to appoint as many sanitary
inspectors as were required.

Other types of preventive or remedial measures were mainly left to
private initiative. Additions were constantly made to the homes and hostels
intended for various groups in need of help of some kind. One such was
the Young Women's Christian Association of Toronto, founded in 1873.
Its constitution read in part:

The purposes of this Association shall be the temporal, moral and religious
welfare of young women who are dependent upon their own exertions for support.
It shall be the duty of the Board of Managers, assisted by all members of the
Association, to seek out young women taking up their residence in Toronto, and
endeavour to bring them under moral and religious influences, by introducing
them to the members and privileges of this Association, securing their attendance
at some place of worship, and by every means in their power surrounding them
with all Christian associates.

147

Two houses at the corner of Duke and George streets were secured for a boarding house which proved an immediate success. In the second year 190 boarders included dressmakers and milliners; nurses, teachers, and students; bookkeepers, saleswomen, and machinists. In 1876 the YWCA arranged for religious services and personal interviews in gaols, and in 1878 started the Haven where young women convicted of petty crimes could board on release from gaol. In 1885 the YWCA sponsored the Girls' Industrial Institute which served hot meals and at which classes were held in stenography, dressmaking, singing, reading, writing, and spelling.[8]

In 1887 the Humane Society of Toronto was established for the protection of children and animals, and when the humans were separated from the other creatures the Children's Aid Society was organized in 1891. For the treatment of disease three new hospitals were added. The Hospital for Incurables, intended for indigents, opened on Bathurst Street in 1874 and moved to Dunn Avenue in 1878. The Hospital for Sick Children, unique on the continent when it began in 1875, resulted from the energy and generosity of John Ross Robertson, publisher of the *Telegram*. It had various small quarters until it moved into its new building on College Street in 1891. Grace Hospital was founded by homeopathists in 1888 as a dispensary for the poor, open for an hour each day. Before long it was accepting resident patients.

Important contributions to both health and welfare were made out of the estate of Andrew Mercer which escheated to the crown when he died intestate and without lawful heirs in 1871. The background is bizarre.[9] Mercer, commonly believed to be illegitimate, migrated from England to York in 1801. He had a good income, mainly from mortgages and other loans, and he was generous – never pursuing debtors and giving to every religious, charitable, or educational cause for which he had an appeal. On the other hand he lived with the greatest simplicity, spending little on clothes and never entertaining. The nagging problem in his life began in 1850 when he employed Bridget O'Reilly as a sewing woman. She lived in his house and was evidently the mother of his son, Andrew. She made his life miserable but he never could persuade her to leave the house although he offered a sum for her support. He kept a record entitled 'Memo. of Biddy's Bad Conduct,' in which he noted that she constantly stole money, totalling $350.30 in 1860 (evidently a serious underestimate). In her 'mad fits' she broke windows and Mercer kept a record of the panes destroyed. By direction of the Court of Chancery a search for heirs was made in Canada, England, and Scotland but without success. Suddenly, in 1875, Bridget and her son claimed that she had been married to Mercer, a claim coldly rejected by the court. They even produced what they said was a will in favour of 'wife and son' but that was ruled to be a forgery.

In spite of these dubious activities the two did well. Bridget O'Reilly was known to have more than $12,000 in savings accounts; and because it could not be proved that that was part of the estate she kept it. Andrew Junior, whose activities did him little credit, was granted a sum of money and land. As the original estate had amounted to more than $140,000 a good deal remained to be disposed of, and in view of Mercer's interests the inspector of public charities was consulted on the disposition of the balance. On his recommendation $10,000 was allotted for the creation of a Provincial Eye and Ear Infirmary in connection with the General Hospital, and $90,000 to establish an institution to be known as the Andrew Mercer Ontario Reformatory for Females. It was built to the south of King Street, a few blocks east of Dufferin Street.

No mirror reflects as much of the complicated life of a city as does the press. Events and developments of innumerable kinds are recorded, and if incompletely or in a partisan spirit that too is suggestive. The character of the publications, the subjects that they cover, the points of view they take, and the reception they meet all are evidence of the interests and attitudes of the time and place. Why a particular publication starts and why it succeeds or fails is in itself illuminating. Or the case may be seen the other way: more especially before the invention of radio the press was the daily or weekly or monthly fare of a large proportion of the population. Its weaknesses were in part attributable to readers, and their mental blocks in part to what they read.

No better period can be found for examining the press of Toronto than in the 1870s by which time the list of publications was long, the types varied, and experiments common.[10] Doctors were served by three specialized publications and lawyers by half a dozen. Reminders that Toronto served an agricultural area were the *Canada Farmer*, a fortnightly published since 1864 by the *Globe*, and the *Farmers' Monthly and Agricultural Review*. Commercial affairs were covered in some six or seven periodicals. One, and at times two, monthly magazines were for family reading. Bengough's famous political cartoons appeared in *Grip* (1873–94).

The churches were active in publications relating wholly or in part to religion. The doyen was the *Christian Guardian*, organ of the Wesleyan Methodists since 1829 and made famous by Egerton Ryerson who was editor for three periods. The Methodist Book Room also brought out the monthly *Canadian Methodist Magazine*. From 1857 to 1884 the Primitive Methodists published the *Christian Journal*, a weekly which carried general news and claimed to be not 'intensely denominational.' The Presbyterians had a weekly, the *Canadian Presbyterian*, and the Baptists the *Canadian Baptist*. The division in the Church of England between high and low church was shown in the fact that for twenty-five years before they merged the *Dominion Churchman* was paralleled by the *Evangelical Churchman*.

Sunday school papers and improving home reading such as *Golden Hours for the Young* and *Pleasant Hours* were numerous and often short-lived. On a subject that deeply concerned some of the churches and all in some way was the *Canada Temperance Advocate*.

An important development in this period was the rise of periodicals of quality devoted to learning, literature, or opinion. The *Canadian Journal*, published in alternate months by the Canadian Institute, was older (1852) but it was discontinued in 1878. *Saturday Night* began a long career in 1887, founded by W. C. Nichol and E. E. Sheppard, the former having been editor of the *News*. Before long the two men separated. Nichol undertook a new and similar weekly, *Life*, but it shortly proved to be ill-named. Three periodicals were associated with Goldwin Smith and together constitute a milestone in the progress of literary and political criticism in Toronto. Smith, regius professor of history at Oxford and professor of history at Cornell, came to live in Canada in 1871. In 1875 he married the widow of William Henry Boulton and thereafter lived in the beautiful Boulton house, the Grange, set in the midst of spreading lawns and old trees. The house was a meeting place for residents of Toronto and visitors alike, for graceful manners and good conversation. For a decade or two it was in these respects unequalled.[11]

Goldwin Smith added a wing for his library and there he spent long hours, not in writing history – though in the past he had done that well – but in expressing on paper his views on a range of contemporary events and trends. His understanding of the forces that made up Canadian opinion was limited and his forecasts of the country's future were frequently wrong. He had strong views, ones that were sometimes so unpopular as to infuriate contemporaries. Yet all that he wrote was honest and interesting and expressed in simple but flowing prose. Whatever his defects he was a writer of exceptional talent. A. V. Dicey, author of the classic *Law of the Constitution*, stayed with the Smiths and lectured to a class in the university. 'One thing only,' he wrote to his wife, 'made the speaking rather formidable. Goldwin Smith went with me, and his habitual command of absolutely perfect language made me sure he must feel at every turn the imperfection of my expression.'

The *Canadian Monthly* (1872–82) arose out of plans made before Smith moved to Toronto. He refused the editorship when it was offered to him but wrote regularly under the nom de plume of 'Bystander,' and as in the other publications with which he was connected gave substantial financial help. The name he had adopted in writing for the *Monthly* was carried over as the title of a periodical which he founded in 1880. The *Bystander* was described as a 'monthly review of current events, Canadian and general,' and the current events had largely to do with politics but strayed into literature. Smith wrote the whole of it himself. It was published in

Mashquoteh, the residence of W. A. Baldwin, Deer Park, about 1878

three series of about a year each and with intervals between. The *Week*, which began in 1883, overlapped with it. This was of Smith's founding too, and he called it an 'independent journal of politics, society, and literature.' The articles in it were by various contributors who did not necessarily share Smith's opinions. The first editor, Charles G. D. Roberts, then a young man of twenty-three, published in the *Week* some of his own poems and those of Archibald Lampman, Bliss Carman, Wilfred Campbell, Charles Mair, and Pauline Johnson.

Remote from such sophisticated journals but representative of a powerful group in Toronto was the *Sentinel and Orange and Protestant Advocate*. The editor was E. F. Clarke, Irish by birth, printing apprentice of the *Globe* and the *Mail*, arrested in the strike of 1872, mayor of Toronto from 1888 to 1891, and later member of parliament for West Toronto. In spite of the close association of Clarke himself and of Orangemen in general with civic affairs the *Sentinel* usually had little to say about events or issues in the city. As the organ of the Orange Order it devoted the largest part of its space to the activities of lodges at home and abroad. For the rest it carried on ceaseless warfare against 'popery,' the power of which it saw as seeping in everywhere. Editorially it battled with the Roman Catholic newspapers and with the *Globe*.

The *Canadian Freeman*, for long owned and edited by J. G. Moylan, was a Roman Catholic paper that opposed the Orange Order but which faded out in 1873. The *Irish Canadian*, however, remained to promote the interests of Irish Roman Catholics. The *Nation* (1874–6) was the mouthpiece of Canada First and as ephemeral. One paper, the *News*, edited for a time by E. E. Sheppard, claimed to be politically neutral; while the *World* started in 1880 as an independent Liberal paper and later switched to independent Conservatism.

One of the most interesting themes is the connection between daily newspapers and political parties.[12] A subject on which some Liberals found common ground with all Conservatives was dislike – and at times something approaching fear – of the *Globe*. Robust and confident that paper had a circulation large in total and wide geographically. It handled increased output by introducing the latest techniques in printing and its distribution by imaginative use of the facilities of transportation. In 1887 an accelerated delivery system began by means of a special train consisting of a locomotive and one car. Leaving Toronto early in the morning and travelling at the rate of up to sixty miles an hour, it reached London at 6:40 AM, Stratford at 8:40, and Sarnia at 9:45. At these and other stations newsboys were waiting and other bundles were passed to connecting trains.

On the Liberal side of the fence a rival paper, the *Liberal*, was started in 1875 by Edward Blake, Goldwin Smith, David Mills, and Thomas Moss. Smith, himself a temperate partisan, wrote bitterly of George Brown: 'Those who thwarted Mr. Brown's will or incurred his enmity, were not merely assailed with the abuse which is bandied in our party frays, and often shows more heat than malice; they were systematically hunted down.' Although well written the *Liberal* could not seriously compete with the *Globe* and only caused division in the party. It lasted for a few months.

The Conservatives were united in their anxiety to offset the influence of the *Globe*. In spite of its triumph in the printers' strike and of having absorbed the *Patriot*, *United Empire*, *British Colonist*, and *Toronto Watchman*, the *Leader* did not carry enough guns and the Conservative leaders determined to found a new party organ to be called the *Mail*. Macdonald passed the hat to the party stalwarts who bought shares in the new company sufficient for it to get started though not enough to avoid financial stress. He and others then invited T. C. Patteson to accept a position which in effect made him editor. Patteson had been born in England, educated at Eton and Oxford, immigrated to Canada and studied law at Cobourg, practised for a time, and was one of the first civil servants of Ontario. In consequence of resigning from the last appointment he was promised a comparable position if after serving the *Mail* for a time he decided to resign. For some reason the Conservatives thought it useful to issue a high-sounding prospectus, which Patteson wrote, but in reality the *Mail* was designed as a partisan paper, to be as tough as the *Globe*. Charles Lindsey, son-in-law of W. L. Mackenzie and for a time editor of the *Leader*, was delighted by the appearance of the new champion. 'You have already,' he wrote to Patteson in July 1872, 'delivered the country from the despotism of one all controlling paper [the *Globe*] and thereby performed an incalculable service.' He sealed his congratulations with a cheque for $100.

It was less easy to impress those who complained of the gulf between the noble sentiments of the prospectus and the actual content of the paper. In October 1872 Patteson answered very frankly criticisms by George Macdonnell of Kingston of articles on Oliver Mowat.

In handling our political opponents it is necessary to deal with them after the fashion which you are wrong in supposing peculiar to the *Globe*. My experience is that it is perforce that adopted by every prominent paper on this side of the Atlantic: and the recent presidential contest affords the best instance of it on the other side of the lines.

It is a matter to which, I assure you, I have given anxious and prolonged attention and when I wrote the Prospectus for the *Mail*, to which you are good enough to refer, I fully believed in the possibility of changing the tone of political discussions in the Canadian press. It was not long before I found myself confronted by facts which destroyed all the theories in which I had indulged. It was useless to swim against a tide of the overpowering strength I found opposed to me. Strong food had created strong appetite. If I was respectable the people called me dull, if literary and argumentative I was heavy. A dish spiced with personalities, on the other hand, I was not slow in finding from the exchanges exactly suited the palates of the public ... When you and I and a few thousand others are prepared to pay four times the present cost of our daily paper, such a paper as you and I and the others would desire to see can be provided. Meanwhile supposing that 3,000 people daily read the *Mail* 2,500 of them disagree with us; and the very first principle of shop-keeping involves the necessity of our pleasing the majority of our customers. If the *Pall Mall Gazette* were published in Toronto it would be bankrupt inside of six months.[13]

In correspondence with Goldwin Smith, Patteson protested that he could not write as he thought, which brought the retort that 'your principles would spoil your own trade which Macdonald's never do. You are no more on the stump or in Parliament than I am; and the same may be said about Editors and writers all round.' Easy to say, and in the case of a man of independent wealth and no party affiliation, possible to practise. That was one reason why Smith was able to make a unique contribution. But Patteson, though not like Brown a controversialist by nature, was the prisoner of a system. His job was to denounce the mammon of political unrighteousness. This he did, holding the fort even through the thin days

153

of the Pacific Scandal. He did complain, however, that this faithful party organ 'in the headquarters of the enemy' was too much neglected and not supplied with news from Ottawa. On some occasions he was scooped by the *Globe* on Conservative moves.

After Patteson left the editorial chair in 1877, soon to become post-master of Toronto, the paper, which had been losing circulation, was sold to a creditor, John Riordon, a manufacturer of paper, and Richard Farrer became editor. Under him and his successors the *Mail* strayed from Conservative rectitude to the point where it was publishing editorials by Goldwin Smith in favour of commercial union with the United States. This was too much, and in 1887 the party flag was hoisted on a paper founded to carry it, the *Empire*, which Hector Charlesworth later described as the first and last Canadian newspaper to be completely owned and controlled by a political party. In the fulness of time the *Mail* returned to orthodoxy and was merged with the *Empire*.

The *Evening Telegram*, which first appeared in 1876, followed unexpected paths. Goldwin Smith had departed from his esoteric glades to provide the financial sinews for a popular daily of which John Ross Robertson, formerly business manager of the *Nation* and joint publisher of the defunct *Daily Telegraph*, was the proprietor. The two men were in some ways unexpected allies and their political views did diverge as the *Telegram* became more conservative; but they had in common concern for efficiency and honesty in municipal government. Indeed of all the newspapers published in that age in Toronto the *Telegram* gave most attention to the affairs of the city.

It would seem from even this partial list that the people of Toronto could well have spent all their spare time reading newspapers and periodicals, but they had access to books as well. In 1876 the *Telegram* commented sarcastically on a report of the directors of the Mechanics' Institute – 'a title which doubtless owes its retention to the fact that there are only 16 mechanics who are members of it' – which noted with regret that of the 34,205 books lent by the Institute's library in the previous year 27,164 were novels. 'This,' remarked the *Telegram*, 'is a very suggestive fact, and certainly speaks volumes for the intellectual tastes and aspirations of the reading portion of the community.' Although an understandable reaction that seems a hasty one. Novels could be a high form of literature, and no account is taken of books bought or borrowed from other sources. But even if a large proportion of the novels were of the lightest variety a comparison with modern times would be inappropriate because of the invasion of alternative mechanical entertainment – radio, motion pictures, and television. In any case the directors did not have to worry for many years more about the public taste since the first free public library in Toronto was established in 1883 and inherited the books of the Mechanics' Institute.

One innovation that affected nearly everyone was regular delivery of mail by letter carriers, which started in 1875. Pillar boxes, placed on the streets fifteen years earlier, had proved to be a successful experiment. A more radical improvement in communication was the introduction of the telephone. A Toronto doctor, A. M. Rosebrugh, was a friend of the Bell family and keenly interested in the invention made by Alexander Graham Bell. He secured early instruments and in 1877 operated two-way and four-way circuits without an exchange, and at first without any bells. He obtained an exclusive licence for the use of the telephone in Toronto, and in 1878 letters patent from the province for the Toronto Telephone Despatch Company. In April 1879 the company opened the first exchange and in June issued the first directory.

In 1881 the company was purchased by the Bell Telephone Company of Canada, which had been incorporated by a Dominion statute of 1880. The number of subscribers grew quickly – from 400 in 1881 to 993 in 1884 and to 3,400 in 1890. The first exchange, Main, was followed in 1884 by North and in 1890 by Parkdale. Multiple switchboards and calling by number were introduced in 1884.

Photography was not a new invention by any means but it was still in a relatively early stage. The first form of dry plate was not invented until 1871. When the firm of Notman and Fraser opened its doors on King Street in 1867 it was one of several, but is of particular interest. William Notman, the famous photographer of Montreal had given employment to John Fraser, trained as an artist in England before migrating to Canada, and then sent him to open a branch in Toronto. At that time it was customary to colour and improve a photographic print by hand, and for that purpose it was necessary for a firm to employ artists. Horatio Walker, Homer Watson, and John Hammond were three of those in this Toronto branch, and Fraser himself was an expert. Based on this group meetings were held in Fraser's house to discuss the formation of an art society, leading to the decision to establish the Ontario Society of Artists. Among the early members were Daniel Fowler, O. R. Jacobi, F. A. Verner, and Robert Harris. The society's first exhibition was appropriately held in Notman and Fraser's Galleries in 1873.[14]

Displays of art had long been included in the exhibitions sponsored by the Provincial Agricultural Association, and the Ontario Society of Artists was one of the bodies called in to discuss the project of an annual exhibition in Toronto in place of one held there periodically. The initiative had come from the Toronto Electoral District Society which secured the concurrence of a committee of the city council. It was then that the two called in the OSA, the Mechanics' Institute, the Horticultural Society, Manufacturers'

Arrival of the governor general, the Marquess of Lorne, and Princess Louise, September 1879, opposite the Queen's Hotel

Association, and Poultry Association. This enlarged gathering agreed that the first annual exhibition should be in 1879, and secured the passage of a provincial statute incorporating the Industrial Exhibition of Toronto.[15]

The old site south of the lunatic asylum and immediately west of Strachan Avenue had become too small. After obtaining authority to sell this, on condition that the proceeds be devoted to the maintenance of parks, the city moved the exhibition south to a property of over fifty acres leased from the Dominion government. This new and second home was shaped in the form of a triangle, with the Great Western tracks on the north, Dufferin Street on the west, a short frontage on the lake, and the rifle ranges on the eastern and slanting side. The Crystal Palace was taken apart and rebuilt on the new grounds in a larger and modified form. Twenty-three buildings were ready for the hundred thousand visitors who came, but until 1882 the absence of any artificial lighting, indoors or out, confined the show to the daytime. Transportation from the city was also at first difficult. The boats were overcrowded as were the Great Western trains; but in 1884 an electric train carried people from Strachan Avenue

156

into the grounds. The cars were small and open, with benches bolted on, but fortunately the speed was not such as to make the riders fall off.

The Marquess of Lorne, governor general, and the Princess Louise came to Toronto for the great opening in September 1879. Every kind of band and military unit turned out, and so did representatives of the city, the province, and the churches. Schools had a holiday for the occasion. Everyone paraded to the Allan Gardens where the princess planted a tree, and then on to the exhibition. In the evening all was gaiety in the city. 'Everywhere one went,' wrote the *Globe*'s reporter, 'he found himself mingling with dense, singing, noisy, good-humoured, happy throngs . . . At any step he could not avoid asking himself where in the world all these people came from? Not only Toronto but a large part of the Province seemed to have come out of doors . . . As for the illuminations no description could convey an adequate idea of their beauty, extent, or brilliancy.'

On a subsequent evening a concert was arranged in the Horticultural Gardens, to be graced by the presence of the Lornes. After a long wait for these distinguished guests it was decided to fill in time. The Philharmonic Society sang the *Hallelujah Chorus*, very badly according to the *Globe* reporter, and a lady sang *Home Sweet Home* with a tremolo which annoyed him. Still no governor general. Undaunted, the chorus made a false start on *God Save the Queen* and then retired while the Buffalo Orchestra played the overture to *Martha*, the reeds and horns being sharp. Finally the Lornes arrived at nine-thirty, so back to the beginning with the *Hallelujah Chorus* (apparently rather better this time).

Perhaps the reporter was unduly critical, since everything, he admitted, was applauded. In any case the music – good or bad – and the parades were only incidental to the opening of the exhibition, and that was well and truly done. As the years went on the fair grew larger and to get more space there were purchased for it the remaining two hundred acres of the Garrison Reserve (that including what it already had under lease) on condition that the old cemetery be cared for and the fort preserved. In 1904 the name was changed to Canadian National Exhibition.

The exhibition from the first was a mixture of commerce, education, and entertainment. From the city's point of view it meant imported money spent in hotels and shops. For exhibitors it was a chance to show their wares, whether machines, grain, or paintings. Those who attended gained a smattering of knowledge and could inspect a display of merchandise far wider than they would ordinarily see. The midway was fun and the risks of lost children and pickpockets could be borne. In days when forms of entertainment were not so many the exhibition was an occasion to which thousands of people looked forward from year to year. In order that everyone in Toronto might be able to go the city council agreed to a petition of employers that a half-holiday be granted.

For the months between the people of the city organized many ways of spending leisure hours. A great variety of clubs existed for longer or shorter times. Some were in the London tradition, silent and solid, with large leather chairs dotted over reaches of thick carpet. The Toronto Club was the oldest of these, situated since 1864 on York Street. The National Club was fast losing the character given it by the Canada First movement, but the Albany Club had a political flavour. Some other clubs, less sumptuous but equally sedentary, were devoted to chess and draughts; but the majority were in some form athletic. Skating and curling made up the largest group, with one or two for snowshoeing and another for tobogganning. The Toronto Golf Club was the only one for that game. Founded in 1876, it was the third in North America (after those in Montreal and Quebec). At first it had no property of its own, using a 'golfing green' on vacant farm lands north of the Woodbine race track. Nor did it have a club house until 1894, but then the fees for the thirty-five members in 1888 were not excessive: $5 entrance fee and $5 annual subscription. Other clubs were for lacrosse, baseball, fencing, bicycling, horse racing, sailing, and rowing. For non-clubmen there were six public skating rinks and three roller skating rinks.

It is common to think of the waterfront as having been spoiled by the railways and to some extent it had been, but the lake still had much to offer for the people of Toronto in the summer months. Some families had cottages on the island, going back and forth on the ferries. Others stayed at Hanlan's Hotel, a large and rambling wooden building opened in 1882. Edward – more commonly Ned – Hanlan was certainly the best known Torontonian of his time and probably of all time. In 1873 he became champion amateur oarsman of Toronto Bay. Turning professional in 1876, he became champion Canadian sculler in that year, champion of America in 1878, and of the world in 1880. For those not staying on the island an easy trip gave them a day's or some hours' recreation, playing games, fishing in the lagoons, or just taking the cool breezes. An alternative for a Sunday outing for the family was a cruise in one of the lake steamers.

To the west of Toronto a new playground close to the lake was opened to the public in 1876. John George Howard – teacher, artist, architect, and surveyor – had built Colborne Lodge on his large property in 1836 and had long interested himself in gardening, forestry, and the other tasks in a rough forest. Early in June 1873 he wrote to the city council, saying that several times he had been asked by William Boulton on what terms he would be prepared to convey his estate to the city. His proposal was that a transfer be by stages. For three years he would retain the entire 165 acres. At the end of that time 120 acres would pass to the city, Howard retaining the house and the surrounding forty-five acres until the death of himself and his wife when the gift would be completed. He suggested

J. Duck's Hotel and Pleasure Grounds, erected in 1878, mouth of the Humber River

that the city for its part should pay for the lifetime of himself and his wife an annuity of $1,200, adding that as he was seventy and his wife seventy-one the total could not be great (as it turned out he lived until 1890). Here was another park ready to fall into the city's lap and – like Allan Gardens and Queen's Park – through no foresight of the city fathers. Frozen into inactivity by the very thought of a park, the council did nothing until late in July when it accepted with little grace an obligation small in the case of a man who had done so much for the city and who was prepared to resign a property of great potential value.

It is fair to add, however, that the council's mental block was removed soon afterwards. In 1877 the city was persuaded to buy 170 acres of the adjoining Ridout property, and in 1928 added the Chapman estate of seventy-one acres. In due course, then, High Park extended over more than four hundred acres. As soon as it was opened people began to use it for picnics, and many schemes were considered for building roads, making fences, planting, and draining. No large operation was at first undertaken but Howard was tireless in directing what was done.[16]

Further west again was Duck's Hotel, built on the lakefront near the Humber in 1874. It was a popular place for bathing, dining, and square dances; and small boats or canoes could be rented for expeditions up the Humber as far as the Old Mill.[17] Visitors from the city could go by the ferries that plied along the lakeshore or by bus. In 1878 the Great Western began to run a local service as far as Mimico, one greatly appreciated, said the *Mail*, by citizens. A 'neat little engine' pulling a single car made frequent trips. The regular stops were High Park – now, the paper added, equipped with swings, see-saws, and picnic tables – the Humber, and Mimico. It was indicated, however, that this friendly little train would stop almost anywhere between.

In Toronto a swimming club existed, but outdoor bathing was severely restricted, it being still held that exposure of arms and legs was somehow immoral. 'No person,' ran a by-law of 1868, 'shall bathe or swim along or under the piers, wharves or shores . . . between the Rolling Mills on the east and the Queen's Wharf on the west, from the hour of seven o'clock in the morning to nine o'clock in the evening.' No one seems to have introduced that ultimate curiosity of Victorianism, the bathing machine, and it was not until 1890 that the rules were relaxed to the extent that citizens might bathe provided that they wore 'a proper bathing dress covering the body from the neck to the knees.'

Safer places than within the city for bathing were the neighbouring lakeside spots that have been mentioned or still further from the city. For those with means summer holidays gave the opportunity. In the dog days of 1877, in early August, the *Evening Telegram* chatted about those who were away and where they had gone. Some people were in England, several at Rosseau in the Muskoka Lakes, others on Lake Huron near Goderich, but a surprising number at Lake Superior, especially at Thunder Bay. It meant a long trip, one that had in part at least to be by boat, but evidently there was more interest in visiting northern Ontario than in later days when it became so much easier. Late in August the *Telegram* reported 'splendid weather for Lake Superior tourists.' And that was in days before the mines of the north poured their wealth into Toronto.

# 7

# Pride and prejudice

In the last decades of the nineteenth century Toronto could be seen at its best and at its worst. The first was evident to the inhabitants and the second to outsiders. Size, population, and economic strength gave easy assurance of supremacy in Ontario. In an age weighed down by economic depression many people still lived comfortably, and if not all did that was the way of the world. Manifest physical progress was a source of justifiable pride, and behind the bricks and mortar were manifestations of the mind and the spirit.

For himself and his fellows a Torontonian might paint a rosy picture, but the chances of impressing others were less certain. Toronto was not popular. It was accused of smug satisfaction with worldly success. Perhaps that could be written off as envy, but the charges mounted: boring because of outmoded puritanism; bigoted in matters of race and religion; more British than the queen. The description becomes a caricature, but like all good caricatures had a modicum of truth. The moderates of the day were as inconspicuous as moderates incline to be and many quiet people pursued their gentle paths. But it was the words of the crusaders that were noised abroad as the voice of Toronto, and the image that they created was open to disagreeable accusations of intolerance and prejudice. The circumstances of the eighties and nineties aroused and exaggerated points of view entrenched in Toronto; and by an unhappy twist of fate extremes in Quebec and Ontario fed on each other.

The revival of ultramontanism in Quebec, following that in Europe, brought with it a conception of the relations of church and state that was wholly unacceptable to majority opinion in Ontario. 'The church,' read a joint pastoral of the Quebec bishops in 1875, 'is not only independent of civil society, but is superior to it by her comprehensiveness and by her end,' and the state is 'in the church and not the church in the state.' In politics in the seventies individual priests intervened with what was described as 'undue influence' and 'spiritual and temporal intimidation' to such a degree that some elections were declared void by the courts. The Irish archbishop of Toronto, J. J. Lynch, was much more cautious and moderate in defining the relations of church and state.

Honoré Mercier, closely associated with the extreme ultramontanes and a new voice of Quebec nationalism, was swept into office as premier of Quebec on the wave of indignation that followed the execution of Louis Riel, whom many people in Toronto had loudly denounced as a murderer. One of his early actions was to sponsor a bill to incorporate the Order of Jesus and in the following year, 1888, another to compensate them for the loss of their lands. It was this pair of acts, and particularly the second, which touched off the Protestant reaction in Toronto. The extensive Jesuit holdings in Canada fell to the crown after the pope had suppressed the order in 1773. Re-established in 1814, the Jesuits again took up their work in Canada. Their estates passed to the province after confederation and they made claims to them as soon as they had been incorporated. Mercier's bill was to authorize payment of $400,000 in lieu of estates valued at $1.2 million; but it was left to the pope to determine the distribution of that sum and his decision was followed. At the same time the grant to Protestant schools in Quebec was increased by $60,000. Of twelve Protestants in the Quebec legislature only two questioned the bill.[1]

A demand, chiefly by the Ontario Protestants, was then made that the act be disallowed. It was true that it was clearly within the competence of the provincial legislature and that it imposed no financial or other obligation on anyone outside the province and therefore could not be declared *ultra vires*; but the current doctrine of disallowance, especially as interpreted by the prime minister, J. A. Macdonald, was that the veto could be exercised on grounds of general interest. Neither political party would touch it, however, and a resolution in the House of Commons in favour of disallowance was supported by only thirteen members.

Two of them were from constituencies in Toronto where the Jesuits' Estates Act evoked everything from mild criticism to hysteria. The *Globe* launched into a series of editorials condemning the act but for a long time held out against disallowance as contrary to Ontario's conception of provincial rights. It interviewed a number of clergymen. Principal Caven of Knox College censured the act as a flagrant violation of the principle of the separation of church and state and as increasing the domination of Roman Catholics. At that point he conceded that not all Roman Catholics were undesirable, but certainly the Jesuits were. The minister of Carlton Street Methodist Church argued that the order should never have been incorporated, and that there would be no peace in Canada with Jesuits present. The minister of the Central Presbyterian Church said that incorporation should be vetoed, and the minister of Knox Presbyterian Church called for strong opposition to the Jesuits. The pastor of Jarvis Street Baptist Church said that the act was a menace to civil and religious liberties, while the minister of the Metropolitan Church demanded that Protestants should rise against the abhorrent Jesuits. The minister of St James' Square Presbyterian Church said that in the light of the bloody history of Rome Protestants should unite as one man and threaten the politicians with withdrawal of support. The Reverend William Patterson, preaching in Cooke's Church, announced that Romanism had been one of the greatest evils ever to exist. Although he would not prevent its practice it should not have preferential rights. In Western Congregational Church F. H. McGregor warned his listeners to avoid the crafty inroads of the Romans. Of two Anglicans approached by the *Globe* the rector of Grace Church expressed disapproval of incorporation but deprecated inflammatory writing. The rector of All Saints' withheld his opinion since a committee of the Anglican synod was examining the matter.

The Toronto Orangemen decided to call a mass meeting to be addressed only by Orangemen. A citizens' committee of some thirty men with W. H. Howland as chairman circulated an address to the people of Ontario. The Jesuits' Estates Act, they said, was unjust, unconstitutional, and disloyal (the last two adjectives apparently being drawn out of a hat). It was another attempt by ultramontanes to control legislation and should be disallowed. They decided to call for June a public meeting representative of Ontario for the purpose of creating an organization to secure religious equality. Meanwhile they convoked a meeting in April (1889) at the Granite Rink which, with three thousand people, was filled to overflowing. Howland was in the chair, backed on the platform by seventy-five men, many of whom were clergy.

Those of the 'glorious thirteen' members of parliament who were present received an ovation and then the flow of oratory began. W. T. McMullen, moderator of the general assembly of the Presbyterian Church in Canada, worked his way through a rambling discourse to a resolution of thanks to the thirteen for 'their noble defence of the true principles of religious liberty enshrined in the British Constitution,' a curious reference which he wisely did not try to explain. Emerson Coatsworth, Jr., future member for Toronto East, made an even more incomprehensible reference, this time to the Magna Carta, in the course of an argument that the people should decide whether they were to be ruled from Ottawa or Rome. D'Alton McCarthy, a Toronto lawyer and member of parliament for North Simcoe, in a speech of vast length outlined the history of the Jesuits' estates, noted the vices of the political parties, and argued the case for disallowance. He ended by warning of the growing strength of the French Canadians. 'Do you realize that if Canada is to be a nation we must stop

French aggression? Do you know that tracing history from the time of Lord Durham, who united the country to assimilate, that the French have been becoming more and more French? They are opposed to national unity and are determined not to become British subjects.' Dangers loomed for Ontario where the French Canadians wanted two languages and better provision for Roman Catholic schools. John Charlton, the next speaker, was enthusiastically greeted. He also wanted to know whether Canada was to be a British country. The Jesuits' Estates Act, he announced, was unconstitutional and should be disallowed. Altogether it was a long evening with signs of exhaustion at times, but at least there was evidence of a prevailing state of opinion in Toronto.

In tune with remarks that have been quoted a group of men led by D'Alton McCarthy organized the Equal Rights Association, although words used in the Granite Rink might have raised some question as to what rights were to be equal and for whom. The association, which attracted some eminent members throughout Ontario, later turned its guns on the school question in Manitoba. Another organization, the Protestant Protective Association, was an alien from the United States, coloured by anti-Catholicism so sweeping as to antagonize all but extremists. For a time it made some impact on provincial, and more especially on municipal, politics; but both the regular provincial parties regarded it as objectionably biased. The torch of militant Protestantism was most strongly carried by Orangemen.

The history of Ontario is full of references to the Orange Order but usually in connection with Orange-Irish street battles on the Glorious Twelfth or with its political influence. Curiously, little other information is available. For many years the order played an important part in the government of Toronto, but the reasons for its concentrated effort in this field are unexplained. Writing in 1923 H. C. Hocken, a leading Orangeman and former mayor, pointed out that since 1834 only thirteen men who were not members of the order had been elected as mayor. In the year in which he was writing only four out of twenty-nine members of the municipal council were not connected with the Orange Order.[2] For the late nineteenth century, however, published numbers of lodges vary so greatly that no reliance can be placed on them; nor would such figures in any case have much meaning without a knowledge of the size of each lodge.

Admitting such lacunae, no doubt exists that the Orange Order was a very powerful force and that its membership included many influential citizens. Its views in the latter years of the century can be found by reading its official organ, the *Sentinel*. To that paper the Jesuits' Estates Act was but another manifestation of the spreading menace of Roman Catholicism, in which, it repeatedly said, the Jesuit Order was the power behind the throne. 'At no period since the Reformation,' it had warned in 1883, 'was the necessity for a close bond of union among Protestants more evident than at the present.' On all sides could be seen threats to 'pure evangelical Protestantism.' Payment for the estates of the Jesuits was barefaced robbery. 'What a shame! What a disgrace!'

Day after day and year after year the *Sentinel* repeated its warning that Protestantism was in danger. Added to that was a racial element since French Canadians were Roman Catholics. Even when the goalkeeper of a Toronto lacrosse team was attacked by spectators after a game in Montreal that was both 'a sample of Romish bigotry' and 'Montreal blackguardism.' The *Sentinel* concluded that French Canadians were not desirable immigrants to Ontario. They were, admittedly, frugal, industrious, and not given to any great vices,

But the trouble lies in their lack of education and their subserviency to the Romish Church, not only in spiritual but in political matters, and the impossibility of assimilating them into the dominant English race ... The greatest danger to be feared from the French-Canadian invasion is the powerful political lever it will give to the Romish church in Ontario. As it is, through its Irish Roman Catholic vote and the French-Canadian vote already here, Rome is nearly mistress of the political situation ...

The French Canadians are the most foreign of all the non-English races that immigrate to the English provinces of the Dominion ... The environments of enlightenment and liberalism which surround them have little or no effect in dispelling the dark gloom in which the Jesuits have plunged their understanding.

A detached observer might have wondered where to find the enlightenment and liberalism about which the *Sentinel* wrote and whether bigotry was peculiar to Roman Catholics. Protests were voiced against these and other demonstrations of extreme Protestantism. The *Globe* wrote with bitter sarcasm of the 'fearlessness' of those in Toronto who assailed 'popery' and cast aspersions on the character of nuns. Writing to Laurier in mid-1889 J. S. Willison expressed the opinion that the ultra-Protestant movement had reached its height.[3] Perhaps it had, but the complex of religion, race, and language formed a subject still bitterly contested. Not long after the date of Willison's letter D'Alton McCarthy was calling on the people of Ontario 'to take in hand our French-Canadian fellow subjects and make them British in sentiment and teach them the English language.' He warned that votes now were better than bayonets later.[4]

Twenty years after the confederation of the provinces of British North America one of the principal pillars on which it rested was showing cracks. During the debates of 1865 the two men who best reflected opinion in Lower and Upper Canada, George-Etienne Cartier and George Brown, had praised the terms of union as allowing room for different races, languages, and creeds. The federal design of 1867 was a frank recognition that the union of 1841 had led not to assimilation as Durham had intended but to increased friction between disparate cultural forces. The fences drawn around the provinces under the new order helped the development of differing social philosophies, but they were not high enough to prevent the crusading Protestants of Ontario from leaning over the top.

In spite of generalized and sometimes fiery oratory no serious body of opinion in Toronto would have advocated either the legal disabilities for Roman Catholics that once had obtained in England and Ireland or closed doors against immigrants from Quebec, but remedial action would be taken within the city. As a means of absolving French-Canadian immigrants from the stigma of Roman Catholicism a group of people in Toronto set up in 1889 a mission for French-Canadian Protestants, some of whom were converts. Both the English and French languages were used at services and meetings, at one of which the pastor of the People's Methodist Church spoke of 'the efforts put forth by the Roman Catholic Church to keep the French-Canadian Catholics in the city from Protestant influences,' and declared that the priests 'were already denouncing the mission and warning the French Canadians against it.'[5] The results of this competition for souls are not recorded.

The most practical questions had to do with religion and language in education. In the university problems were being resolved by converting it into a federation. Theology was left to denominational colleges and other subjects divided between the colleges and the university. The high schools, relatively few in number, had never been affected, but in the public schools religious teaching and language were controversial.

'Separate' schools in the case of Toronto were Roman Catholic. Before confederation the church had expressed dissatisfaction with the situation of the schools and amendments were made, the most important in the act of 1863. Although it did no more than make minor concessions to separate schools the act was important as defining the rights which, under the British North America Act, could not be prejudicially affected by later provincial legislation. That was not, however, as had been hoped, a final settlement, and dispute actively revived. Some contemporaries thought that the whole system was wrong: that confessional schools should not be supported by public funds. Others would have the privileges restricted; and others again asked, and to some extent secured, more favourable conditions for the separate schools.

In 1888 Archbishop Lynch issued a pastoral letter on education. For the clergy no duty was more important than teaching. On the laity rested the responsibility for sending children to the Roman Catholic schools. 'Parents sin grievously who prefer a non-religious education for their children. Here in Toronto, where bigotry is still too rampant, the atmosphere of the non-Catholic school is dangerous to children.' Those who did attend such schools, he added, were more or less tinctured with Protestant ideas. The history taught was biased, leaving the impression that the popes and the Jesuits were bad. On the other side of the argument the pastor of a Congregational church spoke in opposition to separate schools, arguing that 'the State has no right to acknowledge religious caste, thus legalizing division and perpetuating alienation.' He refused to describe the public schools as Protestant: they were rather those that belonged to the public. 'You will notice,' A. H. U. Colquhoun, editor of the *Empire*, wrote to J. P. Whitney, 'that even Toronto school children are fighting over religious differences in the good old 16th. century style.'[6]

For many years the minority involved in disputes about education was almost wholly Irish, but as migration from Quebec increased a second issue was added, that of the language of instruction in public schools. In 1890 a provincial Conservative circular soliciting votes for Whitney in an Ontario riding mentioned as matters of prime importance,

First, the question whether the separate schools receiving Provincial aid are to be continued practically under the control of the authorities of the Roman Catholic Church, and

Second, the question whether the English language is to be the language of the Public or Common Schools all over the province – in effect whether Ontario is to continue an English province or community in every respect.

The first question was of immediate concern in Toronto. In 1886 eighteen out of forty-eight schools were separate, with the Christian Brothers, Sisters of St Joseph, and Ladies of Loretto as teachers. In 1897 the proportion had changed to seventeen out of sixty-seven but the issue was not for that reason regarded as disappearing. Toronto schools were little affected by the question of language, but the more general challenge in the second part of the circular brought a ready response from those who regarded both Roman Catholicism and the French language – even the French-Canadian people – as alien to their conception of a Protestant and British province. For an unknown number of years French and German had both been used as languages of instruction in certain districts of the province where one or other language was spoken more commonly than English, but without statutory authority and without protection comparable to that given to confessional schools in the British North America Act.

The use of German faded out of itself but controversy continued over French. The *Sentinel*, tireless in its Protestant vigil, remarked in 1910 that 'our French-Canadian fellow citizens argue that only by the use of their language in the schools can their children acquire an education. This is but a subterfuge to gain their ultimate goal of turning the public schools into French confessional schools.' That organ of the Orange Order also worried

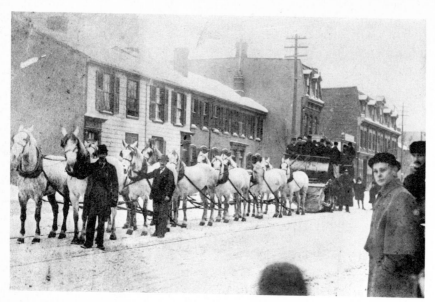

Snow plough in use in 1891–2

about the method of electing members to the Board of Education, by which, it charged, several members had 'come to think that they could ignore the Protestant sentiment of the city and put Roman Catholic teachers in permanent positions in the public schools.'

Other religious rifts appeared. A shrewd young observer, Helen Macdonald, noted in 1891 that 'during summer the Queen's Park has been disgraced on Sunday afternoons by all sorts of preachers, whose opposite views strongly expressed led to rioting. Park preaching consequently forbidden.'[7] A different and somewhat later dispute was that between the supporters of fundamentalism and modernism in the Baptist Church. Several churches in Toronto were affected, but the storm worked up its height in the twenties in the Jarvis Street Baptist Church whose pastor was T. T. Shields, an able orator and relentless controversialist. Questioning the orthodoxy of teaching in McMaster University, Shields intervened in appointments to the staff and in the election of chancellor. Having failed in these moves he and other members of the fundamentalist party set up a separate Pastors' College. The congregation of Jarvis Street, of other churches, and the Baptist convention were split down the middle; and in 1922 the Park Road Baptist Church was founded mainly by those opposed to Shields' doctrines and actions.[8]

Such was the principal evidence for the case that Toronto was intolerant and narrow-minded. Charges less serious but as common were that it was bound down by a heavy-handed code of public behaviour. To the extent

168

that the object was peace and quiet the régime might be defended. A by-law decreed that

No person shall advertise any sale of merchandize, furniture, or other articles, or matter, by the ringing of a bell, blowing of a horn, crying, hallooing, or creating any other discordant noise, in the streets of the City, or on the steps of a house or other premises open to the public street, whereby the public are liable to be subjected to inconvenience and annoyance: Provided always, that nothing contained in this section shall be construed to extend to any person duly appointed and authorized by the Council to follow the calling of Police Crier or City Bellman.

Relenting a little, a later by-law allowed the silence to be broken by licensed hawkers or pedlars, who might 'moderately cry their wares,' or by a milk dealer who, on any day but Sunday, might ring a bell in front of a house to which he was delivering. Steamers' whistles might be blown only as danger signals and those of locomotives as authorized. Public parks were to be cleansed of 'all drunken and filthy persons, vagabonds and notoriously bad characters,' and parks might not be used as pastures for horses or cattle.

The ban on begging on the streets might be accepted by even a critical visitor, as might one on profane swearing or 'any other immorality or indecency.' The proscription of gambling, indoors or out, would be regarded as in a different category, as would rules forbidding lewd books and immoral plays. Sabbatarianism had strong support. When the Lord's Day Alliance was formed in 1888 it had the backing of most of the churches; and the churches of Toronto, with some 117 congregations, constituted a formidable force. The effective public opinion of Toronto discouraged both work and play on Sunday. For some years no street cars were permitted to run and boys were arrested for playing on the streets. In 1895 three members of the Toronto Golf Club appealed against conviction by a magistrate of illegally playing golf on Sunday, but when a higher court found in their favour it was on the ground that 'golf is not a game of ball similar in any sense to the games enumerated in, or intended to be prohibited by, the statute, and also that it is not a noisy game.' The principle was not by this decision abandoned, but the forty or fifty men who played golf could do so on Sundays.

Most of the characteristics which have been noted would have applied to other cities and towns of Ontario at the same time, but Toronto was large and powerful, and therefore conspicuous. Montrealers or Europeans were inclined to find it at best dull and at worst unreasonable. All that must be on the record if the Toronto of the late nineteenth and early twentieth centuries is to be understood. Whether it was good or bad can be judged only subjectively. What to some honest men was the maintenance of essential principles was to others intolerance and bigotry. What is certain, however, is that all the aspects of the city of that day which have so far been depicted represent only one part of the mood and life of Toronto.

Toronto was not as yet a big city, but big enough to embrace many kinds and conditions of men. Plenty of them were detached from the kinds of controversy that were conspicuous beyond the city limits, either because they had more practical problems to think about or because they were attached to other values. J. V. McAree, columnist of three Toronto newspapers, wrote delightfully of his youth in the poor area east of Parliament Street, where for many families existence itself was sufficient problem. He was brought up in his uncle's little grocery store, one that for the most part was patronized by those whose personal finances ranged only between bad and worse.[9] The conception of credit held by both the uncle and his customers tumbled the store into bankruptcy in the end, but not before it had fed the hungry and penniless. It was a hard life in a way, but McAree's picture is not a sombre one, and from the milieu of his youth came men of ability.

Leafing through the petitions addressed to the city council brings out a series of partial photographs as unrelated to each other as would come from turning the dial of a radio. Why, asked a number of petitioners, should cows not be kept on Borden Street and Hope Street? Would the city, asked residents east of the Don, kindly abate the nuisance caused by the cow byres belonging to Gooderham and Worts? Would the city pay compensation for damage suffered by two women who fell into a hole in the sidewalk on Queen Street East? Multiplied hundreds of times the sum of day-to-day practical questions should dissipate any idea that all the residents of Toronto devoted their time to debating religious and educational questions.

The worldly-wise have laughed at the implications of such tags hung on Toronto as 'city of churches' or 'city of homes' – at what they envisaged as a dull, plodding, bourgeois régime. Yet other moderns wonder how to recapture something of the family life of those days. Quiet, shady streets were seen from rocking chairs on front verandahs. Small gardens were carefully nurtured. On Sundays the family, heavily draped in Victorian costumes, set off for church once or twice a day. Was their life dull? If an observer could have seen through the thick and frequently ugly curtains he would often have noticed shelves of good books, perhaps the family engrossed in round games, or clustered about a piano. Such people – and there were many of them – had the enterprise to make a considerable part of their own recreation.

There were, however, other opportunities. As had long been the case most of the leading professional musicians were church organists, thus

Grand Opera House, 1874

ensuring a high standard in the churches and leadership for secular organizations. Edward Fisher, an American by birth, became organist of St Andrew's Church in 1879 and in 1887 founded the Toronto Conservatory of Music. Arthur E. Fisher (who was no relation) played the viola in the Toronto Chamber Quartet and established the St Cecilia Choral Society. F. H. Torrington was organist of the Metropolitan Church from 1873, conducted the Philharmonic Society, and founded the Toronto College of Music. Elliott Haslam started, in the late eighties, the Toronto Vocal Society which excelled in unaccompanied singing. Perhaps the highest point was reached by A. S. Vogt, organist of Jarvis Street Baptist Church, in the Mendelssohn Choir which he began in 1894. Performance of music was enhanced through the gift by Hart Massey of Massey Hall in 1892, a building which proved to be almost perfect acoustically. The theatre, too, was active in Toronto. Hector Charlesworth wrote happily of the Grand Opera House within whose baroque walls were to be seen most of the noted actors and actresses of the last quarter of the nineteenth century.[10]

Nothing could have been more remote from the strident cries of controversy than the quiet lives of the gifted few who were brought together by common interest in music, literature, and the arts. Amateurs among them came from the ranks of business, teaching, medicine, and the law. Professional musicians associated in their gatherings as did the artists of the day, such as George A. Reid, president of the Ontario Society of Artists, Edmund Wyly Grier, the portrait painter, and Sydney Tully, daughter of the architect. Members of the staff of the small university fitted into the social and cultural life of the town more than they did in later days. James Loudon and Robert Ramsay Wright were scientists, Maurice Hutton a classicist, James Mavor a political scientist, George M. Wrong an historian, and W. J. Alexander a professor of English literature.

Men and women such as these joined in what were known as salons, held in private houses. Helen Macdonald wrote of some that she attended. Music usually took up a good deal of the evening. A male quartet included a physician and a painter. At other times papers were read on literary subjects, one, for example, by Pelham Edgar of Victoria College on Walt Whitman. Pauline Johnson read one of her new poems. It was all highly civilized, and the more so because it was inexpensive and required no more equipment than a piano. Such gatherings had been traditional and continued into the twentieth century. By their very nature they were unadvertised and seldom recorded, but the performances by such groups of amateurs and professionals were of very high quality.

The city in which such diverse types of people lived, in which the best features were all but concealed by the worst, was growing in size and in physical comfort. Residential areas were moving away from the waterfront, or perhaps it would be more accurate to say that distinctively residential districts were evident and were necessarily north of the business section. Looking at the streets in 1897 it seems evident that some were, like Church Street for example, being abandoned to commercial activities, but parts of other older streets, such as Beverley and Jarvis, were more than holding their own. Admiral Road was pretty well filled up but Spadina had more vacancies than houses. St George Street had many large houses, Rosedale only a thin scattering.[11] Queen's Park was now in the centre of the best residential districts, and, in competition with the old King Street parade on foot, 'some carriage people here,' to quote again from Miss Macdonald, 'are trying to establish driving 2 afterns. a wk. in the park as a fashionable

Bloor Street, north side west of Yonge, about 1898

event.' Soon after she had written that (in September 1891) she 'went tearing up across park to Bloor Street suddenly to my disgust found myself entangled in a mass of carriages, children, maids and a few promenaders. Quite a number of very good horses in pairs, two or three tandems and carts, several fairly showy single horses in Gladstones and a drag and four-in-hand turning in from Bloor Street as I reached there.'

Commercial and public buildings were appearing on a larger scale. The Bank of Montreal at the corner of Front and Yonge streets was built in 1885 to a design by the firm of Frank Darling and S. G. Curry. Together with charm of form it reflected something of the confidence and solidarity peculiar to Montreal. Darling also planned the Toronto Club's new building on Wellington Street in 1897. St Paul's Roman Catholic church on Queen Street was designed by Joseph Connolly in the style of the Italian renaissance, with an interior that would recall happy memories to those who had visited Italy. The chief monuments of the nineties were the main parliament building and the city hall. The first was begun in 1886 and finished in 1892. A massive building in a heavy style, it was the work of R. A. Waite, an English architect living in Buffalo. It had a fine setting in the southern part of Queen's Park. What became the city hall was originally intended to house only the courts of justice. The site, on Queen Street opposite the lower part of Bay Street, was expropriated in 1884. Before the plans were drawn by E. J. Lennox it was decided to provide accommodation also for the municipal government; and the completed building of red sand stone had a total floor space of 5.4 acres. It was ready for occupancy in 1899 when those going through the front door faced a great

173

Water works, late nineteenth century

stained-glass window, designed and made by Robert McCausland of Toronto and entitled 'The union of commerce and industry.'[12]

Increasing attention had been paid by the city council to types of construction, the principal consideration being to guard against fire. At intervals the regulations were consolidated, in each case becoming more comprehensive and strict. The code of 1890 was embodied in a by-law (number 2468) of twenty-six pages. Buildings were not to be erected on streets less than thirty feet wide or without a vacant space of at least three hundred square feet. Furnaces, stoves, and chimneys had to meet certain standards and the ladders of early York must still be in place. Inflammable liquids and gunpowder were restricted. Churches, hospitals, colleges, schools, halls, and theatres must have such stairs and doors as in the opinion of the director of buildings were required. No seats were to be put in the aisles. Theatres had to have fire hoses plugged in. The city was divided into four fire limits, the first being approximately bounded by Jarvis, Queen, and Simcoe streets and the Esplanade. That limit was to have the maximum protecton, including fireproof walls and roofs.

Nothing is more basic to the well-being of an urban community than a plentiful supply of pure water, and no need of Toronto was less well met. Long before water pipes were in use constant complaints were made that the bay was becoming hopelessly contaminated. When water came to be pumped out of it sewers were at the same time drained in. A comment by the *Globe* in 1882 was characteristic: that the whole sewage of Toronto flowed into the bay, unpleasant in itself and dangerous to the water supply. The municipal government could not be other than painfully aware of the gravity of the situation and it did make efforts to solve the problem, albeit with limited success.

In 1872 the city decided to replace private with publicly owned water-works. A provincial statute of that year gave as reason for the change the unsatisfactory performance of the Toronto Water Works Company, and while this was true enough it was only one side of the story, for it was not the company that was making the water impure. In 1873 the city bought the company's plant at the foot of Peter Street and ran a four-inch wooden pipe into the lake. For a time this gave a steady if inadequate flow but in 1890 it became plugged with sand. In 1891 a new five-inch steel pipe was carried into the lake to a distance of 2,500 feet, but it developed leaks and rose to the surface, causing a serious epidemic of typhoid fever. In 1895 the same thing happened again and the citizens had to go back to the ancient practice of buying water from carts.

The city then called in an expert, a hydraulic engineer from England. He rejected the suggestion of using Bond Lake on the grounds that the water in it was both insufficient and impure, and recommended instead bringing water from Lake Simcoe, overcoming the height of land by means of a tunnel and siphoning. The alternative, favoured by the city engineer, was a tunnel under the bay together with improved pumps and reservoirs. This was broadly the method followed but it did not bring water of unimpeachable purity since the intake could never quite escape the outlets of the sewers. For many years thereafter citizens continued to buy water by the bottle brought from springs outside the city. Under the circums-tances by-laws that required that each house was to have wholesome water and that wells should annually be cleaned had a hollow ring.

The invention of electricity suggested many conveniences for a city. At the end of the seventies experiments with interior electric lights, supplied by small generators, were made successfully; but the first concern of the city council was with street lighting. Several companies sought contracts for that purpose. In 1879 the Consumers' Gas Company secured a pro-vincial statute authorizing it to expand its operations, including the manu-facture and supply of electricity. 'Whereas,' the preamble read, 'the com-pany alleges that other modes of artificial light have been discovered and that gas may be beneficially used as a cheap fuel for heating and cooking purposes,' the company was to be permitted to launch into these two fields. In one it did, and the application of gas to cooking was to have very wide results. The company, however, seems to have dropped the idea of supply-ing electricity, partly, perhaps, because of the amount of new business created by gas stoves, partly because gas lighting was not automatically ruled out by electricity.

The city council and its committee on fire and gas found the whole new problem puzzling; and certainly they have puzzled later historians by a series of moves and counter-moves confusingly and incompletely recorded. One alderman was so unimpressed by the electric lights installed in the

St George Street, 1898, Gooderham house, now the York Club

council chamber that he proposed that the whole thing should be removed as nothing more than a nuisance. The city fathers as a whole had no such devastating criticisms of the new-fangled device but neither were they at all sure what to do. They were not convinced that gas lighting was obsolete or clear as to what company or companies should be permitted to provide whatever electric lights were to be on the streets. On the first point they hedged, renewing the gas company's franchise for a limited time only.

That left two electric companies, Canada Electric Light and Manufacturing Company and the Toronto Electric Light Company, moving on and off the stage like Cox and Box, and two others – the J. J. Wright Electric Company and the Royal Electric Company of Montreal – hovering uncertainly in the wings. It was not taken for granted that any one company should have a monopoly and indeed it was decided that one, for a financial consideration, might use poles erected by another. After consulting American cities the committee on fire and gas concluded that, 'owing to its superior brilliancy,' electric light was used in the central parts of most of them. Meditation on the respective claims of the companies in the field led to the proposal that the two principal ones should each exhibit twenty-five lights, and whichever showed the better results would be chosen.

Whether that was done is not clear; but out of a scrappy record it appears that both the Canada Electric Light and Manufacturing Company and the Toronto Electric Light Company secured one-year contracts in 1883, used each other's poles, and provided lighting on different streets. In 1884, after

176

some debate, the franchise for the first company was terminated and the Toronto Electric Light Company seemed to be left triumphantly alone until five years later out of the blue came the Toronto Incandescent Electric Light Company of which the manager was Frederic Nicholls, later the president of the Canadian General Electric Company. An agreement of 1889 between that company and the city noted that it was the intention of the company to manufacture and supply electricity, and that for the latter purpose it was empowered to lay underground wires. Whether it was to provide street lighting and if so on what terms are, incredibly, not even mentioned. It appears, however, that this was but a glimpse of a beautiful future in which poles would be no more, but that the agreement was never implemented. Meanwhile electric lighting gained in popularity as is indicated by petitions addressed to the city council asking for its extension to additional streets. Some houses and other buildings were wired but for years gas lighting continued to be used in others. At the end of 1890 the Consumers' Gas Company was awarded another five-year contract for street lighting.

The eventual ascendancy of the Toronto Electric Light Company is suggested by the contract it was granted in 1890, following its tender. The period was five years. The company was to provide not less than eight hundred arc lamps of at least one thousand candlepower each. For that the city was to pay twenty-four and a half cents per lamp per night, that being considerably below the earlier rate.

Transportation was the third of the essential public services. Shops and other commercial organizations used horse-drawn vehicles. Many of the old houses still surviving have stables, now converted into garages or flats. The coachman usually lived on the floor above the horses' stalls. To have a private carriage was in itself a mark of economic, if not always social, distinction, as indicated by the common phrase 'carriage trade.' For those not within this exclusive class forty-five cab operators advertised their services. The tariff was based on zones. Within the central one – bounded by Peter, Sherbourne, and Carlton streets and the bay – the rate was twenty cents for a one-horse cab and twenty-five cents for a two-horse one. From midnight until six in the morning the fare was double. The roads were steadily improved, but no technological change came until the automobile was introduced in the twentieth century.

The street car system, on the other hand, was radically altered by the adoption of electricity. In 1891, when the franchise of the Toronto Street Railway expired, the company had sixty-eight miles of track, 1,372 horses, 361 wheeled vehicles, and one hundred sleighs. It averaged fifty-five thousand passengers a day.[13] Rather than renew the franchise the city acquired ownership of the company's assets for $1,453,788, the value determined by arbitration. Apparently, however, the council – or perhaps the public – soon tired of public operation, for later in the year tenders for repurchase were invited. That accepted was from a new corporation in which the principal, briefly described as 'William Mackenzie of the City of Toronto, contractor,' was one of the great figures of transportation in Canada. The Toronto Railway Company was only one of his many enterprises, which included some of the radials that will be mentioned and his greatest achievement – in partnership with Donald Mann – the Canadian Northern Railway.

Under the agreement between the city and the company, confirmed by provincial statute in 1892 (55 Vict., c. 99), the latter was to reimburse the city for the cost of its previous purchase, adding the value of new works and improvements during the months of public ownership. In addition the company committed itself to an annual payment of $800 per mile of single track, $1,600 of double, and graduated percentages of gross receipts. The wide gauge (four feet, eleven inches) was to be retained; night cars to be run as deemed necessary by the city council; cars, of the most approved design, to be heated and lighted; no cars to be run on Sunday unless and until approved by a vote of the citizens (passed in 1897). Horses might be used at first but electrification was to be begun within one year and completed within three.

And so the thirty-year span of the Toronto Railway Company began. The electric cars made possible greater speed and service. The heating system, consisting of a coal stove at one end of the car, was not perfect but a distinct improvement. When open cars were introduced for the summer, families could go for rides all round the new Belt Line (within the city this time), and children watched with fascination the conductor swinging with his fare box along the continuous steps at the side. Double-truck cars came in 1895, to the regret of schoolboys who had already discovered that entertainment could be derived from rocking the single-truck ones. Air brakes were not installed until 1905.

In the agreement the price of tickets was set out, followed by a clause which read: 'The payment of a fare shall entitle the passenger to a continuous ride from any point on said railway to any other point on a main line or branch of said railway within the city limits.' Transfers, which had not existed in the régime of the old company, were therefore available. Later on the company took the position, upheld by the courts, that 'city limits' meant those of 1891, the date of the agreement, and refused to extend the one-price system beyond them. There is some reason for believing that the consequent cost of travel discouraged people from living in the newer districts.

Toward the end of the nineteenth century it becomes particularly important to think of Toronto as an urban area as well as a city. Population figures for the city itself certainly show the number of persons for whom

Yonge Street, 1890s, looking north from Front Street

the city council was responsible, but as they jump whenever an adjoining district is annexed any analysis of density becomes difficult; and it is not always possible to distinguish between the number of people in the urban economic complex and the number under one political jurisdiction. The word 'suburb' introduces as much confusion as light, since it can apply to an area touching the city limits or another twenty miles away.

All that can be said with any confidence is that on all sides of the city were people, connected with it, who were looking for some city services and always for transportation. The island was a special case since its residents – estimated at three thousand in 1900 – were seasonal. In 1894 they formed an Island Association the objective of which were better roads and sidewalks, improved sanitary conditions, adequate ferries, and gas and telephones. To some extent they succeeded. North, west, and east lived people who wanted better means of reaching their daily employment.

One early attempt to meet this need was by a steam railway, the (original) Belt Line, more famous for relics than performance. Already the city had taken steps to improve the valley of the Don, once beautiful but now sadly defaced. A provincial statute of 1886 was passed 'in view of the necessity which exists for improving the Don River and securing the sanitary condition of that part of the City of Toronto contiguous to the said river,' which was a polite way of saying that the Don had been turned from a salmon river into a drain. The river was to be deepened, the banks cleared, and agreements made with railway companies that used the valley for access to Toronto.

The Belt Line Railway Company, incorporated in 1889, was designed to serve outlying areas then without satisfactory public transport. For the southern part of the large circle or belt it was apparently always intended to make use of the Grand Trunk tracks, perhaps by running rights over them. On the western end the Belt Line was to run north from those tracks by way of the Humber Valley, cut across on a line north of Lonsdale Road and through the Rosedale ravine, and then down the Don Valley to rejoin the Grand Trunk. For that last stretch it was necessary to fit into the general improvement scheme. Terms were not easily reached. Arbitrators named by the city and the company failed to agree and finally a settlement was made by an umpire. The city was to lease in perpetuity a strip of land twelve feet wide, receiving in return compensation determined at intervals of fifty years. The company was to make crossings and to accept other obligations such as contributing to the cost of whatever bridges were necessary.

Construction went ahead and during it an arrangement was reached with the Grand Trunk under which the latter would operate the line on completion through a forty-year contract at an annual rental. That point, however, was never reached for the Belt Line Company got into such serious financial difficulties that it could not proceed with laying the track. In 1892, therefore, the local company unloaded the white elephant on the Grand Trunk on terms that could hardly have led to other than loss. With its considerable resources the Grand Trunk was able to complete the line later in that year and open it for traffic, but the scheme was a failure and operation was abandoned after two years. For long afterwards portions of the track were used as freight spurs, while citizens explored abandoned sections and gazed at empty stations resembling Swiss chalets.

Electric railways were more promising. Instead of a complete train with its crew one electric car could rapidly convey passengers and light freight over limited distances. Most of the country around Toronto was relatively flat and so construction was not difficult. The Metropolitan Street Railway Company, incorporated in 1877, had pioneered in suburban transport with horse-drawn cars as far as Eglinton Avenue. Electric ones were introduced in 1889, with permission to increase the speed to twelve miles an hour, but only if that did not cause alarm or injury to horses and vehicles on Yonge Street. The new motive power made possible a series of extensions northward: to York Mills in 1890, Richmond Hill in 1896, and Newmarket in 1899. The farthest point reached was Sutton, in the twentieth century. Some freight was carried, the delivery of milk being so important that in

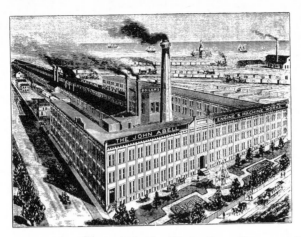

John Abell, Engine and Machine Works, Queen Street near Parkdale, erected 1886

1895 the ban against Sunday cars was lifted for that purpose only. Eastward the Toronto and Scarborough Electric Railway, Light and Power Company, incorporated in 1892, built a line beside the Kingston Road, reaching Victoria Park Avenue in the following year and West Hill ten years later. Along the lakeshore to the west a radial under various ownerships ran from Sunnyside to Long Branch in 1894 and in 1905 to Port Credit. To the regret of the public the gap between there and Oakville, to which a line went from Hamilton, was never filled. The Toronto Suburban Railway built northwest to Weston and much later on to Guelph. All in all the radials provided a valuable service, a rapid and pleasant means of travel when roads were extremely bad and motor cars, when they existed at all, few in number.[14]

Citizens of Toronto were proud of the advances made by their city but aware too that progress was limited by the economic depression which slowed up agriculture and industry throughout Canada. With other Canadians they hoped always for improvement, and some of them were prepared to examine any plan designed to that end. The current one was tariff reciprocity with the United States. That was an ambition never far below the surface, and efforts had earlier been made to restore and perhaps widen the agreement that had existed before confederation. By 1887 two alternatives were being commonly discussed: unrestricted reciprocity, that is complete free trade between the two countries, and commercial union, a *zollverein* with a common tariff against third countries. The distinction between them, real enough, was sometimes made, sometimes deliberately blurred, often misunderstood. The Liberals, traditionally inclined to low tariffs, debated among themselves as to which, if either of the two, might

181

fill the need of a party long out of office and seeking a platform with appeal to the electors. In the end they chose unrestricted reciprocity, but it served the interests of their opponents to represent their policy as the more vulnerable commercial union, which indeed some leading individual Liberals were known to prefer.

Within Toronto one of the main supporters of commercial union was Goldwin Smith, but as he was more than suspected of being unsound on both Canadian nationalism and the British connection he was as much a hindrance as a help to that cause. He founded the Commercial Union League with G. Mercer Adams, a journalist associated with his literary enterprises, as secretary. From Toronto the league spread its operations through nearby counties where, with some reason, it was anticipated that the principal support might be found. Prices of agricultural products were low and farmers had seldom seen any advantage in protective tariffs. It was quite a different thing to convince the business community. H. W. Darling came very close to persuading the Toronto Board of Trade of which he had been president. The board did endorse the maximum freedom of commercial intercourse with the United States, but only if that did not place Great Britain at a disadvantage or weaken the bonds of empire. Under no circumstances would it go as far as commercial union which it saw as a threat to Canadian autonomy.

The newspapers were divided. The *Empire* maintained the Conservative party line, which was opposition to any form of reciprocity not designed by Conservatives. With Edward Farrer holding the pen the *Mail* fell completely from grace, having no doubt about the virtues of commercial union. In supporting that policy it was automatically called upon to refute the common arguments that commercial union would damage the United Kingdom by putting her in an unfavourable trading position, weaken the imperial relationship, and even lead to annexation. 'The argument in favour of reciprocity,' it wrote, 'has originated, we firmly believe, as much in a patriotic desire to preserve the integrity of Confederation as from the more material consideration of dollars and cents.' This was a little hard for some people to swallow, as was the thesis that Britain would actually gain by being able to extend her investment in a more prosperous country.

Although in the end it had to accept the phrase 'commercial union' the *Globe* preferred to talk about 'free trade,' with the United States or better still with all countries, that being not a new position for the paper to take. In phrases that recall the imperious reign of George Brown it expressed its disapproval of George T. Denison. 'Since the Unrestricted Reciprocity discussions began he has been insolent enough to accuse all those who favour free trade with the state of being annexationists, traitors, renegades and what not. By implication he uttered his slanders against this journal.' Insolent was not a word that Colonel Denison would expect to be applied to himself, but certainly he had talked with unbridled candour, describing commercial union as 'veiled treason.'

Thus in Ontario, where commercial union or unrestricted reciprocity seemed to arouse the greatest interest, two principal sources of opposition became evident. One was that the financial and manufacturing groups were more than reluctant to see the end of protective tariffs which they had long demanded and enjoyed. The other objection was political: that such policies would lead to the destruction of the empire or complete absorption by the United States. Those who had been seeking to recast the empire in some federal form attacked the commercial unionists and in so doing were backed by numerous people. Denison claimed that Toronto was the most loyal city in the empire, and certainly it was in part because of its British sentiment that it rejected either form of reciprocity.

It did not follow, however, that the Imperial Federation League as such became a popular movement. Toronto was not even the first Canadian seat of a branch. When it did get one all three members of parliament and some other citizens of repute stood up as sponsors, but the league continued to have an esoteric ring which it could never overcome. Because the league in Canada was a continuation of that set up in London in 1884 it was interpreted by some critics as no more than quiescent colonialism. This, in fact, was not the temper of its leaders. What they hoped to do was to strengthen the solidarity of the empire but at the same time to give to Canada a voice in its direction.

The project of a federation faded out for the present but not the political debate to which the league had turned its attention. The Liberal party chose to fight the general election of 1891 on what they called unrestricted reciprocity but what their opponents usually called commercial union. J. A. Macdonald, great politician as he was, announced that he hoped to die as he had been born, a British subject. Another great politician, Oliver Mowat, said the same thing but without the resultant publicity. In Toronto two Conservatives, F. C. Denison and G. R. R. Cockburn, retained their seats, and a third, Emerson Coatsworth, Jr., was elected. Against the embattled ranks neither Washington nor Liberalism had prevailed, and the Conservative lines in Toronto seemed to be intact. Yet public life in the city was not forever to run in such predestined grooves. During the political campaign of 1896 it was proposed that Wilfrid Laurier hold a meeting in Toronto, a suggestion thought most unwise by the Liberal candidate for Toronto Centre, William Lount (who was subsequently elected). The meeting, nevertheless, was held and Laurier was greeted with enthusiasm that could hardly have been excelled. Hundreds of people who could not squeeze into Massey Hall waited outside and escorted Laurier to a second, overflow meeting in another auditorium. 'Is this Tory Toronto?' Laurier asked as he moved in the midst of a cheering crowd.

The end of the nineteenth century saw the zenith of imperial Britain, dramatically symbolized in 1897 by the diamond jubilee of the Queen and Empress who had come to the throne in the year of the Canadian rebellions, so long ago. In London princes and kings assembled in glittering ceremonies and throughout the worldwide empire the Queen's subjects applauded the stern old lady who had restored the prestige of the throne and presided over the unequalled progress of her people in territory, wealth, and power. It was heady stuff, not least in British Toronto; but imperial triumph was soon to be tested in blood.

The newspapers of Toronto kept their readers well informed of the course of events that led to the outbreak of the South African war.[15] News despatches from London, explanatory articles, maps, and editorials occupied much of the space in the daily press. For contemporaries they provided information and for later readers impressions of how the people of the city reacted to the crisis. Martial spirit rose high even before hostilities were inevitable. On 2 October 1899 the *Globe* wrote,

The proposal to offer to the Imperial Government a Canadian contingent for service in the event of hostilities in the Transvaal has aroused considerable enthusiasm among militiamen throughout the country. In no other city in the Dominion has the proposal received more hearty approval than in Toronto, and at a general meeting held in the Canadian Military Institute on Saturday night it was endorsed in an emphatic manner.

On the following day the editor, J. S. Willison, expressed the opinion that 'The despatch of a Canadian contingent would be in the nature of a national declaration of Canada's stake in the British Empire.' Such a force, he went on, should be as obviously Canadian as possible, in personnel and insignia. On 11 October news of the probability of a Canadian contingent was received at the armouries with loud approval. On the following Sunday thousands of citizens lined the streets as the 48th Highlanders paraded to St Andrew's Church, and in several Methodist churches sermons demonstrated sympathy with the position taken by the British government.

In Monday's editorial Willison laid out the position he was to maintain, and he had considerable influence. The situation, he argued, with the Orange Free State supporting the Transvaal, was serious enough to justify unusual steps. Canada should fulfil its obligations but also claim a voice in questions of peace and war. Canadians sought a united empire, but a united Canada too; and he deplored irresponsible talk of French domination in Ottawa and other remarks calculated to make a breach between the two races.

The mayor, John Shaw, called a public meeting to discuss arrangements for a send-off for the contingent and suggested collecting money for

Ontario Jockey Club Park, Queen's birthday, 24 May 1898

clothing, food, and medicines. At Government House a gathering of ladies considered what comforts could be sent to the troops. Events moved rapidly. A recruiting office for the Military District was opened on 21 October and was thronged with applicants. On 25 October those accepted left for their ship. At the armouries they were addressed by the mayor and the chairman of the committee. The officers from Toronto were presented with binoculars and other ranks with silver match boxes. Tens of thousands of people, packed like sardines, were all along the streets and showered souvenirs and flowers on the soldiers while bands played *Rule Britannia* and *God Save the Queen*.

Never [wrote the *Globe*] has Toronto been more enthusiastic in honouring her valiant sons. The heart of the people went out to the men who marched forth to devote their strength, if need be their lives, to the defence of the empire and the expansion of her power . . . The departing soldiers saw on either side a solid bank of crowded faces alive with admiration and enthusiasm, and they marched through one continuous patriotic cheer that followed them along the route. Such a demonstration, unprecedented in our history, shows the sincerity of Toronto's military spirit.

Unprecedented then but to be repeated over and over under circumstances far more serious and compelling. In some ways it seems now, as it must have seemed at the time, more than a dozen years between the Boer war and the first great war, for in that interval Toronto had grown and prospered. New factories had sprung up, motor cars introduced the atmosphere of a new age, and the population had more than doubled. But if the people were far more numerous the prevailing attitude toward the British empire had changed hardly at all. In reality they thought of the empire in terms of the United Kingdom, which in time of need must be supported at all cost. Whether the motive was gratitude for the past, advantage in the future, or undefined sentiment is of little consequence since the result was the same. The rule of Britannia must not be weakened, whether by distant rebels or Teutons aiming at world power.

The Toronto newspapers in 1914, while again serving their readers well by their accounts of events leading up to the war, were editorially of one mind on where Canada should stand. The *World* held that the country should contribute at least fifty thousand trained men to the imperial forces. The *News* called for co-operation between political parties to help the mother country. 'This country,' said the *Star*, 'must do all it can to support the arms of Britain.' On 31 July an editorial in the *Globe* declared that 'Canada must do her part as an integral part of the Empire, and assuredly must discharge the imperative first duty of self-defence. When Britain is at war Canada is at war.'

As in 1899 the first few months were full of good, if misleading, news. The war had hardly begun before banner headlines exulted over the sinking of the German navy. In land campaigns the allied armies suffered occasional reverses, but they were declared to be only temporary. On the eastern front the German forces were having a very bad time against Russian power. Such a tone was by no means intended to discourage recruiting, nor did it. The militia regiments of Toronto enrolled new men with regularity and awaited calls from Ottawa for specified numbers of personnel for the battalions going overseas. The 3rd Battalion (Toronto Regiment), drawn from the Queen's Own Rifles and the Royal Grenadiers, and the 15th Battalion (48th Highlanders) were included in the first contingent. Others followed as large numbers of Toronto men enlisted in the army and in the navy. Since Toronto was the headquarters of No. 2 Military District, however, it is not possible to identify the exact numbers who came from the city itself.

Osgoode Hall Library interior, 1897

In 1914 the *Mail and Empire* daily recorded the activities of both the militia regiments and other organizations which trained for possible service: the Toronto Homeguard Sharpshooters' Association paraded 769 men, of all ranks, and twice weekly had classes for officers; the Board of Trade Rifle Club drilled at the armouries; the College Heights Association decided to join forces with the Toronto Military Training Association; the Toronto Rifle League was formed by twenty-one civilian rifle associations in the city.

Men and more men were needed as the hopes of early victory faded and the way to Tipperary proved to be long and hard. Toronto continued to respond to the calls of the armed forces, and others of its people did what war work they could as daily – amid the mud and horror of Flanders and France, at sea, and in the air – toll was exacted to bring both sorrow and pride to hundreds of Toronto families.

# 8

# *Progress and poverty*

The progress made by Toronto in the late nineteenth century, while substantial, was limited by conditions which were beyond its power to alter. The dominating one was the long economic depression which, hardly relieved, bore down on North America and the whole western world. Canadian exports increased only marginally until the very end of the century, agriculture suffered in consequence, and nearly every kind of business was held back.

The Dominion from sea to sea was little more than a political entity. For a long time Canadians had looked sadly at the empty spaces of the vast new west, where – to misquote the Bible – the harvest was not plentiful because the labourers were few. Instead of the anticipated thousands of sturdy yeomen from Britain and western Europe only scattered settlers were to be found and many of these were from Ontario, thus weakening the rural population of that province. Central and eastern Canada were also losing heavily by the emigration to the United States of those who sought better opportunities there. Immigrants had come in quite respectable numbers, but many of them were but birds of passage who moved out before long. Never from confederation to the turn of the century, with one minor exception, were immigrants as numerous as emigrants. The worst year was 1890 in which there was a net loss of 111,164 persons.[1]

One conspicuous sign of the better times that came with the new century was that, while emigration remained a worry, immigration was multiplied many times. The highest figure for the latter was 406,065 in 1913, and that gave a net gain of 217,914. In the early years of the twentieth century the largest number came from Britain: the majority of these from England, with Scotland next and Ireland a poor third. On the average about one-quarter of the newcomers came to Ontario, although they may not all have stayed there; but they were far from outnumbering the native-born. Toronto

Timothy Eaton residence, 182 Lowther Avenue, hall, about 1900

had a much higher percentage of persons born in Britain than had the rest of the province, a little over 100,000 out of a total population of 376,538 in 1911. Thus Toronto, without losing its racial character, was strengthened within its own walls; but more significant still for its economic progress was the creation of a new market in the west following the peopling of the prairies.

In the decade of 1900–11 the population of Manitoba nearly doubled and during the same years those of Saskatchewan and Alberta were multiplied by about five. The atmosphere of boom was apparent in advertisements in the Toronto newspapers. Winnipeg real estate was represented as 'an investment safer than stocks and will yield bigger returns.' A full-page spread displayed the attractions of a residential area in Portage la Prairie. In Saskatoon a residential lot in Pleasant Hill could be bought for $125 to $150, which was really not much, it was explained, for the fastest growing city in Canada. Moose Jaw also had a full page, and the fact that the land agent was staying at the King Edward Hotel suggests that buyers for western real estate were being found. The Eastern Saskatchewan Land Company, owning eighteen thousand acres, offered fall and spring wheat lands (in southern Alberta in spite of the name) at $2 an acre cash or more on terms. Another opportunity was to buy from five to five hundred acres

Downtown Toronto about 1919, looking northwest from below Richmond and Yonge, just before any high buildings

of fruit land in the Kootenay. Undoubtedly some Torontonians bought western lands as a speculation and others went to live on them; but far more derived benefit from staying at home and selling goods and services to the farmers whose numbers multiplied year by year.

Another advertisement in a Toronto paper was for land in Fort William, described as 'the gateway of the West.' So indeed it was, but what in northern Ontario was more important for Toronto was its economic development as a new hinterland. At first the great north was cast for the wrong role, just as the Muskoka-Haliburton district had been earlier. The clay belt had good soil, suggesting to the provincial government that new agricultural areas could be established through organized settlement. It was to make this possible that the Temiskaming and Northern Ontario Railway was built. From the point of view of the original intention the railway was a failure. The land was undoubtedly arable but the season was short and the conditions forbidding. The clay belt attracted few pioneers, and some of those who did go into it had later to be removed to more southerly lands. In unanticipated ways, however, the railway was a great success, for it encouraged prospectors and provided transportation for the results of their discoveries.

That minerals were to be found in northern Ontario had long been known, but before the twentieth century little success had attended the efforts of those who sought to exploit those resources. The Bruce Mine on the north shore of Lake Huron produced some copper as early as the 1840s, and miniature Silver Islet in Thunder Bay made a flash in the pan in the 1870s. In the Kenora area a number of mines were opened and closed. In the course of construction of the Canadian Pacific Railway nickel was found at Sudbury. Prospectors in search of gold in 1897 found instead a rich iron deposit on the Michipicoten River.

The period of active mining was ushered in by a fox at whom a blacksmith threw a hammer in 1903. The fox deservedly escaped but the hammer knocked off a piece of rock under which a vein of silver showed. His monument was the town of Cobalt, a striking example of a mining town mushrooming out of nothing. Porcupine and Sudbury arose equally rapidly. The mining industry suddenly assumed substantial proportions, production in 1929 being valued at about $120 million. This was one of the two principal economic assets of northern Ontario. The other was exploitation of the tremendous forests. Beginning with straight lumbering, this second industry added pulp and paper which, somewhat later than mining, came to be of major importance.[2]

Advertisements in Toronto newspapers of mining shares were as enticing as those of prairie lands. Penny stocks were represented as the road to wealth. One Toronto firm offered shares in the East Bay–Larder Lake Gold Mines Syndicate at two cents a share, explaining that soon they would be selling at fifty cents or a dollar. Shares in Lucky Boys Gold Mine were available at the modest price of six cents, and Bonanza Gold Mine of Larder Lake at fifteen cents. Such attractions were only curtain raisers to the orgy of speculation in the late twenties but indicative of a new element in the economy.

The third factor which affected the economy of Toronto was the war of 1914. The depression of 1913–14 led to unemployment and unused industrial capacity, and Canadian manufacturers expected that both problems could be solved by making munitions. War orders, however, were slow to come. In November 1914 the prime minister telegraphed to the acting high commissioner in London his concern that Canadian firms were being ignored by the British and French governments. 'A very powerful and even bitter feeling is being aroused throughout the Dominion. Men are going without bread in Canada while those across the line are receiving good wages for work that could be done as efficiently and as cheaply in this country.' In December the Canadian government sent a long list of goods that Canadian manufacturers were prepared and eager to deliver.[3] The same pleas carried into 1915, but meanwhile production of munitions for the United Kingdom had begun, under the direction first of the Shell

Committee and then of the Imperial Munitions Board, the latter being under the chairmanship of Sir Joseph Flavelle of Toronto.

With a population of 208,040 in 1901 Toronto was by far the largest city in Ontario, the nearest being Ottawa with 59,928 and Hamilton with 52,634. More than that it was, in population at least, the only city in Canada that was in the class of Montreal (267,730), instead of being half that size as had been the case thirty years before. In the century before the fleur-de-lis had been hauled down in the face of superior force, Montrealers had become leaders of a continental commercial system that extended through the St Lawrence River, the Great Lakes, and connecting waterways to the far northwest and southwest. After the conquest a succeeding group of merchants continued and expanded commercial and financial undertakings, reigning confidently over British North America. And so, as it seemed to the men of St James Street and of the great houses below the mountain, it would ever be.

That situation had long been a challenge to the businessmen of Toronto, even when it was too small to be respected by its near neighbours. They struggled to attain home rule and to some extent they succeeded. But the question posed in the early years of the twentieth century was more than how to score against a superior opponent: rather it was how to become itself an economic unit on a national scale.

In terms of grand strategy Toronto was in an ambiguous position geographically. It was an ocean port only at one remove, and for that reason never failed to encourage the improvement of the St Lawrence canals. It did, however, have a good inland harbour, and upon that fact hung much of its conception of long-distance transportation. When the 'west' was the far country of the fur trade based on Montreal, Toronto had tried, with almost no success, to divert the channel of transportation through its harbour. When the 'west' meant only western Ontario and the adjoining American states a similar effort was made. In that middle period attention was focused on continental rather than national lines, for the idea that the St Lawrence was the proper and natural outlet for the American middle west died hard. The Welland Canal, the Northern Railway, the Great Western, and the Grand Trunk were all intended to serve that purpose and in so doing to profit greatly. Even when rail communications with the Canadian prairies and the Pacific coast were established on a line to the north of the upper lakes Toronto continued to pursue this objective of a waterway that would bring business to its harbour, arguing correctly that bulk freight was always going to move in the main by ship.

Of three routes, actual or potential, each had its proponents in Ontario. One was by way of the Welland Canal. While this was generally seen as having obvious advantages two objections to it were raised: it was roundabout and it led past the Erie Canal, involving the danger of the traffic being pulled away to New York. The second was a canal between Georgian Bay and Lake Ontario. The route to be followed was hotly contested between the towns on the lake. Whitby proposed to take advantage of the Kawartha Lakes, but the Toronto choice, of course, was for a canal to its own harbour, roughly corresponding to the old Toronto portage. The third route would be by way of the Ottawa River to Montreal. When a royal commission appointed in 1870 condemned the Toronto scheme of a canal to Georgian Bay,[4] the Toronto Board of Trade had then to switch from advocacy of that to support of the Welland Canal – clearly the lesser of two evils since the Ottawa River would completely bypass the city.[5]

The continued importance to Toronto of its harbour is evident. In the late eighties the numbers of steamers and schooners loaded had risen quite rapidly, but over the years outward volume was small as compared to inward. The latter was considerable in the first two decades of the twentieth century and continued to rise, amounting to more than a million cargo tons in 1930, the year in which the new Welland Ship Canal was opened to all but the largest vessels. The grain trade, once very active, declined as a result of the destruction of the elevators by fire, but in 1928 Toronto Elevators Limited opened a concrete building with a capacity of two million bushels. In 1931 a high point was reached with the export of 8,935,622 bushels.

By the turn of the century the harbour's facilities had been improved, including about thirty-nine wharves of various kinds. Much, however, needed to be done, and with that in mind a new form of administraton was introduced. By a Dominion statute of 1911 (1 and 2 Geo. v, c. 26) responsibility was placed in a new Board of Harbour Commissioners. Of five members three were to be appointed by the city council and two by the federal government, one of the latter on recommendation of the Board of Trade. In order that one body should have jurisdiction over development as a whole a provincial statute transferred to the commissioners Ashbridge's Bay and other waterfront properties owned by the city.

The board drew up sweeping plans, approved by the city council and the Canadian government, designed both to improve the old harbour and to make use of undeveloped land. The largest undertaking was the conversion of a thousand acres of marsh in Ashbridge's Bay to shipping and industrial purposes. The result was to be 682 acres of industrial sites, 131 acres of streets and railway reservations, and 150 acres of improved waterways, including a ship channel and turning basin. In the central part of the harbour more land was to be reclaimed for industrial use and dock facilities improved. The whole harbour was to be deepened to twenty-four feet with an ultimate depth of thirty feet. Altogether nine hundred acres on the mainland and island would be set aside for parks and recreation. To the west a drive and boulevard were to be built along the lakeshore. Unlike some others these plans were implemented. Sunnyside Beach was formally opened in 1922, and by 1929 a considerable portion of the industrial land had been taken up, bringing revenue to set against an expenditure originally estimated at more than $19 million, divided between the commissioners, the federal government, and the city.[6]

When the Canadian government pledged itself to construct a railway to the Pacific as an inducement to British Columbia to join the Dominion the only large company in existence was the Grand Trunk, and it was prepared to build into the west only through American territory. If that plan had been acceptable Toronto would have been on the main line. Since, however, the Canadian government was determined to have its transcontinental railway wholly on Canadian soil the route was bound to be far to the north of Toronto. Nor were the financiers of Toronto able to make their presence felt in the negotiations leading to the creation of the Canadian Pacific Railway Company. In vain they argued that such a company should be representative of Ontario as well as of Quebec. The CPR was firmly rooted in the Bank of Montreal. It was not until the construction of the third transcontinental, the Canadian Northern, that Toronto organizations and individuals were financially and administratively connected with any great railway.

Geographically, and for the most part in other ways, Toronto was remote from the late nineteenth- and early twentieth-century scheme of railways that crossed the Dominion – the first because the city was too far south of the line from tidewater to Winnipeg, and the second because it was only beginning to compete with the financial power of Montreal. On the other hand Toronto generated too much business to be ignored by any important railway, so that links were forged to join it to the transcontinental lines, partly by the use of old local railways absorbed by the large companies, partly by new construction. As a consequence Torontonians did have access not only to the new west but also, because that was on the route, to the developing mining country of northern Ontario. So the road was open for the enterprising traders, financiers, and manufacturers.

As late as 1917 a local publication, the *Toronto Annual*, remarked that 'Toronto's prosperity is largely due to the rich surrounding agricultural district.' No doubt that was a useful reminder, but it was also true that solid growth in the scale of business called for the maximum extension territorially. Advertisements in the newspapers of the new mining towns of northern Ontario show how quickly the principal shops of Toronto reached into that field. The part played by the Toronto wholesalers is not so obviously displayed but may be assumed to have been considerable. One striking example of the empire-building of Toronto retailers is the growth of the T. Eaton Company's mail order business.[7] Beginning in the later eighties the store's catalogue – or later its series of catalogues – spread throughout Ontario and progressively beyond it. Care was taken to envisage the needs and modes of life in particular areas. Miners in northern Ontario and the Klondike were offered those clothes, foods, medicines, and tools which study had shown they needed. Settlers on the prairies could buy prefabricated houses and barns, while their wives might order clothes for themselves and their children, furniture, and almost anything needed in a house. In the maritime provinces the shop was accused of undercutting local ones. Goods were sent by train from the Atlantic to the Pacific, by stage coach into the Cariboo, by dog team into the far north.

Similarly the financial institutions – banks, insurance companies, mortgage firms – spread their business, in some cases throughout the whole country. Again an example will indicate this development. In 1893 the Canadian Bank of Commerce opened in Winnipeg its first western branch. When the prosperous years came it moved rapidly ahead, so much so that between 1898 and 1910 it had put its name on 140 new branches, including those in Dawson City and Whitehorse. At the same time the bank expanded into northern Ontario to take advantage of the new business there. It opened in Rainy River in 1903, in Cobalt and Port Arthur in 1905, Fort William in 1906, and in Porcupine in 1910. Some of the offices, it is true, were in tents and shacks for, like their customers, they were pioneers.[8] On the home front the Standard Stock and Mining Exchange, which dealt in less conservative securities than did the Toronto Stock Exchange, flourished for a time on the new flood of mining stocks. In 1934 it amalgamated with the older organization.[9]

Manufacturing, which for long had lagged behind trade and finance, was a supplier to the first and was nourished by the second. It too derived stimulus from the twentieth-century boom, and the following table[10] will show how it had come to take a more important part in the economy of the city.

| Year | Population | Capital | Employees | Salaries and wages | Value of products |
|------|-----------|---------|-----------|--------------------|-------------------|
| 1881 | 96,196 | $11,691,700 | 13,245 | $3,876,909 | $19,562,981 |
| 1891 | 181,215 | 31,725,313 | 26,242 | 9,638,537 | 44,963,922 |
| 1901 | 208,040 | 52,114,042 | 42,515 | 15,505,466 | 58,415,498 |
| 1911 | 376,538 | 145,799,281 | 65,274 | 36,064,815 | 154,306,948 |

By 1911 manufacturing claimed more personnel than any other occupation, but it should be noted that the census list of manufactures included such items as bread and confectionery, clothing, and printing and publishing. Within Toronto the heaviest concentration of industry was in the southern part, as had always been the case. Light industry was more common but shipbuilding continued at the Polson Iron Works and the Canadian Ship-building Company. In 1917–19 four Toronto firms constructed twenty-four vessels suitable for the St Lawrence canals. Although orders for munitions did not come at once they amounted, according to the Toronto *Directory* for 1921, to $200 million. The same publication gave the statistics of manufacturing for the year in which it was published and they may be added to the list above: 85,000 employees, about $250 million in capital, and annual production valued at $300 million.

These last figures give some indication of how the momentum gained in the war continued after it, and of how the skills learned by labour and management were turned to postwar industry. The whole economy of Canada, and of Toronto as a major urban centre within it, had been strengthened and diversified. It was the longest and quickest step away from the exchange of staples for imported manufactured goods.

Even before these developments in the war years and immediately after Toronto had committed itself to a degree of economic nationalism. The project of reciprocity put forward by the Liberal government in the election of 1911 was opposed actively by the Toronto business interests which, as has been shown, had found a place in countrywide commerce and finance. The concept of east-west trade that was built into the confederation agreement had been long in maturing, nor indeed could it do so until the basic conditions had been fulfilled: transcontinental railways, substantial native industry, and national finance. But in 1911 all these were facts and accepted to the extent that three railways across the continent were con-sidered as not too many to carry the people and goods that moved across the Canadian scene. A resolution opposing reciprocity was put before the Board of Trade, which much earlier had argued against high tariffs,and passed by the decisive vote of 289 to 13. The Canadian Manufacturers' Association was more in its own tradition when it set its face against reciprocity.

A number of Liberals in the city, led by the 'glorious eighteen' as someone labelled them, were firmly against reciprocity, and the eighteen signed a letter to the newspapers expressing their opposition to the measure. The proposed agreement, they said, would impair Canada's prosperity, injure some parts of Canadian trade, interfere with empire trade, and threaten Canadian nationality. They were a formidable group, representing finance, manufacturing, transportation, and trade: B. E. Walker was president of the Bank of Commerce; H. S. Strathy, director of the Traders' Bank; G. T. Somers, president of the Sterling Bank; J. L. Blaikie, an investment dealer; E. R. Wood, managing director of the Central Canadian Loan and Savings Company; W. T. White, managing director of the National Trust Company; L. Goldman, managing director of the North American Assurance Company; G. A. Somerville, managing director of the Manufacturers' Life; R. S. Gourlay, piano manufacturer; R. J. Christie, managing director of Christie, Brown, and Company, manufacturers of biscuits; H. Blain, of Ely, Blain and Company, wholesale grocers; W. Francis, director of the Consumers' Gas Company; J. D. Allen, manufacturer of hats; Z. A. Lash, vice-president of the Canadian Northern Railway; W. K. George, head of the Standard Silver Company, W. D. Matthews, grain dealer; J. C. Eaton, president of the T. Eaton Company; and Sir Mortimer Clark, lawyer and former lieutenant governor.

These men conferred with others in business and the professions – of whatever political persuasion – and took part in a campaign to stop reciprocity, which entailed defeating the Liberal government at the polls. A public meeting was called in Massey Hall, the Canadian National League founded, and articles and interviews published in the press. Each of the six Toronto constituencies returned a Conservative by a large majority.

Physically the signs of prosperity in Toronto were many. The value of building permits was multiplied about five times from 1904 to 1913 and nearly doubled again between then and 1928. Because of the changing value of the dollar such figures are in reality only relative but they give sufficient idea of magnitude. In the downtown area high buildings were making a new skyline. The union station, although delayed first by the war and then by an argument over the arrangement of tracks, was large and handsome. The general hospital on University Avenue and the third St Paul's Church on Bloor Street belong to these prosperous years.

One house could have been imagined only in a period of sudden prosperity. Casa Loma, Henry Pellatt's unfortified castle, was on the rise of the hill close to the site of Dr Baldwin's Spadina. The architect, E. J. Lennox, worked from sketches made in Europe and from Pellatt's recollections of what he had seen and admired. Some parts of that vast house of ninety rooms were exact reproductions of portions of European buildings. Some of the floors were of teak, panelling was in oak and mahogany, woodwork was carved in England, and three pairs of bronze doors were made in New York. Immense stables for twenty horses with living accommodation for coachmen and grooms were reached by an underground passage. Begun in 1911, the house was completed outside some two years later and for a time the Pellatts lived in part of it.[11]

In their early days motor cars were considered to be signs of wealth. In 1904 Hyslop Brothers notified the public, through the daily press, that they were agents for Oldsmobile vehicles, including a delivery waggon that in the illustration looks exactly like a horse-drawn one without shafts. No prices were given. By 1907 advertisements had become more common. The Canada Cycle and Motor Company, with its factory at Toronto Junction, offered Russell automobiles for sale. A two-cylinder, eighteen

First Sauer truck bought by the T. Eaton Company Limited, probably May 1908

horse power Russell sold at $1,000; a four-cylinder, thirty-five horse power model was $2,500; and the large seven-passenger, forty horse power car was $3,750. Polson Iron Works were agents for the British Thornycroft cars, described as first class only, and which rose to the magnificent seventy-five horse power car at $10,000, an investment of no mean dimensions. The Cadillac, sold by Hyslop Brothers, was only $1,300 but with a claim that it had all the excellence of more expensive machines. The Dominion Automobile Company at the corner of Bay and Temperance streets had a galaxy of cars with names then famous and now forgotten: Clement-Bayard, Stevens-Duryea, Peerless, Packard, Thomas, Winton, and Napier.

Cars were expensive, and even the Ford runabout at $750 in 1907 was beyond the reach of most people. Only a few private cars chugged sedately or uncertainly along the streets of Toronto until mass production, pioneered by Henry Ford, forced prices down and numbers up. Taxis and trucks came into use and cars gradually ceased to be luxuries for the rich. In 1916 Toronto had 11,169 automobiles – twice as many as Montreal – and 1,994 trucks. The speed limit in a city, set by a Dominion statute of 1912, was fifteen miles an hour, and perhaps that was not inappropriate to uncertain machines and imperfect roads. The latter, however, were improving. Of 265 miles of streets in 1905 more than one hundred were paved with asphalt or macadam and another fifty with cedar blocks. In 1928 the streets ran for 562 miles and 82 per cent had hard surfaces of some kind, wooden blocks having almost disappeared.

In the dozen years before the war of 1914 Toronto made marked progress in size, in population, in its buildings, and in the sum of its wealth. Nearly every form of financial and commercial enterprise flourished, a few people having large incomes and more having comfortable ones. Many others, however, hovered on the boundary line between adequate means and poverty. A slight rise or fall in the demand for labour could push them above or below that margin. One compelling factor was a steep rise in the cost of living, unwelcome companion of the advent of prosperity. Prices were rising all over the world but not at the same pace. In one group of countries which included the United Kingdom the advance was between 15 and 20 per cent. In a second group, in which were Germany, Australia, and New Zealand, it was between 25 and 35 per cent. Canada and the United States were among the countries in which the increase was close to 50 per cent. The analyses made of Canadian prices were based on different lists of commodities and services, some including rent and others not. No single and authoritative figure can therefore be given, but it would not be far out to say that foods and materials rose by 42 per cent between 1900 and 1912 and house rents by 62 per cent in the same period.

Looking at a few individual items, clothing was rising steadily, and in the case of first class men's suits by 50 per cent. Shoes were up considerably and so was furniture. Most, but not all, types of food were higher priced. Bread was fairly constant until 1912 but then doubled by 1917. Milk was more expensive and the prices of eggs and butter about doubled from 1896 to 1911. Flour hardly changed and tea not before 1910. On average the price of meat doubled between 1900 and 1913. Potatoes and apples became much more expensive. Hard coal rose, particularly after 1911, but electricity dropped substantially.

The cost of housing was the chief villain of the piece. An unofficial study showed these results: the mean monthly rent of ninety-three houses in 1897 was $7.45 and in 1906 was $13.94; of another forty-one houses the mean rent was $5.71 in 1897, $10.09 in 1906, and $12.85 in 1907. For another ninety-five houses the figures were $7.63 in 1897 and $14.40 in 1906; and of another group of forty-three, $6.20 in 1897 and $13.19 in 1907. In two of these groups the increase was more than 100 per cent. In no case were the houses improved between the dates mentioned.

In the eight or nine years being examined per capita consumption of common foods increased. The total sale of luxuries was greater, that of malt and spirituous liquors by 60 per cent and of tobacco by 66 per cent. More money per capita was spent on life insurance: $4.87 in 1913 as compared with $2.81 in 1900. It was generally considered that the standard of living had risen but it is not easy to pin that down to figures, or to say who was better or perhaps worse off. As to incomes the rentier might be doing well or badly since stocks were considerably up and bonds down.

Delivery waggon, about 1910

Solid information is available for only two categories of salaried workers. Salaries of Baptist, Church of England, Methodist, and Presbyterian clergymen were on the average raised by 30.3 per cent from 1900 to 1912. That was somewhat less than the additional cost of living, but male and female school teachers, with a 46.7 increase, were ahead in the race. For other white collar categories no generalizations can safely be made except that many of them spent more and therefore presumably received more.

For wages in Canada generally the index figure of 143 (1900 = 100) was suggested for 1913 by the official body studying the cost of living, with the added comment that a 45 per cent increase in nominal wages would be needed to maintain the same standard of living.[12] The figure 143, however, is an average; some skilled workers being better off than formerly and unskilled workers in particular worse off. The extent and regularity of employment would affect both.

The housing situation in Toronto was complicated. In 1910 the number of vacant houses per thousand was 8.27. Then the figures were lower until 1915 when a high point of 11.51 was reached. In no year between 1911 and 1917 were half the houses occupied by the owners. Of 13,574 houses constructed for single families only 36 per cent were so used in 1918. Doubling or tripling was not due to an overall shortage but to cost. The City of Toronto's housing commission emphasized the need for small houses at modest rents. The Toronto newspapers painted a far darker picture. The *News* published in November 1906 an article headed 'Evolution of a Slum.'

The exorbitant rate charged the very poor is the immediate cause of much suffering and too often of crime. Overcrowding is made possible by the fact that the demand far exceeds the supply ... Every room which is situated near the centres of employment is eagerly competed for, and the landlord is sure of

An immigrant family, about 1910

tenants no matter how wretched the rooms may be. Repairs and improvements are, therefore, seldom if ever made.

One (smelly) house, the article went on, was rented as follows:

| | |
|---|---|
| 4 rooms with 7 people | $ 9 |
| 1 room with 2 people | $ 4 |
| 1 large room with 4 people | $ 8 |
| 2 small rooms with 6 people | $ 8 |
| 2 large rooms with 2 people | $12 |
| 1 large room with 2 people | $ 8 |
| shop and room, 5 people | $19 |
| Monthly revenue | $68 |

So twenty-eight people (eighteen adults, ten children) lived in thirteen rooms. With that rent, the *News* pointed out, the property was worth $20,400, although it was assessed at $1,500. 'Owing to conditions like this speculators are buying up these properties. They make a small payment down of, say, $100 or $200. The rents which they exact from the poor tenants furnish the future payments, and, in a case like the one quoted,

Yard common to four dwellings, about 1910

the house is paid for in a couple of years.' That, said the writer, would go on until cheap, sanitary houses were built. The conditions that existed, he was satisfied, led to drunkenness and bad health.

The *Globe* spoke with two tongues. Editorially it voiced the traditional bourgeois self-defence that you could build houses for the poor but they would not live in them. In the news columns, however, was an interview with a man who had been investigating conditions of housing and who said that it was almost impossible for a large family to find a home on a labourer's wage. Landlords were prejudiced against tenants with many children, but in any case a man earning $9 to 10 a week and paying $10 for a house per month would find it difficult to buy food and clothing. His examination had led him to conclude that you could not even tell how many people slept in a house, since men were on the floor and children in hammocks slung from the ceiling. Many houses were unsanitary and infested by rats.

In 1907–8 concern over the cost of living led to a study of living conditions and family budgets directed by James Mavor, professor of economics at the University of Toronto.[13] An investigator visited many houses with a long list of questions and found everything from extreme poverty and sordid conditions to comparative prosperity. All the cases were of wage-earners. Here are a few characteristic results: a family of eight lived in a three-roomed house on Agnes Street which rented for $11 a month. Water came from a well but the pump was broken. One of the rooms had no window. In a seven-room house on Chestnut Street was a family of three with eleven boarders. In another house on the same street, with eleven rooms, were two families of two each and boarders. It was described as dirty but warm. A house on Centre Avenue accommodated a family of two with thirteen boarders.

And so it went, with many similar cases. 'High rents in Toronto,' wrote the *World*, 'force many people to build their own houses in the city's outskirts,' and drew attention to photographs of shacks covered with tarpaper. One area that suddenly experienced this development was from Davenport Road toward St Clair Avenue, west of Poplar Plains Road. On the southern part of this district workmen were building 'hundreds of little cottages, many of them not much more than shacks' as the *News* noted. Roads were crude, houses in irregular rows, and sidewalks in the early design of two planks laid lengthwise. Men worked on their houses after six in the evening and in some cases the country bee was revived. Moving away from the city centre, however, produced in some cases intolerable costs of transportation. In 1907 the city's housing committee first met and discussed whether the city should itself build houses, but concluded that that would be unwise.

A valuable part of the inquiry made by Mavor and his associates was into family budgets of wage-earners. The details have to be treated with reserve since different prices were given for standard articles like bread and eggs, and in some cases it appears that information on expenditure on pleasure was withheld. However, the returns give the dimensions of budgets, showing that some wage-earners were able to live well within their means while others were constantly in the red.

A presser, his wife, and two children rented for $8 two rooms in a six-room house that held altogether three families (fifteen persons). His income was $5 to 6 a week and average expenditure $5.53.

A picture framer with a wife and six children earned on the average $8 a week. They took in two lodgers at $10 a month for the two. The children paid for their own boots by running errands and the mother obtained her clothes through charity or buying at mothers' meetings and paying by instalments. They admitted no expenditure on amusements or holidays. Their total average income was $10.50 a week and expenditure $10.69.

A foreman carpenter owned his own house and eight others. He earned $16.72 a week when working. The family spent in a year $75 for holidays, contributed $5.20 to a church, and had insurance premiums of $25.64. Their apparent saving in a year was $822.05.

A machinist, a painter, the foreman in a shop, a brass finisher, and a brewer's labourer could all show surpluses. An illiterate Irish labourer was driven by high rents to build outside the city a shack for himself, his wife, and six children. By that means his annual expenditure of $631.84 was more than met by an income of $705. A piano worker with irregular employment had a small deficit, a bricklayer a small surplus, and a motor-man broke even. Except in a few cases the margins were so narrow that temporary unemployment or sickness could bring disaster. Of the nine hundred Chinese who lived in Toronto in 1907 most were laundrymen. They lived in clean well-equipped houses, with bathrooms quite common, and were able to eat well.

On balance the information available on the conditions of living of low-income families does not necessarily suggest a standard lower than that which obtained in some earlier and later periods. Hours of work were long and wages low in modern terms. The former were slowly being improved under pressure from the trade unions; but, while wages were rising, it was touch and go as to whether they were ahead of or behind the cost of living.

The welcome return of prosperity at the turn of the century lifted Toronto from a local to a national level, but brought with it uncertainties. Rising prices threatened to overtake incomes and intermittent declines in business to create unemployment. Serious as the resultant situation might be for individuals, a limited number were adversely affected and for limited periods. When the boom seemed to be at an end in 1913–14 it was more than revived for the last four years of the war. Apprehension that such improvement was artificial and that the cessation of wartime demands would bring a serious slump proved on the whole to be ungrounded. A decline did set in after 1920, but by 1922 it had done its worst, and from 1925 to 1929 new high levels were reached.

The 1920s were years of increasing extravagance. Reaction from the serious mood of the years of hostilities was all the more understandable in that it was generally believed that the job had been done for once and for all – there would not again be a war. Toronto was gay, dancing to the new forms of jazz music, while the young adopted new fads in costume and habit. Economically there was some solid base. The mining and the pulp and paper industries, of considerable concern to the business community of Toronto, were expanding. Manufacturing in and near Toronto pro-gressed. But there was unreality too.

Through 1928 and the first three-quarters of 1929 the boom continued to gain momentum and in Toronto people saw nothing but a rosy future, one which would provide for itself without cautious saving in the present. Perhaps the best example of this state of mind was the widespread specula-tion in stocks, particularly by hundreds of men and women who had never before done so and who often had no understanding either of what they

Visit of Prince Arthur of Connaught, 1906, Sir John Eaton driving car, in front of University College

were buying or of the terms on which they bought. Buying on margin (paying only 10 per cent of the purchase price) was agreeable and relatively safe so long as the market continued to rise; and amateur investors counted imaginary fortunes from the current values of securities which they did not in fact own.

The stock exchange was a barometer which could register storms as well as fair weather. At the beginning of October 1929 dark signs showed in a world economy that few people had realized was unsound. On 3 and 4 October prices collapsed but rebounded. After a pause the same thing happened on 21 October. The *Globe* carried on its front page the news that 'stock market panic threatens New York in last hour's trade . . . avalanche of selling orders . . . small dealers wiped out.' For 24 October it was much the same story: 'Stock speculators shaken in wild day of panic. Record for all time is set by Wall St. in a frenzy of selling.' Again some recovery was made possible as bankers intervened to support the market, but neither their efforts nor the assurances of Canadian bankers and brokers that general conditions gave no cause for alarm could stop the rot. On 29 October all trading records were broken on the New York and Toronto exchanges as in waves of frantic selling an 'utter collapse in the stock market,' as the *Globe* reported, 'was narrowly averted.' Even that cautious phrase was an understatement.

Such was the alarming news on Toronto breakfast tables; and that it was not a passing phase became apparent as month after month gloomy stories came in from all over the western world. Economic depressions had plagued Canadians before 1900 and again in the early twenties, but that which began so suddenly and so violently in 1929 had a set of features which gave to it its peculiarly devastating character. It was not just a temporary lapse affecting a limited number of people. The effects were extreme and spread widely throughout the community. No relief, moreover, was to come for years, although, happily for their peace of mind, most people did not at the outset anticipate such a long grind. The storm, too, hit without warning in a time of great prosperity, so that the drop was from a very high to a very low point. As one dark year followed another people began to wonder whether the whole fabric of twentieth-century society was disintegrating.

As a trading nation Canada was badly hit by curtailment of purchasing power in other countries. A severe fall in demand for agricultural products and drop in price were exaggerated in the western prairies by drought. Throughout the country manufacturing was heavily reduced and the construction industry suffered almost equally. Thanks to a diversified economy Toronto was less seriously affected than were some of the cities of Ontario and far less than many areas in the west, but such a comparison was poor consolation for those who lost their savings, their expectations, and often their jobs. Employers in trade, industry, and finance looked for means of retrenchment in a buyer's market that had few buyers. Hopes of making fortunes were replaced by calculations on how to minimize loss. Two inescapable conclusions were to reduce the number of employees and the pay of those who could be retained.

In describing an earlier and more hopeful period the rising value of building permits in the city was cited. Similarly the fall in value, even more rapid, indicates the blow to the construction industry and everything dependent on it. From a high point of more than $51 million in 1928 the total dropped to some $30 million in 1930 and to a grim low of not much more than $4 million in 1933, the worst year of the depression. Manufacturing was hit hard too, the number of persons employed in it falling by more than twenty-six thousand or about one-quarter of the pre-depression work force.

In some skilled trades wages were reduced little if at all, but with benefit only to those who had and retained jobs. The unskilled workers were hardest hit, both by reduction of employment and by wage cuts, the latter sometimes below the level of subsistence. The professional and clerical classes had the lowest rates of unemployment, but even if they did keep their jobs the great majority saw their salaries reduced or promotion deferred. New school teachers started at lower rates; doctors and dentists could not always collect their fees; lawyers found clients elusive. A stock-broker's office echoed to the sound of a single footstep. The overall index of employment in Toronto (1926=100) stood at 126.3 just before the depression began, at 110.3 in 1931, and at 84.4 in 1933. It is probable, however, that the situation was even worse than the statistics indicate since any person who could be said to be employed might be on short hours or on less than a living wage.

Some remedial steps could be taken by those whose incomes were cut or ceased altogether. A small proportion had savings but in most cases they did not last long. Families doubled up to save rent, sold non-essential possessions, and did what else they could to economize. A general decline in the cost of living was a real help. The index (1935–9 = 100) stood at 121.6 in 1929 and at 94.3 in 1933. In the same way the consumer price index dropped by 17 points between 1929 and 1933. Since living was thus markedly cheaper a few people, including a small proportion of skilled wage-earners, actually gained; while some rentiers and salaried persons experienced little change.

Such factors afforded some protection to a limited number of people but to a great many others were of little avail. The examination earlier in this chapter of family budgets in the first decade of the century gives sufficient indication of the narrow margin between having and not having the capacity to pay rent and buy food. Some families in the thirties were close to starvation in freezing houses. Penniless men begged in the streets or lived in tarpaper shacks on garbage dumps. Those in the worst straits were not all residents. Of forty-four thousand single men registered for relief in Toronto between 1931 and 1936 transients accounted for twenty-three thousand.

Apart from ending the world depression – a feat which no one could perform – nothing could be done for those whose hardships did not amount to physical suffering; but something had to be done for the thousands who lacked food, clothing, shelter, or medical attention. If the free enterprise society had run without brakes in the boom years of the late twenties it now threatened to come to a dead stop. In its modern meaning the welfare state had not been born. Some provision had always been made, in the main by municipalities and private organizations, for the poor and unemployed, for the physically and mentally ill, for orphans and neglected children; but not on a scale that would bear the overwhelming demands of the thirties.

Dominion, provincial, and city governments all accepted some responsibility for those hit hardest by the depression, as did a number of unofficial bodies, but together they had not the financial means to do more than a part of what needed to be done. The absence of unemployment insurance was serious, and when the Bennett 'new deal' foundered on a constitutional rock the gap remained until the depression was over. In any case it was a measure that could only with difficulty have been started in such hard times.

The government of Toronto was hampered in its efforts to pursue remedial programmes by a decline in tax revenue, its main source of funds. With falling values assessments of property had to be lowered and a portion of the householders were unable to pay even reduced taxes. At the beginning of 1930 tax arrears amounted to $5.5 million. Some expenditures could be deferred but essential services could be pared little. Meanwhile the total cost of relief multiplied to such an extent that in place of surpluses there were deficits, that of 1932 being well over a million dollars. Even so Toronto was in a better financial position than most of the nearby municipalities.

At one point in 1934 the number of unemployed persons on relief in Toronto was close to 120,000. In the light of experience the relief agencies of the city, official and unofficial, were better co–ordinated, thus allowing for more efficient operation, avoiding overlaps, and identifying the proper recipients of relief. In connection with the last it could be expected that some individuals would make improper claims. A test in one area of the city revealed that 10 per cent of those applying for relief were not entitled to it, and it also became known that some men made a practice of going from one soup kitchen to another. On the other hand it was difficult to locate others who needed and were qualified for relief but too proud to ask for it.

Food for families was supplied from city funds through the House of Industry which had had long experience in this respect. Parcels of groceries were made up and called for by the recipients. Perishables, such as milk, bread, butter, meat, and vegetables were delivered direct by dealers. In 1933 a change was made by transferring the operation of unemployment relief to the Department of Welfare which issued vouchers that would be honoured at shops. Whether the ration was sufficient to maintain health was questioned by those who cited the higher level recommended by the Ontario Medical Association and the still higher one set by the Nutritional Committee of the League of Nations. On the other hand it could be pointed out that the general standard of health in Toronto showed only a slight deterioration during the depression.

Another traditional method of assistance was through public works. The Ontario government adopted a programme of road building in the north of the province, recruiting mainly unmarried men from different parts of the south and establishing them in camps. On the whole the scheme was a success, but it could cover only a limited number of men from Toronto and could not go on indefinitely. Municipal relief works proved to be not very satisfactory. They were expensive since their purpose called for manual rather than machine methods; foremen were dissatisfied with the type of labourers assigned to them; and little imagination was shown in selecting projects.

Principal attention at the time and since has, properly enough, been directed to the plight of the unemployed wage-earners and of others actually suffering.[14] At the same time it should be recognized that the depression was a dominating force in Toronto for ten years: not just something that enlarged the requirement for poor relief. Little sympathy need be wasted on the amateur speculators who, after playing a gambling game that they did not understand, saw their paper gains buried beneath the welter of ticker tape on the floor of the stock exchange. But pity was due to those many people who came to have a sense of frustration and helplessness, who watched numbly the defeat of personal plans sensible in 1928 and impossible of achievement in 1930; to the hardworking and thrifty persons, too, whose savings were sapped away and who desperately looked for places in the economy for their sons and daughters. Young people seeking initial employment could find few gaps in a blank wall.

The generations growing up after the thirties, living in an affluent society and protected on every hand by social security, cannot, with the best will, understand what disciplines the depression imposed, how people were driven to the old-fashioned virtues – or what had once seemed to be virtues – of frugality and competitive work. Perhaps its results were not all bad, for in it grew up the men who wrote the name 'Canada' on many battlefields.

If, however, the depression dominated and circumscribed life in Toronto it was not the sole subject of conversation, nor was it a barrier against a wide range of intellectual and artistic advances. Funds were limited, as they were for improvements in public services, in buildings, and for almost any purpose; but the community was not static because the economy was. Toronto was badly hit but it was not a desert. It was, in fact, very much alive.

# 9

## *The end of an era*

A description of Toronto as it was in the generation before the second world war might still bear the title of Henry Scadding's classic, *Toronto of Old*; for, large as it had become, the city had still much of the ancient character that was to be diluted and modified in postwar years.

Between 1905 and 1939 the city grew from about seventeen square miles to thirty-five. The change was due to a series of annexations of which the principal were North Rosedale (1906), Deer Park (1908), East Toronto (1908), West Toronto (1909), Midway, well beyond the Don (1909), Dovercourt and Earlscourt (1910), the very large North Toronto (1912), and Moore Park (1912). By the time of the first war Toronto had reached approximately its present boundaries, with the exceptions of Forest Hill and Swansea, which were added by the provincial government in 1967.

Within this expanding territory the city was sorting itself into quarters: wholesale trade, retail trade, finance, manufacturing, and the different classes of residential districts. Here and there were individual houses beyond the limits and further out the suburbs, most of which were still small. Already at the beginning of the century Toronto was a substantial city, but its new-found prosperity nearly went up in flames.

Fire, caused by defective wiring, broke out on the evening of 19 April 1904 in E. and S. Currie's neckware factory on the north side of Wellington Street west of Bay. Chief Thompson entered the building with a small detachment, was trapped, and in escaping injured his leg and was taken to hospital. The fire was already fierce and out of control. Fanned by a gale from the northwest it swept down Bay Street, jumped across Front Street at about eleven o'clock, and spread westward at the same time. The Toronto Fire Department was putting up a good fight, but the water pressure was not good and men and equipment were insufficient to deal with this overwhelming march of flames. Appeals for help brought reinforcements from Hamilton, Buffalo, London, and Peterborough.

It was a frightening scene, with sparks and debris blowing wildly for hundreds of yards. Dynamiting was tried but to little avail as the wind blew fire across the spaces thus made. Boats pulled out of the docks into the bay while citizens crowded downtown to see the spectacle and children were held up to distant windows to watch the glow. A few companies were able to rescue their records and other valuables and in several cases employees entered the battle with such hoses as were in their buildings and often strove to good effect. In the Queen's Hotel, close to the centre of the fire area, guests and staff draped wet blankets over the window frames and kept dousing them as the hot wind dried everything. Several times the roof caught fire but watchers put it out. 'Acts of daring and strategy as any feat of arms' was the way in which the *Globe* described the stands made at the Customs House and the Bank of Montreal. Up Bay Street the *Telegram* building was saved, and with that the prospect of destruction of more vulnerable buildings was averted. For a time it must have seemed that it would be impossible to stop a fire so widespread and so violent, and it was a tribute to the local fire department and its allies that the danger was over by the morning.

'Standing at the corner of Front and Bay Streets,' wrote the *Globe* reporter early on the next day, 'one begins to realize the extent of the awful destruction that has been wrought, on every hand are ruins almost as far as one can see. Within the whole burned area there is not a single wall intact.' Fourteen acres with eighty-six factories and warehouses, much of the commercial strength of Toronto, were devastated. Insurance experts estimated the loss at $13 million and five thousand employees were thrown out of work. The companies concerned were enterprising in making temporary arrangements, and before the embers were cold architects were at work on plans for new buildings. But for decades afterwards blocks of ruins along Front Street reminded Toronto of its great fire.

Destructive as the fire was it never got beyond one area, thanks to the efforts of the firemen and the direction of the wind. Part of the main business district escaped as did all the residential ones. At the time 226,365 people lived in Toronto. Ten years later the number had risen to 470,151, and at the time of the second war to 649,123. The last was not far below the point at which the population was stabilized by the metro system and by withdrawals beyond the city limits. Toronto had more immigrants than any other Canadian city, and in 1931 they made up more than a third of the whole. For the most part, however, the newcomers were – as in the past – from the British Isles, so that the population was predominantly British. Migration into the province from Quebec became considerable, but most of it was to the northeast. The thin end of the European wedge

Macdonell Avenue, Parkdale, 1917, characteristic of middle-income districts

was beginning to show in the census of 1941. Germans, Italians, Poles, Scandinavians, and Ukrainians were all to be found in Toronto but as yet in numbers too small to affect the balance.

Some of the wealthy and comparatively wealthy continued to live on such established streets as Beverley, the lower part of St George, and Jarvis. North of that the Annex was filling up with numerous semi-detached houses, solid and capacious but lacking in style, and larger houses interspersed among them. On the hill, above and below St Clair Avenue, neighbours were remote at the beginning of the century but building continued in all that part. By the twenties apartment houses were still not common but numerous enough to constitute a recognized category of dwellings.

Little headway was made in providing houses for low-income families. One stage of the problem has been described in some detail in the previous chapter. Under the authority of a provincial act of 1913 the Toronto Housing Company was incorporated and the city guaranteed its bonds. The company built and operated Riverdale Courts on Bain Avenue (east of Broadview) and the Spruce Courts on Spruce Street. They contained cottage flats of three to six rooms with separate entrances and together could accommodate 334 families. The rents were $23 to $40.

In 1920 the Toronto Housing Commission was established by statute and was authorized to build houses for working men of moderate means. The commission, made up first of private citizens and later of municipal officials, erected 236 houses in the eastern and western parts of the city, and sold them on condition of monthly payments covering principal and interest. In the depression years the owners found difficulty in meeting their commitments.

In 1934, at the suggestion of the lieutenant governor, H. A. Bruce, the city appointed a commission, not to build houses, but to examine the housing that existed in poorer districts. Its findings on slum areas make grim reading. Of 1,332 dwellings covered in the survey 96 per cent fell below the committee's standard of amenities and 75 per cent below its standard of health.[1]

Early in the war, Board of Control appointed two men to examine housing in general. They reported 'the most acute housing situation in half a century. More than three thousand dwelling units were needed. They gave as causes of the shortage the city's failure to act on any housing plan in the years 1922–42, decline in building, increase of employment in Toronto, higher earnings which enabled some families to have separate dwellings, and movement of suburbanites into the city because of gasoline rationing.[2]

Within the average house radical changes took place in the first thirty years of the twentieth century. Already at the beginning of that period central heating by coal burning furnaces was fairly general. Hot air, steam, and hot water systems were all used. Indoor plumbing, too, had been accepted by even the most conservative. Since the city sewers did not always keep up with the spread of houses, septic tanks had sometimes to be installed. Electricity was slower to be generally employed for lighting but then gas already gave satisfactory results. Mechanization was not rapid, but neither was it as essential when domestic servants were available. Electric clothes washers were not on the market until the early twenties, electric sewing machines before the middle, or vacuum cleaners before the end.

Many houses had furniture of an older and better period, but if additions were needed or new houses required to be equipped it would ordinarily be necessary to draw on what was made at the time. Through the first two decades of the century anything not especially designed by an enlightened few was of unequalled ugliness. The contorted styles of the late Victorian era faded out after the first war, but unhappily the pieces were solidly made and lasted all too long. Complicated patterns and a general impression of heaviness were evident in curtains and blinds of the same years. Comfort was not ignored but aestheticism had no priority.[3]

The churches continued to play an important part in the life of the community, not only because the average family attended religious services on Sunday, but because the churches were active in organizing social activities and in welfare work. According to the census of 1921 the Church of England still had a substantial lead, with the Presbyterians next, then the Methodists, and the Roman Catholics somewhat fewer. The Jewish population of Toronto had increased considerably. The exact numbers of adherents of any church are not known, but the important fact is that the churches were filled and new ones were built as the city grew. Few contemporary records can be found of the range of activities of any of the churches, perhaps because they were taken as a matter of course. One interesting diary is that of Mrs Mary Robertson, wife of a Scottish beadle at St Andrew's Presbyterian Church on King Street, for she jotted down her 'experiences and anecdotes.' In 1917 the church was busy with war work. Women came to spend all day at such tasks. 'How these women work, and how they gabbled.' In 1919 the church's finances needed to be restored after expenditures on soldiers' comforts, and to that end sixty men spent five evenings planning a campaign to raise money.

January of 1920 was bitterly cold and many calls came in from those who were without food or fuel. Members of the congregation, Mrs Robertson recorded, were marvellously kind in meeting needs. In December Christmas tree parties were held for the children, Mrs Robertson filling two hundred bags with candy for the occasion. Then came receptions for new members of the church, dancing classes for the children, and Irish banquets – complete with jigs – for the boys of the Sunday school. Supper parties, too, were organized for children from various missions.[4]

Mrs Robertson was violently opposed to church union, being in step with the minister, Stuart Parker, also a Scot, who was actively in opposition to the proposed merger of the Presbyterians with the Methodists and the Congregationalists. In the case of the Presbyterians the decision was to be made by individual congregations. The vote at St Andrew's – according to the diarist – showed only one woman in favour of union and Mrs Robertson declared that she was really a Methodist. St Andrew's and a number of other Presbyterian churches rejected the union proposals and became known as 'continuing Presbyterians,' but the United Church was none the less founded in 1925.

Public schools, separate schools, high schools, and private schools together formed a complete pattern. For pupils, and more especially for adults, the library system was adequate. The reference library at the corner of College and St George streets, the central circulating library on Adelaide Street, the municipal reference library in the city hall, and twelve branch libraries scattered throughout the city were ample for the reading public. Books issued for home reading in 1922 amounted to 1,854,579.

After years of stress and uncertainty the University of Toronto was settling down to solid growth under the wise guidance of two successive presidents. Sir Robert Falconer (1907–32), who had come from Pine Hill College in Halifax, had been a Presbyterian minister and a scholar whose

Mendelssohn Choir, 1911, conductor Augustus Vogt, performance of 'Children's Crusade' in Massey Hall

own attainments led him to encourage advanced studies in the university. He was succeeded by H. J. Cody who as rector had filled the great church of St Paul's, was minister of education in 1918, and member of the board of governors of the university since 1917. He became president in 1932 and held that office until elected chancellor in 1944. Over a span of nearly forty years the university became considerably larger and known for advanced studies in several fields. To take a few examples: J. C. (later Sir John) McLennan was a distinguished physicist whose researches included the magnetic detection of submarines. Dr (later Sir) Frederick Banting and Dr Charles Best discovered insulin. H. A. Innis, economist and philosopher, inspired a whole new school of scholars in their approaches to economics, history, and communications. E. J. Pratt became recognized as an accomplished poet from the time of his first publication in 1923. The

COPYRIGHT 1911
PRINGLE & BOOTH
TORONTO.

smaller McMaster University moved from the shadow of its large neighbour in 1930 to develop rapidly in Hamilton.

An important addition to education and culture in Toronto was the Royal Ontario Museum. Formally opened in 1914 it had for several years been in the planning stage with some gathered works of art. Early in the century C. T. Currelly, who became the museum's first director, had been sending material from the middle east to Victoria College, but consultation led to the conclusion that it would be best to establish one museum for the university as a whole. Sir Edmund Walker, chairman of the board of governors of the University of Toronto, had long advocated museums, and he now took a leading part in organizing the foundation by the university and the provincial government of a museum that quickly attained international rank.[5]

In the field of communications it was a question whether the spread of radio broadcasting would overshadow the press. Receiving sets were coming to be the rule rather than the exception in Toronto by the late thirties. As it proved, the newspapers survived the rivalry but they themselves were going through changes. A relatively large number of dailies, each expressing the personality of the editor, were being caught up in the trend toward large-scale business. Fewer papers with larger circulation took over. They might be politically partisan but were no longer dependent on the financial support of political parties and were more commonly associated with the publisher (often the owner) than with the editor. In 1936 the *Globe*, long since dissociated from the Brown family, was bought by a businessman, George McCullagh. He, with financial support from a mining man, W. H. Wright, also bought the *Mail and Empire*. The two were then merged under the name of *Globe and Mail*, a paper professedly independent politically. Thus Toronto readers were left with one morning and two evening newspapers.

Toronto was rich in musical performance if not in composition. Families and groups of friends, amateur and professional, continued to enjoy evenings of music in their houses. Old and new choruses flourished. A. S. Vogt disbanded the Mendelssohn Choir for three years, reconstituting it in 1900 on a different basis. In 1902 the choir began its joint concerts with American orchestras, the first being the Pittsburgh Symphony under Victor Herbert. Combined concerts were given in both Canada and the United States, notably of Beethoven's *Ninth Symphony* in New York in 1907 and of Brahms' *Requiem* in Cleveland in 1910. In 1917 Vogt was succeeded by H. A. Fricker, an English organist, and in 1942 by the Canadian organist, E. C. MacMillan. Albert Ham, organist of St James' Cathedral, directed the National Chorus from 1903, and Edward Broome the Oratorio Society. Healey Willan, who came to Toronto in 1913, was still another of the distinguished organists of Toronto. Before and after his arrival he composed church music, symphonies, radio operas, and a piano concerto.

Most of the leading musicians in Toronto had come from the United Kingdom, but there were European influences as well. Vogt was born in Ontario, the son of a German émigré of 1848, and himself returned to Germany to study. The three Hambourg brothers – Mark, Boris, and Jan – came to Toronto from Russia in 1910, already having achieved fame as an instrumental trio. They founded the Hambourg Conservatory of Music, and Boris was the cellist of the Hart House Quartet when that was founded in 1924. The Conservatory String Quartet, active in the same period, included another distinguished cellist, Leo Smith, who was professor of music at the University of Toronto.

Individual artists, including the incomparable Caruso, other leading singers and instrumentalists, and a number of orchestras performed in

Toronto. A local symphony orchestra was founded in 1908, one with seventy to eighty professional players and with Frank Welsman as conductor. Suspended during the war, it was revived in another form in 1924. Luigi von Kunits was the conductor. Only twilight concerts were given, that making it possible to enlist musicians who in the evening played in theatres. The third form of the orchestra began in 1932. Evening concerts were brought back, with Ernest MacMillan as conductor. The Promenade Symphony Orchestra, under Reginald Stewart, gave summer concerts from 1934, providing pleasure for the audiences and employment for professional players.[6]

For a dozen or more years of the new century the professional theatre, free of the rivalry of motion pictures, flourished as before. Many excellent touring companies came throughout the season to the Grand Opera House, the Princess, and the Royal Alexandra. The last, too, had for several years a repertory company during the summer. A leading lady who came for several summers, Percy Haswell, was a particular favourite. Amateur theatricals gained increased vigour and support, some of the companies competing in the Dominion Drama Festival which began in 1933.

One of the most interesting and least visited corners in Toronto was the Studio Building in a Rosedale ravine where three of the new Group of Seven painters – J. E. H. MacDonald, A. Y. Jackson, and Lawren Harris – had their winter quarters. Tom Thomson refused such luxury so an old shack behind the building was partially restored, and in it he impatiently awaited spring and Algonquin Park. The Group's subjects were peculiarly but not typically Canadian, since they were for the most part scenes in the pre-Cambrian shield with hardly a glance at the softer lands of the south in the style which had appealed to the late nineteenth-century landscape painters. At first the new style of painting was regarded as strange, almost revolutionary, but in time its character was appreciated, and the wealthy began to look doubtfully at the Dutch pictures which almost invariably adorned their walls.[7]

In any late summer pictures could be seen too at the Exhibition, in company, of course, with innumerable other things. The popularity of the fair was increasing, both for residents and visitors. It was estimated that the latter annually brought $5 million to the city. Attendance first edged past the million mark in 1928 but fell again under the weight of the depression. Toronto has never been famous for its parks but the exhibition grounds had been kept free. The official list of parks and playgrounds in 1928 gave a total of 1,662.51 acres. As many as eighty-three baseball diamonds showed how that game had gained favour at the expense of lacrosse, which was allotted only five. Similarly 261 tennis courts indicate another conquest. Several cricket clubs played on every Saturday afternoon of the season. For skating there were sixty-two rinks and for hockey sixty.

High Park toboggan slides, 1925

Some, though never enough, playgrounds were open for children. A small zoo at Riverdale Park, exhibits of flowers, and the pleasant spaces of the island were all spread out for the people generally. In 1931 the Maple Leaf Gardens were ready for the hockey team of that name. It was at this time that the great amateur hockey teams and football teams of the twenties were being eclipsed by professional ones.

In the variegated life of a city the ideal is a partnership between public and government in which, according to subject, one takes the lead, helped as need be by the other. At the same time it is necessary for the citizens to participate in the process of government, if only in elections, supporting such improvements as they deem appropriate. Without reaching perfection this kind of relationship did exist to advantage in the first thirty years of the century.

The form of municipal government was little altered, nor was there, apparently, any appreciable demand that it should be. On the other hand the provincial agencies concerned with municipal affairs were reconstructed in such ways as to place greater authority in the hands of specialized bodies. The Ontario Railway and Municipal Board was created by statute in 1906 and given powers in certain fields, particularly the financial, and of course over railways. In 1917 the Bureau of Municipal Affairs was set up to deal with public utilities. In 1932 the Railway and Municipal Board was renamed the Ontario Municipal Board, the Bureau of Municipal Affairs placed under it, and its powers widened then and later. A Department of Municipal Affairs began in 1935, designed to have a general oversight of municipal questions.[8]

The system of taxation went through some changes. In 1904 the personal property tax was, by provincial statute, replaced with a business tax, which was on premises used for carrying out any trade or profession. That delighted the Board of Trade which had described the old method as 'inequitable and inquisitorial.' For a time a municipal income tax was imposed but that too was abolished in 1936. The tax on real property remained the principal source of revenue. For example, in 1937 it was 88 per cent of the total.[9]

Expenditure of public funds was obviously a question on which the public might properly comment. Estimates before the depression of 1929 showed as major items debt charges, schools, police, and a variety of public services.[10] The last particularly affected the daily life of citizens. The humble but necessary sewer had become almost general but disposal was not satisfactory (or ever was to be). The city works produced an adequate amount of water, but the public did not all share official confidence in its purity. The fire department had been reorganized, although, as will be seen, it was still the object of criticism. For street lighting gas was used to some extent until 1911 but electricity was steadily taking its place.

Electricity for both light and power was introduced, as has earlier been noted, in the late nineteenth century. Technical difficulties, however, limited its usefulness. The arc lamp was too bright for most interior purposes and, being wired in series, all such lamps had to be on or off at the same time. Originally all electricity was generated by steam engines in local plants and passed short distances, by direct current and in unchanged voltage, to the lights. Three innovations gave to electricity its more general usefulness. Generated by water power, it could be transmitted in alternating current and at a high voltage over considerable distances, with the current then reduced to a safer level by means of transformers, and fed into incandescent lamps.

It was, then, possible to convey electricity from the Niagara rapids to Toronto. The Toronto group headed by Frederic Nicholls, Henry Pellatt, and William Mackenzie absorbed the Niagara Power Company – the transmission agency – as a feeder for the Toronto Electric Light Company and the Toronto Street Railway. In these first years of the century, however, municipalities in Ontario were demanding an investigation of the possibility of public suppliers which, they thought, could charge lower rates. A provincial act of 1903 authorized municipally owned works on condition

Fashion parade, 12 March 1919; one of the early Eaton fashion shows during the company's fiftieth year celebrations, auditorium of the Furniture Building (later the Annex)

that an advisory commission first explore the field. Such a one was established in the same year with Adam Beck as a member. It did prepare a report recommending that municipalities proceed with a joint programme, but before that was finished a Conservative government came into office, in 1905, and followed a modified course. Beck became a member of Whitney's cabinet and chairman of a second commission of inquiry.

Meanwhile cities and towns continued their cry for cheap power, dramatizing it by a parade of fifteen hundred delegates to the Toronto city hall and the parliament buildings. In the same year, 1906, the legislature passed an act 'to provide for the transmission of power to municipalities' and for a Hydro-Electric Power Commission of Ontario. Toronto responded by signing with the commission a contract for the purchase of power, brought from Niagara, to be distributed by a civic agency created for that purpose, the Toronto Hydro-Electric Commission. By 1911 rates had been cut almost in half. Until 1920, however, the Toronto Electric Light Company continued to operate, in competition with the municipal body. The former had the advantage of using 60-cycle current, whereas the Ontario Hydro had ill-advisedly selected the flickering 25-cycle (which later they abandoned).[11]

Up to a quarter-century ago citizens of Toronto charged, with some reason, that their city was being allowed to grow in a haphazard way without thought for the future, and indeed without solutions to pressing current problems. It was sprawling across a widening area, so it seemed to them, without proper attention to health, appearance, or convenience. Streets were not broadened or cut through before expensive buildings stood in the way, and highways leading out of the city were wholly inadequate. A maze of overhead wires defaced the streets. No substantial steps were taken to eliminate slums. Land that could have been reserved for parks was allowed to be used for other purposes. The waterfront was shut off by railway tracks, commercial buildings, and smoke.

And yet if the city had been judged by the quantity and quality of paper plans it would have been seen as one of the most advanced of its time. A whole library of studies, all containing excellent recommendations, accumulated. Planning began when the Town of York was first laid out. Most of the bad and few of the good features survived. For the first fifty years of the city's existence nothing resembling modern plans were made, but the local government did conduct a series of *ad hoc* struggles over the preservation of the waterfront, the use of the Garrison Reserve, and those parks that did come its way.

At the turn of the century, however, the initiative of a group of public-spirited citizens marked the beginning of a period of hard thinking about the future of the city. For a time the effort was principally unofficial but developed into that alliance of public and government that has been suggested as a sign of health in an urban community. The Toronto Guild of Civic Art was organized in 1897 by a number of men who sought to promote the improvement of the city in both its artistic and utilitarian sides. By 1908 it had nearly four hundred members and an able committee. At the time of its first report, in 1909, the advent of the motor car, increase in population, and swelling boundaries were all signs, as the Guild remarked, that the city was at the parting of the ways. It was, indeed, to remain stuck at the parting of the ways for a long time, oblivious of the excellent suggestions for arterial roads cut diagonally, wider streets, and more parks.[12]

The Guild made further reports at intervals, but in the first one proposed the establishment of a body to prepare a plan for the improvement of the city. Acting quickly, the city council set up a Civic Improvement Committee in the same year. The new body was almost inactive for two years, but after being reorganized began to face its job. Membership included the mayor, three controllers, seven aldermen, and a number of well-known citizens, including a useful overlap with the Guild. Sir William Meredith, formerly leader of the provincial Conservative party and now chief justice, was elected chairman. Later in 1911 a report was issued that covered a wide field. The emphasis was again on transportation. From a proposed civic centre, the boundaries of which were defined, diagonal roads should be cut northeast and northwest. A long list of existing streets should be widened and connected wherever there were breaks. A bridge over the Don Valley was needed, to be connected with Bloor Street (which stopped at Sherbourne) by a diagonal from the corner of Howard and Parliament streets.

Particular attention was drawn to transportation to, and within, districts then outside the city. The 'piecemeal and haphazard development of the suburbs' left an 'inconvenient maze of uncoordinated streets, which, by the greatest stretch of the imagination cannot be called thoroughfares.' Bearing in mind this deplorable situation in relation to the future of the city, the report called for the creation by the provincial legislature of a metropolitan district and 'a competent body clothed with the necessary powers for carrying out a broad, sane and comprehensive scheme of Civic Improvement.' Specifically on transportation the report asked for rapid transit to the suburbs, which, they said, would mean subways.[13]

In making that study the committee had the advantage of an analysis of public transport prepared by two American experts who were called in by the municipal government. The resultant report was based on two convictions. One was that 'the growth and standing of cities are enormously dependent upon transit facilities,' and the other that municipal operation was 'usually incompetent and wasteful and unsatisfactory to the public.' They considered that within the city limits the street car service was on the whole adequate, but that the same was not true of outlying districts. Like the contemporary planning groups they recommended diagonal highways, but were also convinced that shallow-depth subways were needed, starting with a line from south to north.[14] In 1911 city engineers prepared plans for a subway, but when the proposal was put before the electors it was rejected. Another consulting engineer advised a subway in 1912.

From that time the idea of subways remained for long quiescent, attention being directed to street railways and radials. For the latter a sweeping scheme of lines was being advocated by Adam Beck.[15] It was with these discussions in mind that in 1915 T. L. Church, the colourful and perennial mayor, asked for advice from a technical group consisting of the city's commissioner of works, the chief engineer of the Ontario Hydro, and the chief engineer of the Toronto Harbour Commission. Two recommendations were made: that the city take over the street railway on the expiry of the company's franchise, and that a new transportation commission be established including representatives of the bodies from which the members of the group came. Such a commission should be vested 'with all necessary power to plan, control and direct all transportation and terminal facilities of every kind whatsoever (exclusive of existing steam railways).'[16]

Since 1911 the city had been operating street cars as supplementary to those of the Toronto Railway Company, which had refused to extend its one-fare tickets beyond the city limits of 1891. These lines, known collectively as Toronto Civic Railways, served the outlying districts of the expanded city, but each of them collected a separate fare. By 1920 there were nine separate transit systems, an inconvenient and expensive situation for anyone travelling in the outer areas. Since the company's franchise terminated in 1921 the future of the railway was put to public vote, the electors deciding to take it over so that it, combined with existing public lines, would form a single street railway, publicly owned and operated.

The Toronto Transportation Commission was ready to assume responsibility in 1921, and immediately began to implement a programme of consolidation and modernization. Better rolling stock was procured and the more important change to a single ticket for the whole system put into effect by 1923. Buses were introduced as supplementary to street cars, the first, appearing in 1921, being double-deckers with solid tires on the London or New York model.[17]

Since the city was so rapidly absorbing the immediate suburbs the system of transportation that had thus been evolved applied to a large area. Beyond those widened limits density of population was low and it was not rising rapidly. In 1921 the Township of Etobicoke had only 10,445 people, that of Scarborough 11,746, and the three Yorks together 57,448. Yet a need existed for travel to these and other townships and the means of doing so left a good deal to be desired. Electric radials seemed for a time to be the solution, but they necessarily left many routes uncovered and were being overshadowed by the automobile, which did not need to follow set tracks. It was true that roads were still inadequate, but from 1914 the province undertook to build better ones radiating from Toronto. The Toronto and York Highway Commission and the Toronto and Hamilton Highway Commission were two bodies set up for this purpose. The cost of works undertaken by either would be shared with the city. The concrete highway built to Hamilton might nowadays be mistaken for a wide sidewalk, but no great trucks spread themselves across it, and to the reluctant mudlarks of fifty years ago it was a glimpse of heaven.

Planning continued along much the same lines. The Civic Guild described how College Street should be widened,[18] and later analysed the difficulties of the Moore Park area;[19] but the next broad approach was left to a new body, the Advisory City Planning Commission, consisting of eight men appointed by the city council in 1928. Its first report concentrated on widening streets, including Richmond, York, and Queen; extending University Avenue southward; opening a new diagonal boulevard to the exhibition grounds; and running a new street between Bay and York.[20] The permanent officials to whom the report was referred recommended the adoption of proposals for widening certain of the streets.[21] In 1930 the Civic Guild made further suggestions concerning streets.[22]

Such is the tale of city planning, prewar style. It was limited in range and down to earth, but it did offer sensible solutions to a number of pressing problems. Here and there throughout the pages of the many documents were imaginative suggestions that later bore fruit, but the immediate results were small. A little widening was done, and a few streets, like University Avenue, extended. Government and public were cautious and the city was little altered as a result of so much mental effort. Finally the depression tied purse strings, and Toronto remained essentially as it had been.

Another type of private intervention had to do with the administration of the city generally and particularly in fields other than traffic. In 1913 an organization of citizens first known as the City Survey Committee commissioned the Bureau of Municipal Research in New York to examine the treasury, assessment, works, fire, and property departments. The report thinly concealed an iron hand in a velvet glove.[23] 'Administrative defects,' the director wrote, 'are primarily those of methods and not of men.' It was a pleasant gesture to officials who had co-operated, but followed by a long list of mistaken procedures and in some cases of inefficiency. In the treasury department accounting was well done but budgetary methods had many faults. Departmental estimates provided inadequate information and a civil list was needed. That revenue from the street railway should be used to reduce taxation while repairs to the railway track pavements came out of debenture issues was beyond understanding. Such are examples taken from seventy-five pages of criticism.

In writing of the assessment department it was pointed out that while density of population in Toronto was exceptionally high and housing conditions poor, owners of property had not been encouraged by their assessment to improve their houses. Insufficient information was made public, although 'publicity and publicity alone will insure equity and fair play in making assessments.' The department of works was already being reorganized, but in any case the bureau made twenty-nine suggestions for change.

The fire department was the object of the most severe censure. Organization, training, size, and efficiency were all below par. Preventive rules were being ignored in theatres and the department had done nothing to enforce the provisions of the by-law. Indeed the situation was considered to be so serious that the bureau had made an emergency report to the mayor. In the property department the conspicuous weakness was the incongruous list of duties for which it was responsible. Several of the functions should be transferred to more relevant departments.

The City Survey Committee, perhaps impressed by the value of the report which it had inspired, reorganized under the name of the Toronto Bureau of Municipal Research. It described itself as

a permanent citizens' organization supported entirely by private subscriptions. Its chief aim is to keep alive citizen interest in the citizens' business during the 365 days of each year between elections. It strives to attain this end by discovering all the meaningful facts concerning city government and keeping the citizens continuously informed as to those facts by concentrated publicity, without indulging in personalities or partisan politics. Its belief is that an untiring pursuit of this end by these means will, within five years, result in large savings and more efficient city services.[24]

The members of the Toronto Bureau, drawn in the main from the business world, were an able group, supported financially by a long and imposing list of commercial, financial, and legal firms. The bureau issued bulletins on particular aspects of city business and an annual report, the first of which was dated June 1915. The bureau, like that of New York, emphasized co-operation with city officials, and one of its early activities was to have a series of conferences on aspects of municipal government. It examined many subjects, for example in 1920–1 it surveyed public and separate schools, motor buses, telephones, and the budget. Like the planning groups it marked an important stage in acceptance of responsibility by private citizens for the well-being of their city.

At midnight on 5 to 6 March 1934 rockets and bombs sent up on the island, a giant bonfire on the western sandbar, and the strokes of the bell in the tower of the city hall proclaimed that Toronto was a hundred years old as a city. Within the Coliseum in the exhibition grounds eleven thousand people took part in a watch-night service. All the celebrities were there: governor general and lieutenant governor, prime minister and leader of the opposition, premier of Ontario, military, religious, and academic leaders. As the new day and the city's new century began the choir sang a *Te Deum* and the national anthem.

In the middle of April a series of concerts were given: by the Toronto Symphony Orchestra, the Hart House String Quartet, pupils of the public and secondary schools, the American Bandmasters' Association, and the Mendelssohn Choir. The twenty-fourth of May was chosen as the beginning of outdoor festivities since, as the official programme remarked, Victoria Day had long been a public holiday dear to the heart of Toronto.[25] In spite of this British beginning the one new note in the proceedings was then struck – a parade of 'national groups' in native costumes. Then came the veterans of wars, and after them floats recalling the history of York-Toronto. The objective of the procession was Fort York, to be reopened after restoration. On the following Sunday games were arranged in all the parks, again with a bow to the allegedly international character of Toronto's population. It was well meant but not descriptive.

Toronto, as the programme and the speakers did not fail to point out, had grown greatly in territory and population. It had become a modern city with the amenities that pertained to that status. It was as prosperous as the depression allowed, if without the great wealth of later years. People and government had given much thought to the steps needed in relation to future growth. Yet Toronto still retained much of its traditional character. Even physically it inclined to the past, since the imagination of the planners had done little more that build a bank of ideas from which to draw in the future. The sharp edge of religious intolerance had been blunted by time but the Puritan Sunday died hard. Visitors complained that on that day nothing was open except the churches. On the whole, too, they still thought it to be dull and provincial. The residents were aware of their reputation. Some of them thought it nonsense. Others remarked lightly that Toronto was an overgrown village, uninteresting, perhaps, to visit, but a pleasant place in which to live.

In politics Toronto was rated as supporting the Conservative party and generally suspicious of anything unorthodox. Such a state of mind has sometimes been attributed to British ancestry, an argument that is invalid since Britain has always been a refuge of new ideas. Indeed, the creed of the principal socialist groups in Toronto was imported from England, as was the experience of organized labour in politics. While it was not necessary to be conservative to disapprove of the philosophy of Russian communism, a predominantly conservative community was particularly sensitive to any sign of an attempt to spread into Canada a doctrine designed to overthrow the political, social, and religious order. The general strike in Winnipeg in 1919 was widely believed to have been organized by imported communist agitators, and as such to be a warning of danger.

To some of those who suffered most from the depression which began in 1929, or to those who studied its effects, it seemed that an order of society which could collapse so badly and produce so much misery must be defective. Such reflections did not by any means necessarily lead to adherence to any particular alternative, but did bring serious discontent and criticism of the existing régime. The communists in Canada hoped to channel such thinking into the stream of their argument that capitalism could bring only inequity and disaster for the masses. Unrest in labour camps organized for the unemployed seemed to some observers to be an indication that communists were exploiting the dissatisfaction of the day. In reply to those who claimed that communists in Canada were too few to constitute any threat the reply could be made that the Bolshevik revolution had been the work of a handful of Russians and that the Communist party in the Soviet Union was a small part of the population.

The question that came before the people of Toronto, as they saw it, was whether to tolerate the public exposition of communist ideas. For a year or more before the depression began, an active controversy had raged over this point, and it gained momentum from the conditions that followed the autumn of 1929. By a strange anomaly the decision was made on behalf of the city not by its elected representatives or by an expression of public opinion but by a body ill-designed for that purpose, the Board of Police Commissioners. By a provincial statute of 1858 such a board was to be established in each city and was to be made up of the mayor, recorder, and police magistrate. The municipal council was, then, represented only by the mayor who, apparently by convention, was elected as chairman. The other two members were provincial appointees. That the board should be independent of council was a main principle followed in the act, the intention being that by this means the police force would be insulated from political pressure and patronage. Decisions of the board were to be by majority vote.

No substantial amendments were subsequently made to the act of 1858. The Consolidated Municipal Act of 1922 (12 and 13 Geo. v, c. 72) substituted a county court judge for the recorder, adding that if there were two or more judges the lieutenant-governor-in-council would name one of them to the board. Similarly an act of 1929 (19 Geo. v, c. 58) provided that if more than one magistrate held office the provincial government would assign one of them. In 1928 the Toronto board consisted of the mayor, Samuel McBride; a county judge, M. Morson; and a police magistrate, Emerson Coatsworth. In 1930 only the mayor changed when B. S. Wemp took office. In 1931 W. J. Stewart became mayor and Morson retired. The chief constable, D. C. Draper, a former army officer with no police experience, was for a time secretary of the board and later attended only in an advisory capacity. The newspapers of those years spoke of a wide split within the board, noting that the mayor was always in a minority of one on questions concerning allegedly communist meetings, and that the course followed by the board, and therefore by the police, was laid down by Coatsworth and Draper, supported by the county judge.

The responsibility of the police force, under direction of the commissioners, was to enforce existing laws and by-laws. It did not have, nor was it intended to have, competence in judging political or social doctrines. The course of events, however, suggests that the distinction between these two functions was blurred. The simple purpose followed by the board was to prevent communists from conducting any propaganda. Two difficulties seem not to have deterred the majority. One was the definition of 'communist.' Members of the party, if they could be identified, were obvious; but there was a tendency – encouraged by the communists themselves – to confuse communism with other forms of socialism or indeed with anything judged to be radical. The second difficulty was that the legal foundation for police action was shaky.

The city council was deeply concerned with the situation that developed. Its sole representative on the board of commissioners, the mayor, was helpless and frustrated. Although the board had been deliberately designed as a non-political body it had in fact become intensely political, and was a law unto itself. Members of the council attempted to take the only remedial action at their disposal, to induce the provincial government and legislature to modify the composition and powers of the board. In November 1930 council agreed that there be referred to its committee on legislation a proposal that the board be in the future composed of the mayor, the senior county judge, and a third man to be agreed upon by those two.

After examining the matter the committee sought and obtained authority from council 'to confer with the Board of Police Commissioners with the view of establishing a closer relationship between the Board and the Council.' If they did so confer – and no doubt they did – the absence of any report suggests that their efforts met with failure. In March 1931 they made the following positive proposal:

Your committee recommend that legislation be sought at the present session of the Ontario Legislature whereby the Police Commission in the future shall consist of the mayor, a county judge or magistrate to be appointed by the Ontario Government, and a third member to be agreed upon and approved by these two for a period of two years, and that provision be made for a member of the Supreme Court to hear appeals against the decisions of the said Police Commission.

That recommendation went substantially further than the original one but was adopted by council. There, however, the printed record ends. Presumably the proposal was sent to the provincial government, but if so there is no indication of how it was received. By negative evidence it must be concluded that the government was not favourably impressed. Certainly no bill was introduced and no discussion took place in the legislature.

Thus the police commission was left to develop and pursue a political course unhindered by any governmental or judicial authority. It continued to do so by majority decisions. The principal device for preventing communist – or what it deemed to be communist – meetings indoors was thinly veiled intimidation of owners or managers of public halls. Their attention was drawn to section 98 of the criminal code under which they were liable to fines if they permitted a gathering unlawful in itself or in which force or violence was advocated. At least on one occasion when such broad hints were not taken the police broke up a meeting by exploding a gas bomb. For outdoor meetings the favourite location was Queen's Park. Existing by-laws restricting open air meetings related only to religious ones (because they had much earlier led to riots) and to such as obstructed traffic. Undeterred by the limits of legal restraints the board, in close communion with the chief constable, either prevented persons whom they considered undesirable from speaking or drove the public from the park.

Eight persons were arrested for failure to stop making speeches and two candidates in the provincial election, who were communists, were taken into custody. Newspaper reporters described dramatically scenes in the park as 'the motorcycles roared their way,' and as, so they said, the less agile of the public were trampled underfoot. Editorially, however, three of the Toronto dailies – the *Telegram*, the *Mail and Empire*, and the *Globe* – consistently supported the police commission, and there is every reason to believe that they reflected a strong body of local opinion, probably a distinct majority. In reply to criticism that freedom of speech was endangered one point was consistently made, as is illustrated by an editorial in the *Globe*:

The absurd effort to make it appear that Toronto's Police Commission is opposed to 'free speech' was denied by Judge Coatsworth in a statement to the *Globe* in language more moderate than the situation merited. 'The Police Commissioners,' he said, 'are in favour of free speech, and will not interfere with such unless conducted by Communists to make unlawful utterances by preaching sedition' ...

To say that it cannot be known that the Bolsheviks preach sedition until they begin to speak is as ridiculous as to say that it is not certain that a gunman whose sole desire and object is to kill will not do so until he has pulled the trigger ...

The aims of the Bolsheviki are not secret. The orders from Moscow are well known ...

Apologists for the Communists claim that they are but a handful of harmless fanatics not worth bothering about. They are, on the contrary, the emissaries of Soviet Russia spreading poison wherever they can do so.

The argument was not wholly without validity but it did have two serious flaws. One was that the persons who were prevented from speaking publicly were not all communists. The other was to argue that, even if sedition were woven into communist doctrine, any remarks on communism were in themselves seditious.

Those people in Toronto who overtly opposed the policy of repression were strange allies. The communists, those who sympathized with them in part, and organizations which had come under their control, formed one group. What they needed was supporters from outside it and for that reason may well have welcomed the actions of the police. Organized labour was divided, influenced on the one hand by the knowledge that communism in practice would mean the end of unions, and on the other by a tendency to favour the left rather than the right, the small man against the capitalist. The Co-operative Commonwealth Federation had a similar problem, for to form even a temporary and limited common front with communists would conflict with its attempt to purge communists from its own ranks. To the extent that any of the churches entered the debate they could not ignore the fact that communism was a sworn enemy of religion, although some churchmen emphasized different aspects of the problem. Other people in Toronto expressed, individually or in groups, the view that freedom of speech was being curtailed without any legal authority.[26]

In their usual patter the communists described their opponents as fascists, with no referee to point out that, from the point of view of human liberty, no difference existed between communism and fascism. And, as if to prove it, the two leading exponents of the authority of the state over the individual, Hitler and Stalin, came together in the summer of 1939 to make an unholy alliance under which peoples were to be bought and sold like cattle.

The burden of the depression was such as to divert attention from the international scene, but for those who could raise their eyes above the problem of their daily bread the outlook was sombre. Individuals wrote articles as to what Canada's stand should be in the face of aggression and groups met to discuss the same subject. Various views were expressed, one body of opinion holding the view that collective security should be sternly enforced – but not by them. Action tore through the words. The Japanese seized Manchuria with impunity and the Italians Ethiopia. Rearmament of Germany was carried out in defiance of the Treaty of Versailles. All plans for opposing force collapsed as members of the League of Nations, Canada among them, shied away from acceptance of responsibility.

The aggressors moved forward unhindered. In 1938 Hitler took possession of Czechoslovakia and blackmailed the western powers into the Munich agreement. After it was signed individuals in Toronto were critical and hinted that they would have battled for freedom to the last ditch, but a sense of relief was the common reaction. On 1 September 1939 the German forces invaded western Poland. On 10 September Canada declared war on Germany. A week later Soviet troops entered eastern Poland and at the end of the month invaded Finland. Minor operations continued until in May 1940 the German mass attack on western Europe began.

The *blitzkrieg* in Belgium, the Netherlands, and France crowded minor events off the front page of newspapers. Freedom of speech was no longer an abstract question, for where the armies of the dictators triumphed no freedom for the individual could survive. Men in Toronto, and women too, enlisted in large numbers in the army and navy and in the newer air force. In the thirties some thinking on public questions had been confused and fumbling; but the people of Toronto could recognize a clear issue when they saw one, and this was a struggle for the survival of a way of life in which, with all its defects, they believed. In flights over Germany and the middle east, in the Battle of the Atlantic, and on the beaches of Dieppe young men were tragically lost who not long before had been searching for reality in a world of puzzling values.

As the tempo of campaigns increased so did the demand for munitions and other instruments of war. As in the first great war unemployment was replaced by a shortage of labour and women were needed in large numbers to fill the ranks in factories that emerged from little or nothing. Ammunition was made in several plants. The aircraft industry expanded rapidly, as did the industries concerned with chemical products, precision instruments, electrical apparatus, shipbuilding, guns, and explosives. Seen in statistical form the rise in employment was as follows:

| | | |
|---|---|---|
| 30 September 1939 – 1 June 1942 | 57.3 per cent |
| 30 September 1939 – 1 July 1943 | 68.8 per cent |
| 30 September 1939 – 1 July 1944 | 74.1 per cent |

In the summer of 1943 the proportion of the working force in war employment was 67 per cent and in civilian employment 33 per cent.[27]

The second world war was a grim, businesslike affair for those abroad or at home. A régime of moderate austerity was imposed through taxation, rationing, and control of prices and rents. Some food items like tea, butter, and meat were strictly rationed. Shortage of electricity because of the demands of industry blacked out houses for some hours in each day, and the citizens scrambled in attics or summer cottages for half-forgotten oil lamps. Streets had a strange appearance with candles flickering in the windows of each house. New cars were unprocurable and so were tires for old ones. Gasoline was so narrowly limited that bicycles had a new vogue. Some of the large shops brought back into service horse-drawn delivery waggons. The number of passengers in street cars and buses rose from 154 millions in 1939 to 303 millions in 1945.

Concentration on the needs of war affected the supply of many consumer goods. It became difficult to buy a shirt, a tea kettle, or a refrigerator. Shops frowned on anyone suspected of hoarding. Some expendable activities were dropped. At the outbreak of war the entire physical plant of the Canadian National Exhibition was offered to the Department of National Defence, which gradually took it over, so that the old Military Reserve came back into its own. Similarly the Royal Winter Fair, which was held on the exhibition grounds, was suspended during the period of hostilities.

For fifteen years conditions had been abnormal. The depression had halted immigration, slowed or stopped private business enterprise, and committed a substantial proportion of municipal funds to relief of the unemployed. During the war immigration did not revive. Austerity continued after 1939 but for very different reasons. Goods were in short supply and incomes were deliberately restricted in order to channel effort into the production of aeroplanes and munitions. On these terms the economy expanded rapidly, creating a new level of industrial capacity and a large labour force trained in its use. So long as hostilities continued the effect was not materially to change the character of life in Toronto but to build up power which later could be turned into the ways of peace. The stage stood ready for whatever new play might follow when the guns were silenced.

# 10

# Problems of greatness

The territorial growth of a city takes two forms. In a literal sense it grows because it covers more ground, because its political boundaries are extended. At the same time, however, there is an expansion, beyond those limits, of the area of which it is economically and socially the hub. The two processes are concurrent but never coincident, since no city can ever absorb all the land which is dependent on it. The faster it grows within itself the greater the speed with which the fringe communities develop.

When Toronto was incorporated as a city in 1834 provision was made for future extension by attachment to it of the liberties, making up a broad and thinly populated belt that included the old park lots. Portions could be added to the nearest wards whenever justified by density of population. The city was not required to provide full public services in the liberties but was able to exercise such control as it chose over their development. When the liberties had been absorbed and the system itself abolished, other means of control had to be found in order that in the districts which might in future be acquired by the city steps be not taken that would compromise the application of civic methods of organization. The provincial City and Suburbs Plans Act of 1912 (2 Geo. v, c. 43) was the second move toward the principle which, fifty years later, was adopted for the fringe townships of Metropolitan Toronto. Any scheme for subdivision of a tract within five miles of the city and having a population of a specified minimum must, under that statute, be submitted to the provincial authorities who would examine it in relation to any general plan approved by the city council.

Between the 1880s and the first great war Toronto had become much larger, but it was then concluded that the price of imperialism was too high. Annexed areas, sparsely populated and producing little revenue, demanded a standard of services comparable to that in the centre. At the same time the population of the suburbs was increasing rapidly, and it was becoming apparent that some new design of government for the Toronto region was needed if roads and other public services were to be adequate.

In 1923 the minister responsible for municipal affairs circulated to the various local governments a suggestion for a 'Metropolitan District of Toronto' which would have a governing body with the powers of a county council. Evidently any response that came was unfavourable since the idea was not pursued. In the early 1930s the County of York established a Metropolitan Area Committee, but it too had a short life. In 1935 the new Department of Municipal Affairs commissioned A. F. W. Plumptre of the University of Toronto to examine the project of a metropolitan area, one to which new urgency had been given by the financial default of ten municipalities close to Toronto. Noting the increased proportion of persons in the Toronto area who lived outside the city, 22.6 per cent in 1932, the report urged consolidation of the municipalities in two groups.[1]

No action was taken before the war, but during it the province began to tighten its control over municipal development. The Department of Planning and Development, established in 1944, was given authority over planning by the Planning Act of 1946 (10 Geo. VI, c. 71). The statute did not require municipalities to make plans but specified that if they wished to do so they should make application to the minister who would define the planning area, approve the planning board proposed, and finally the plan which emerged from it. The move was presumably intended to encourage progressive thinking and to maintain some consistency and standards.

Termination of hostilities allowed more attention to be given to the future of the Toronto region. 'Greater Toronto' was commonly considered to consist of 'the traditional thirteen municipalities' which made up the old townships of York, Scarborough, and Etobicoke. The city was one unit, and there were seven villages: Leaside, Weston, Mimico, New Toronto, Forest Hill, Swansea, and Long Branch. The remainder were townships: Scarborough, Etobicoke, York, and the townships sliced off the last, North York and East York. The size of the municipalities varied from the forty-five thousand acres of each of Scarborough and North York to the five hundred acres of Mimico. A glance at the following table will show that the populations were rising, and some rapidly. Only Toronto was declining. At the 1945 figure it was overcrowded, the cause having been wartime industry. Even as slightly reduced it could be considered saturated as a residential area, or close to it.

| Municipality | Population in 1945 | Population in 1950 | Percentage increase |
|---|---|---|---|
| City of Toronto | 681,802 | 667,487 | -2.10 |
| East York | 43,399 | 60,155 | 38.61 |
| Etobicoke | 21,402 | 44,137 | 106.23 |
| Forest Hill | 13,960 | 16,191 | 15.98 |
| Leaside | 9,800 | 15,255 | 55.66 |
| Long Branch | 5,220 | 8,044 | 54.10 |
| Mimico | 8,785 | 10,460 | 19.07 |
| New Toronto | 10,173 | 10,961 | 7.74 |
| North York | 26,432 | 62,646 | 137.01 |
| Scarborough | 25,482 | 48,146 | 88.94 |
| Swansea | 7,217 | 7,864 | 8.96 |
| Weston | 6,337 | 7,961 | 25.63 |
| York | 82,753 | 95,659 | 15.60 |

People from other parts of Canada, from Britain, and from Europe were crowding into the Toronto area in tune with the strong trend toward urbanization common to the western world. In 1941 Ontario was 67.5 per cent urban, in 1951 it was 72.5 per cent, and in 1966 up to 80.4 per cent. Furthermore the heaviest concentration was in the large cities. In 1951 33.3 per cent of the urban people of Canada lived in cities of over half a million, and in Ontario only Toronto was in that class. People came to the City of Toronto, and many continued their employment there, but a large proportion lived outside the city gates. Attention, then, was necessarily directed to the area as a whole; and continued growth in the fifties and sixties kept it there. The percentage increase in the Toronto area, as defined by the census, was 24.1 in 1951–6 after which it declined slightly; but by 1966 the area had more than two million people.[2] It is this march of people which forms the background to all the constitutional and social planning.

To those who had been studying the situation in the 1940s or earlier the existing network of governments seemed wholly unsuited to the changing scene. Public services – especially transportation, water supply, and sewage disposal – were in many parts inadequate and the separate municipalities could not financially support the needed improvements. Nor could those be effectively carried out in isolation. Some of the municipalities, for example, were cut off from the lake which was the source of water and the recipient of sewage.

All the parties concerned – province, city, and suburbs – accepted the necessity of some new structure. In 1948 the city called a meeting with the other twelve municipalities and secured their agreement to a study 'leading to recommendations for possible improvement in governmental organization and the provision of public services in the area.' The Civic Advisory

Council, which was called upon to undertake the task, struck a representative committee on metropolitan problems the members of which were nearly all non-official.

Their findings mark a turning point in discussions of the future organization of the Toronto region. The committee first explored the existing situation. The City of Toronto, they found, had almost no vacant land, and since the war 90 per cent of all new housing was beyond the city limits. A number of intermunicipal agreements had been made for the provision of public services but together they did not constitute an effective solution. The committee reached two general conclusions: that some senior level of government for the metropolitan area was needed, and that a differentiation should be maintained between the urbanized centre and the outer ground of future settlement. Having evaluated alternative methods of government, including the borough system of London, they indicated a preference for the following: an enlarged city governed by its council; local municipalities to continue; and a regional authority to plan housing, arterial roads, public transport, and major recreational facilities.[3]

When the final report was being written the committee was aware that other initiatives were under way. The first move had been made by Mimico which, under the authority of a section of the Municipal Act of 1946, applied to the Ontario Municipal Board for joint administration of certain services over a wide area. While that was under consideration the Toronto and York Planning Board, which had been instructed to prepare a plan for city and county, published a proposal that the eight municipalities between the Humber and Scarborough should be united.[4] Shortly after that, in January 1950, Long Branch filed an application for amalgamation in a somewhat smaller region. In February the City of Toronto passed a by-law authorizing an application for amalgamation of the city with Forest Hill, Long Branch, Swansea, Leaside, Mimico, New Toronto, Weston, East York, North York, York, and parts of Etobicoke and Scarborough.

In June 1950 the Ontario Municipal Board began hearings of the applications from Mimico and Toronto. The eleven other municipalities, all opposed to the Toronto proposal, appeared as respondents. The findings of the board, dated 20 January 1953 and commonly known as the Cumming Report from the name of the chairman, make up a blue book of exceptional quality and influence. Behind it was evidence amounting to three million words and three hundred exhibits.[5]

Since, the board noted, provision and financing of public services were the primary responsibilities of any municipality, rapid increase in population affected the structure of local government. Major reforms were urgently needed, for 'no system of local government organization which is based upon rigid territorial divisions of municipal jurisdiction and an equally rigid partition of physical and fiscal assets can be expected to provide for

Jarvis Street Collegiate, built in the 1920s

Sewer construction, about 1910

an area such as this the essential local services which must be the responsibility of municipal government.'

Obvious advantages in the Toronto proposal were outweighed by disadvantages. It would produce administrative confusion and raise taxes because of the need to bring services and salary scales up to the city level. An attempt to govern an area of 240 square miles through a single city council would run foul of the Ontario tradition that local government is close to the people and carried on by elected local leaders. The board summed up the Mimico proposal as having some good features but too many weaknesses. Having disposed of both propositions the board was nevertheless convinced that the century-old system of government was no longer appropriate, and proceeded to describe its own solution. In doing so it acted on an intimation from Prime Minister Leslie Frost that any views the board might have would be welcome. Ideas were to be found in earlier studies, some of which have been mentioned; but no precedent existed in other cities, at home or abroad. Tentative proposals for metropolitan government had been made in the United States but not accepted. The borough system as long used in London had been noted by various planning bodies as the nearest parallel, but it was different in several respects.[6]

The plan put forward by the board was for a federation of the thirteen municipalities broadly similar in principle to the federation of Canadian provinces. The central government would be by a metropolitan council, it having responsibility for 'functions and services considered vitally necessary to the continued growth and development of the entire area as an urban community.' The federating municipalities, however, would retain their identities and have authority over local matters. A design for the central council and for the division of powers between it and the local governments was suggested.

In a statute running to nearly a hundred pages, the Municipality of Metropolitan Toronto Act, 1953 (2 Eliz. II, c. 73), a detailed description of the new régime was, with some amendments, drawn from the Cumming Report. The metropolitan council was to be composed of twelve ex officio representatives of the city and twelve of the suburbs. The chairman, additional to them, was to be the chief executive officer. The first incumbent would be named by the provincial government but subsequently the chairman would be elected by the council, either from its own members or from outside. The council was to have exclusive powers in assessment and borrowing, in transportation, and in administration of justice. To the local governments went fire and police services, garbage collection, traffic control, and distribution of hydro-electric power. Several subjects were divided: taxation, education, parks, health and welfare, housing, and community services. Water was to be supplied by metro and distributed by local authorities, and a similar arrangement was made for sewage disposal.

Bearing in mind the various, and conflicting, views expressed by the municipalities and the novelty of its own proposal the Ontario Municipal Board had from the first urged the need for flexibility and for reconsideration in the light of experience. A provincial commission appointed to make a re-examination reported in 1958 that the briefs submitted to it by local governments, school boards, and other groups and associations indicated approval of federalism. It considered that two or three suburbs might be united and that the metro school board might have greater authority.[7] A study made by the Ontario Department of Economics at the request of the metro council drew attention to the discrepancy in expenditures on general services, from $97.11 per capita in the city to $39.67 in Mimico. It pointed also to inequitable representation on the metro council. Both difficulties, it was suggested, could be overcome by grouping the municipalities into four or five boroughs.[8] A comprehensive analysis was then made by a royal commissioner, H. C. Goldenberg, who accepted the federal principle but recommended that metro be reorganized as four cities: Toronto, Etobicoke, North York, and Scarborough.[9]

In the statute that followed the presentation of this last report, an Act to Amend the Municipality of Metropolitan Toronto Act, 1966 (14–15 Eliz. II, c. 96), the legislature concurred in Goldenberg's approval of federalism. It also agreed to a reduction in the number of municipalities, though not by creating four cities (or five, as F. G. Gardiner, the first chairman of metro had recommended). A pattern of six boroughs was chosen instead. Forest Hill and Swansea were added to the city. East York and Leaside were united under the name of the former. Etobicoke, Long Branch, Mimico, and New Toronto together became the borough of Etobicoke, while York and Weston formed the borough of York. Scarborough and North York were the other two. Representation on the metro council was altered in such a way that the city, instead of having half the members, would have twelve as against twenty from the other boroughs. The authority of the council was increased. A uniform tax for schools was to be imposed throughout the metro area. The limits of metro were not altered.

The City of Toronto remained unconvinced of the virtues of federalism, having rediscovered an enthusiasm for empire-building that it had lost thirty years before. The mayor, Nathan Phillips, presented to the commission of 1957–8 a personal brief in which he expressed the view that federalism was a logical first step in view of the opposition to amalgamation by some municipalities, but asked that an inquiry be now made as to which of them had changed their minds. He argued that even a partial unification could be put into effect, in which case metro would be dissolved and a commission set up to deal with remaining services for the area.[10]

That opinion in Toronto has generally supported amalgamation rather than federalism is indicated by the consistent attitude of the three daily newspapers, by a by-law of 1962 authorizing an application to the Ontario Municipal Board for amalgamation of all the municipalities, and by the straw vote taken at the time of the municipal elections in 1969. A superficial explanation would be that those in civic office sought wider fields of power, but a more convincing one is that the increased population and wealth of the other municipalities in part cancelled the previous objection to supporting weak brothers. Once the metro system was in effect the logic could be pushed further: that the principal sources of the revenue to be distributed would in any case be the advanced parts of the city itself.

A scheme of government, once embodied in legislation, must be implemented as a whole. It is specific and tangible. The same is not true of social plans, those aimed more directly at better conditions of living. Some indication was given in the previous chapter of the early stages of modern planning in the first years of the present century. Pioneer endeavours were made with the minimum of manpower and money and had consequently less depth than those of later days. Some of them, however, showed a good deal of imagination, and if their recommendations had been adopted Toronto would have been a very different place at the time of the second war.

In 1942 a City Planning Board, advisory to the council, was appointed. Its declaration of the rights of man set the tone for many later reports. Every citizen had the right to a dwelling suitable for healthy living. In his neighbourhood should be a park, primary school, a limited shopping area, safe and quiet streets; in his district a secondary school, churches, shops, and facilities for recreation; in the city as a whole roads and transport, higher education, large parks and playgrounds, business and industry.

In 1943 this board, like its predecessor a generation earlier, began on a master plan. This was calculated for thirty years. An area of a hundred square miles would be ringed by a belt of agricultural land and have as well a green belt within it. Major traffic arteries (including Spadina, with a tunnel under the hill), widened streets, and rapid transit would facilitate traffic. Parks and playgrounds, low-rental housing, and redevelopment of blighted areas would improve living conditions.

In the following year the board ran into a difficulty which it might have anticipated. The city council approved the plan in principle but without commitment as to its implementation. 'That,' the board retorted, 'has little or no significance . . . With the passage of every day and the growth of the suburbs, the difficulties of planning the city and its environs are bound to increase.' They would increase, of course, just as in 1909 when the Guild of Civic Art had warned of the parting of the ways. The city's reply did have significance, but not in the sense that the board meant. It was, and is, inconceivable that any city council would pledge itself to a timetable for the adoption of all aspects of a plan of this kind, no matter how wise.

After passage of the act of 1953 responsibility for planning was placed on the metro council as well as on the local municipalities. Its area was metro itself and the five fringe townships; Pickering, Markham, Vaughan, Toronto Gore, and Toronto Township. The waterfront came into the metro field because it formed the southern boundary of the whole area. Representatives of the city and other municipalities, together with a number of experts, were called to join in an elaborate study. The resulting Waterfront Plan of 1967 dealt with a lakeshore of some fifty miles, from Ajax to Clarkson, in a comprehensive way, allocating space for residential, commercial, industrial, and transportation purposes; and for marinas, camping sites, picnic grounds, and bathing beaches. If some of the attractive pictures drawn to show the future come to life residents will hardly have to go away to enjoy boating, swimming, and rest in natural surroundings.

Within the city itself an increase in commercial activities together with changes in types of housing made necessary more attention to zoning, a type of protection of residences that was considered ever since the early days of York but little implemented before the 1950s. In 1956 the City Planning Board put its finger on weaknesses in the existing zoning law:

It allows, amongst other things, apartment buildings of huge bulk to rise almost from the side fences of adjoining houses. They disrupt neighbourhoods of satisfactory character, and create conditions in properties adjoining the apartment buildings which are incapable of remedy ...

The present zoning by-law would allow between two and a half and three million persons to be housed in the city. Even if this were not absurd by any calculation it would be a preposterous concept. If such an objective were within the realms of possibility streets would be impassable, and well over a million cars would have to be parked at night.[11]

The board's report proposed five types of residential zones, ranging from low to high density. The city planners adopted a suggestion made by the Community Planning Association of Canada for dividing up the city for planning purposes on the ground that 'every district in a city of Toronto's size has its own characteristics and problems.' With a general warning against any rapid increase in the city's population they turned to individual studies of the twenty-five districts which they had identified.[12] The Annex, once a peaceful district of houses for individual families, had now several hundred rooming houses and many apartment buildings. Traffic was a problem and parks were grossly insufficient. It was recommended that the Annex should remain residential, with offices and institutions only

243

in the southeastern part.[13] The Don district was a problem of another kind. In it were forty-two thousand residents living for the most part in old houses of declining quality. Families were larger than in other parts of Toronto. Overcrowding was common and incomes low. Schools should be moved, more playgrounds provided, some new houses built by the city and others by private enterprise.[14]

A great deal of careful work, of which a few examples have been given, formed the background to the city's broad plan of 1968, replacing that of 1949. The first part, on the general pattern of development, has been published. It is apparently intended as a statement of the lines of proposed action. It indicates the appropriate roles of residential and non-residential districts, zoning standards and means of ensuring their effect, something of the intended improvements in transportation, the desirability of parks, and encouragement of educational and cultural activities.

The distinction between general objectives and platitudes may not always be easy to maintain, but the latter are rather too conspicuous in this first part of the city's plan. After many years of assurances that plans were designed to provide the greatest good for the greatest number it seems hardly necessary to repeat that 'it is the objective of Council that the quality of life shall be improved for each resident.' What other purpose could there be? In a city in which one investigation after another has revealed the continued existence of slums and near-slums the following sentence in the plan sounds like the voice of one who had never seen Toronto; and it is worse than a platitude since it implies a standard of housing which does not exist and never has: 'Council will encourage the building of housing suitable for the accommodation of families with children in the Toronto region to ensure that sufficient is available for the needs of the population so that the pressures of living within the city do not result in undesirable living conditions.' An imaginary picture is drawn of the Rosedale ravines, naturally beautiful certainly, but cluttered for long stretches with rubbish, dead trees, and vagrants. Surely a plan would be the more valuable if it pointed to weaknesses as well as to good features?

Perhaps it is inevitable that at times emphasis on what should be conceals the reality of what is; but in reading the planning reports of the last quarter-century or more much can be learned about social conditions in Toronto: of unsatisfactory housing for those with small means, shortage of parks and playgrounds in the districts where they are most needed, congested traffic, and other evils of urbanization which it is the purpose of planners to ameliorate. It may be that the word 'planning' has too esoteric a connotation.

The hopes and skills of planners are of no avail except to the extent that they lead governments to take wise, and avoid unwise, action. A plan is not an end in itself; and if it lulls the consciences of government or public it becomes a liability. By circulating draft plans to householders and businessmen for comment and by encouraging public meetings on them the planners have gone some way to engage public interest, but it is probable that only a small minority of citizens have ever seen or read plans, or perhaps know that such things exist. The triangle of planners, executive government, and public is not easily drawn. Between the first two understanding and co-operation are needed. The electors for their part must fulfil their traditional roles of encouragement and criticism.

Examining constitutional and social plans, and sometimes reading between the lines, throws a good deal of light on the conditions and problems of the area with which they are concerned. Another, and more direct, approach is to analyse the actual state of the community: Metropolitan Toronto at work and at play.

# Life in Metropolitan Toronto

At no time in its history has Toronto experienced such drastic change as in the years after the second world war. The urban area, spreading far beyond the limits of the city proper, embraced towns, villages, and farms. The people whose arrival caused such rapid growth came not only from other parts of Canada and from Britain but included such a high percentage of Europeans as to diversify an ethnic pattern that had before been simple. The economic capacity built up to meet military needs was turned to the arts of peace and expanded far beyond what it had been in war years. Wealth gained new dimensions, and a higher standard of living was in marked contrast to the Spartan years of the depression and the war. Because of these circumstances and others, modes of living were altered.

The contrast between the old and the new Toronto is in sum peculiar to itself, but many of the individual novelties are common to cities of North America or the western world generally. They are, in fact, not of the place but of the age. Increase in population, and more especially in urban population, is almost universal. The affluent society is a widespread phenomenon. Excess of motor cars over roads on which they can be driven and over space in which they can rest is typical of all advanced countries. The same is true of the high proportion of families who live in apartments, of their mechanized existence, and of their insistence on having goods and services once considered luxuries. Attempts to influence governments or society by mob demonstrations and civil disobedience challenge the traditional understanding of democracy. Increase in crime is a development with which countless other cities would gladly dispense. Secularism is a product of the times.

The word 'Toronto' has, from the 1950s, had three meanings. The city itself is one part of the federal structure known as the Municipality

Downtown Toronto, 1969

of Metropolitan Toronto. That area was further extended for purposes of the census to include Ajax and Pickering on the east, Stouffville on the north, Milton and Oakville on the west. Toronto in the third sense, the total, covering a substantial part of four counties, is defined as 'a group of predominantly urban communities which are in close economic, geographic and social relationship.' In this largest region live more than two million people.

The city, genesis and operational centre of the complex, appears to be busier and more crowded year by year although it is static in population and territory. It is not the residents who fill the factories, office buildings, shops, and streets. The swelling numbers are of those who, living in the suburbs, find their daily work in the institutions and business activities that grow and multiply. Government at all levels – federal, provincial, and municipal – has expanded in personnel and buildings as it has in functions. With great additions of students and staff the University of Toronto has taken over whole blocks once residential. New or enlarged schools, specialized colleges, hospitals, and many private institutions draw their thousands of humans and possess many acres.

On Queen Street, close to the city's first northern boundary, the new city hall reaches high to survey the great domain over which it holds sway. Its predecessor next door, equally a symbol of progress half a century earlier, had become too small and in 1954 three firms of Toronto architects were asked to prepare plans for a new one. Nathan Phillips, mayor in 1955, was not satisfied with the results, but a broader obstacle was a public vote in 1956 against any new city hall, however designed. In the following year, however, the electors relented after plans for joint use of a new building had been concerted between city and metropolitan governments. An international competition drew 532 plans which were examined by a jury of experts from Canada, Britain, the United States, and Italy. The one selected, that by Viljo Revell of Finland, was for two tall and semi-circular towers joined by a lower structure. The graceful result may be seen the better from the wide open square between the buildings and the street; where, too, citizens may sit in summer or skate in the winter.

The city hall is impressive, as are new provincial buildings in Queen's Park, but it is business in all its forms which has been the chief factor in altering the physical character of Toronto. In a few blocks of the undefined district vaguely known as 'downtown' are concentrated much of the wealth and power of the city, the Toronto region, and indeed of the country as a whole. South of Dundas Street and west of Victoria Street banks, trust companies, the stock exchange, and stock brokers are packed in close quarters, as well as the headquarters of companies engaged in mining and other industries and in wholesale trade, and legal firms whose services are utilized by them all. A detailed economic map brings out the nearby location of the two large department stores, Eaton's and Simpson's, dwarfing all other retailers in the Toronto region. To the south of them the Royal York Hotel similarly towers in its service field.[1]

Narrow streets are everywhere all too common in business districts, and the value of land is the enemy of open space. One old building after another falls victim to the desire to provide more square feet of offices on the same amount of ground. Some escape from a series of canyons bounded by dreary straight lines of stone and glass has been found in the simple device of placing a building back from the street, sometimes with benches and small trees between it and the sidewalk, and an occasional mall running from one street to another. At one time the set-back building was frowned on by property owners who could not bear the thought of wasting expensive land, but lately they have been persuaded by architects that the appearance of their buildings is enhanced by allowing a foreground.

To the south is the waterfront whose occupation by economic armies has been described in earlier chapters. Each succeeding generation, unhappy with the results of its own surrenders, has sought to recover something of a natural playground by hurdling the railway tracks and making land beyond them which should be an unspoiled bay shore. Extensive plans are now being considered which, if put into effect, would revolutionize the section next to the bay; but for the moment they are only plans, and ones that would take a long time to implement. Meanwhile the defenders of the island remain on the alert.

Nothing has quite replaced King Street in its day of glory as the one high-class shopping street. Yonge Street, certainly, has been no candidate for that honour. North of the great department stores it tails off into lines of small shops, undistinguished at least in appearance. Expectations of development at College Street have been only partially realized, but Bloor Street has some pretensions – east of Yonge Street stand the relatively new headquarters of some insurance companies and to the west are some good shops and new office buildings.

Except in a few strictly residential districts shops are scattered through-out the city. They include 'supermarkets' and 'shopping centres' which provide spacious parking lots – parking being an important consideration for the housewives who trundle shopping carts (and accompanied on Saturdays by their husbands who no longer escape to offices on that day). Small and independent shops, especially groceries, survive in spite of the big networks. On a street like the Danforth lines of them, block after block, are hardly broken except by service stations. The downtown financial centre has thrown out so many branch banks that they seem to be on every other street. To a lesser extent the trust companies have placed branches at strategic points.

Some aspects of this layout are new and others are not. The little shops, widely spread, were always there and the department stores go back nearly a century; but the supermarkets and shopping centres have shorter roots. The financial centre has only shifted slightly to the west. Factories tend to be away from the most expensive land. What is altogether modern is the magnitude of economic operations of all kinds. It is this – to repeat – that has engaged so many people and been responsible for the use of so much additional space. To a minor extent the pressure has been relieved by placing tall buildings where lower ones stood, but most of the spread has been at the expense of dwellings – hence the shortage of housing in a city with a stationary or declining population.

The vacant lot, once the despair of ambitious citizens, is no longer to be found. The only means, therefore, of accommodating the same number of residents is, as in the case of offices, to have more families on less ground. The conspicuous means of doing so has been by means of apartment houses, of many storeys wherever zoning rules permit. In 1966 the city had 78,548 apartments, including duplexes, and every month there are more. They are in demand partly because of the lack of small and inexpensive houses, partly because of their convenience. The tenant is freed from responsibility for upkeep and housework is reduced to the minimum, the latter being an important consideration in the virtual absence of domestic servants and when so many women are employed.

Houses, however, were still in the majority in 1966, the year of the most recent census. Of them 55,763 were attached and 44,208 detached.[2] New houses can be provided only by subdividing exceptionally big lots and in some cases pulling down large houses no longer practicable. The replacements are usually called 'town houses,' a phrase mysteriously adding prestige to what are simply semi-detached houses.

Alterations do not add to the total of dwellings unless to create duplexes or triplexes, but can add to the number of medium-sized houses which are in short supply. Agencies have roamed older streets looking for houses, usually rather small ones, that are structurally sound but architecturally obsolete. By shearing off the characteristic front verandah, no longer wanted, improving the front door and perhaps the windows, and painting the result in a pre-Raphaelite tone, a pleasant facade can be made. Indoors a large living room appears at the expense of the front hall and dining room. The kitchen becomes smaller and 'modern.' The usual result is to convert a relatively cheap house into a rather expensive one.

Replacement or restoration of houses in the most run-down districts, the state of which varies from slums to sub-standard, is a much more difficult matter. The cost of construction is so high that neither houses nor apartments can be built by private enterprise at a cost within the means of those with lowest incomes. It appears that any low-cost dwellings which meet even minimum standards of health and comfort must be provided directly or subsidized by government at some level. Both the province and the city have taken some action, although the requirement is still far from being met. The former has erected some large apartment houses for this purpose, and a pioneer effort by the latter was in Cabbagetown, in southeastern Toronto. In Regent Park North an area of forty-two and a half acres – six city blocks – was cleared of 628 houses and thirty-five commercial structures. Of the 822 families who had lived there about half accepted offers of accommodation in the new buildings, but thousands of applications were received from others. As completed in 1959 Regent Park had 1,398 living units (the large proportion being apartments) and six years later 5,241 persons were living in them. Rentals were adjusted to ability to pay.

For those who wish to live within the city and have sufficient financial means houses can always be found in such districts as Bayview, Forest Hill, or Rosedale. More moderate incomes are adequate for characteristic houses in such areas as the Annex, High Park, or streets north of the Danforth. The latter opportunities, however, are limited by an absolute shortage of small houses, and of medium-sized ones too. Even after taking apartments into account the situation is that not enough dwellings exist. A great many people, then, must live outside the city. Some do so from choice in any case, and others from necessity.[3]

It would, however, be misleading to describe as suburbs all the parts of metro that are not included in the City of Toronto. Parts of York and East York are, except for administration, indistinguishable from the city. To cross St Clair Avenue or Bayview Avenue does not take one into suburban conditions. Everything looks and is just the same. Probably the majority of residents of the city could not define its limits, and a drive in any direction would not help them since streets and buildings continue in uninterrupted lines without hint of the municipality in which they are located.

A suburb is in part the product of distance, in part of taste, and in part of necessity. Broadly there are two types of suburbs. One is attached to no community previously existing but consists of miles of houses, and sometimes of apartment houses, built anywhere beyond the zone already occupied. It is simply a means of providing more housing wherever it can be placed. Districts of this kind vary in cost and therefore, perhaps, in prestige. The other type of suburb is based on a village or town which began as a separate entity and by degrees despatched more and more of its workers daily to the city. Markham, Aurora, Brampton, and Oakville are examples. At the present time the number of commuters from each varies, reaching in some cases half the gainfully employed. The figures would be affected by the local presence or absence of factories and other large employers.

The population of Toronto had grown to its wartime size through a combination of natural increase, urbanization, and immigration. The changes that came after the war were caused by alterations in the balance and scale of these three factors. For Ontario as a whole (since metro is not old enough to allow for comparisons) natural increase accounted for more than three-quarters of the population growth in the 1930s, declining after the war until by 1966 it was considerably less than half. At the same time the rate of urbanization was rising. Immigration to Ontario swelled to such an extent that it became the leading component in population growth for the province.[4]

For the Toronto region the net result of all this was more people, of whom fewer were native-born. The coming of immigrants was in itself no novelty. York had been started by a group, mainly from Britain, and year after year the arrival of their successors had continued to build up the town and city. Numbers had varied from time to time according to events at home and abroad – war, famine, depression, or prosperity – but the stream had never stopped. From the point of view of Toronto the novelty in the postwar years was twofold: the large total of immigrants and the number of countries from which they came. Until that time Toronto had been known as markedly British in race and outlook. By 1961, however, only about 59 per cent of the people of metro had come from the British Isles or were the descendants of those who had, and that percentage has almost certainly been reduced in the subsequent decade.[5] Of those non-British ethnically the French come third in order of size, but they are in a special position since a substantial proportion are Canadians. They are distributed throughout metro, but the largest numbers are in the City of Toronto, in Scarborough, and in North York.

Asians, Africans, Arabs, and Latin Americans have not migrated in substantial numbers to any part of Canada, and the Americans who come are fewer than at some periods in the past. All the above are represented in Toronto and add to its variety, but the change in the ethnic pattern has been dominated by migrants from a few countries of Europe. Very recently the proportion of Europeans in the total immigration to Canada has become less but meanwhile great numbers had arrived in Toronto. Italians are well at the top of the list with probably close to 300,000 in metro. They have been described as the most segregated element.[6] In 1961 they were heavily concentrated in the city with smaller portions in York and North York.[7] A considerable proportion of them are skilled or unskilled labourers. Some twenty churches have Italian-speaking priests, and in the districts in which they live the Italians can find shops, restaurants, lawyers, doctors, and dentists that call for no knowledge of English.

Numerically the Germans come next, having, perhaps, half as many representatives as the Italians. They too have their largest force in the city, but most of them speak English and they have been more assimilated than have the Italians and have a higher level of income. At the same time they can get together in their own social clubs. Next (after the French) come the Poles, estimated at sixty-eight thousand in 1966. About half live in the city, with substantial groups in North York and York. They tend to stay in their own groups, with their own social organizations and three newspapers. Ukrainians, next numerically, are for the most part concentrated in sections of the city. Their average incomes are relatively low.

The extent to which immigrants find satisfaction in a new land and to which they are able to adjust themselves inevitably varies.[8] Some of the British have been dissatisfied and returned home, finding employment or living conditions not what they had expected; but for the most part their problems are fewer than are those of foreigners. They have no new language to learn; forms of government, churches, and many other institutions are similar to what they have known; and they hear BBC news over Canadian radio stations, and follow the soccer games, the Boat Race, and the Grand National.

253

For others the differences are greater. Asians and West Indians are not accustomed to cold winters or the Canadian diet. Sometimes they, and Africans, encounter – or perhaps sometimes imagine – racial prejudice. The average Torontonian is not yet fully cosmopolitan. The experience of Europeans is mixed. Some of them, notably those of the professional and managerial categories, take readily to another language and different modes of life, making friends with established residents and participating in community enterprises. Among the less educated are many who pick up only enough English for their employment, still speaking their native tongue at home. They miss the social conditions in which they were brought up and tend to remain in groups. This, for example, is true of many Italians and Ukrainians.

It is the first generation that finds adjustment most difficult. The children fit more readily into the Canadian scene. Having no memories of another country, nothing about which to be nostalgic, they mix at school with Canadians and automatically become used to the language, studies, games, and attitudes of their fellow students. Usually, too, the young Canadian takes ethnic variety more for granted because for him it is familiar and normal, not having been brought up in a racially unified society. The ideal situation would be that immigrants of all ages should feel at home in Toronto as members of the local community, and that without losing their inherited gifts. For such a position to be achieved it is necessary not only that they adjust themselves to a new situation but also that they be fully accepted by Canadians of longer standing. Such a happy state does not come in a day. Segregation of ethnic groups is partly voluntary, partly defensive. Some Europeans who have come to Toronto claim that they are criticized by neighbours and acquaintances as different, and they have the impression that they are not entirely welcome. Others have had pleasanter experiences, finding that the ideas, skills, or arts that they brought are well received as adding to the texture of society.

In describing the population of Metropolitan Toronto attention has first been directed to the radical alteration in the origins and ethnic character of the people, but there have been other changes of significance as well. From one point of view the gulf between riches and poverty is greater than ever. More persons have what would once have been seen as great fortunes, while there remain those too poor to live decently. From another point of view the gap is narrower, since between rich and poor are occupational groups, such as teachers and members of some trade unions, whose real income is much higher than at any time in the past.

If the proportion of public funds spent on education be any measure the people of Ontario must be well educated. Higher education does not come under the jurisdiction of the metro government but is an important element in the social structure. Although the University of Toronto expanded after the war so rapidly as to be barely manageable it alone could hardly have accommodated the great number of students. Fortunately a second institution, York University, was founded in 1959. With its main campus outside the city it has increased its facilities so quickly that it can meet a considerable part of the demand for university education. In an age of technology it is appropriate that the Ryerson Polytechnic Institute should also have been greatly enlarged. Some of the young people, too, attend one or another of the universities not far from Toronto. A partial indication of the extent of higher education is, that of males aged 25 to 44 in metro in 1961 about 13 per cent had had some university training. In this respect Toronto does not stand high in comparison with other Canadian cities, coming seventh in the list.

Elementary and secondary schools have long been municipal responsibilities, subject to provincial direction and aided by provincial funds. The principle advocated in the Cumming Report – that education be of a common standard throughout the proposed metropolitan area – was accepted in the legislation of 1953. For the first dozen years the Metropolitan School Board made large capital expenditures, building 250 new schools and adding to five hundred others; but its terms of reference were not sufficient to allow it to effect uniformity through the area. Expenditure per elementary school pupil ranged from $378 in Scarborough to $611 in Leaside. Changes were made in 1967 by which the Metropolitan School Board assumed responsibility for capital debt and operating budgets. The Metropolitan Separate School Board administers all separate schools in metro except four in Etobicoke. In both the public and separate schools enrolment has been multiplied. In line with new provincial policy a French-language high school, the Ecole Secondaire Etienne Brûlé, was erected in North York, the first of its kind in metro and open to children of the whole area.[9]

In addition to the schools of the state system in metro are fifty-seven private ones of which slightly more than half have religious affiliations, Christian or Jewish. Some of the schools are very small, others of considerable size. Most of them accept day pupils only; nine include boarders. A portion cover all grades, the remainder taking only younger or older pupils. The total enrolment is 14,673.[10] A few Toronto pupils attend boarding schools elsewhere in Ontario, their number being probably offset by young people from other places enrolled in residential schools in Toronto.

On the religious affiliations of the people of Metropolitan Toronto the available information is not even approximately correct. The subject was not covered in the census of 1966, and in that of 1961 the results are obviously distorted by the answers given by individuals. The figures are much too high to have any relation to the number of those actively connected with churches in an age when congregations are on the whole thin. The census, moreover – no doubt for some good reason – includes no specific categories for atheists or agnostics. Something, however, can be gleaned from official statistics. The Roman Catholic Church is shown as having the largest number of adherents, with the United Church second and the Anglican Church third. The others are much smaller. On the whole the distribution by districts is not out of line with the total populations in each, except that more than half of those of the Jewish faith in the whole Toronto region were, in 1961, located in North York.

The churches are guardians of morals, but whether they and the secular powers have upheld them cannot be answered in simple terms. Active membership of churches is not necessarily a criterion. Stern puritans of Toronto as it was at the turn of the century would in some respects be critical of the morals of the present age, but contemporaries would find defects in the code and practices of those days. The pursuit of unorthodoxy in belief and in mode of life, a genuine principle to some people, is a cult for others. In a field so governed by personal views one can perhaps make only two sure comments: that ideas of morals have changed; and that the rise in crime and defiance of law are indications of decay.

A much larger and more varied population has spread over a wide area, affecting conditions of living by size, kind, and space. In 1948 the city contained 67.9 per cent of the total population of the thirteen municipalities that later comprised metro. The townships of York and East York had urban densities, but the three outer townships of Etobicoke, Scarborough, and North York were by that test rural. The percentage of population living in the City of Toronto dropped steeply: to 56.69 per cent in 1953, the year of the creation of metro, and to 37 per cent in 1966. It can be expected to go on decreasing, and is now perhaps a third.

In some respects conditions of living are affected by the place of residence. Only the city and immediately contiguous districts are complete within themselves. A family there can be educated, employed, supplied with goods and services, and entertained without trespassing beyond those boundaries. A prime advantage of the suburbs – and the governing factor for many people – is that they have dwellings available, and for the most part ones less expensive than those in the city. In other ways the advantages and disadvantages of the suburbs vary from one to another and according to individual preferences. Some of the new districts appear, at least in early stages, as no more than monotonous lines of similar houses placed on narrow lots. Others have been able to make use of woods or hills. Suburbs based on towns have to some extent their own local life, the core of which is the body of old residents. To live in a suburb does not necessarily bring open spaces and quiet, but it can do so. Not everyone who lives in a suburb goes daily to the city, but a good many men and women make such trips. Moreover, as has always been the case, others go at intervals for shopping or other personal reasons.

Anything like a full comparison between city and suburban life – if, indeed, such could be made at all – would occupy a book in itself. One obvious distinction is that suburbanites go to the city on business or pleasure, but the city dweller has little occasion to visit the suburbs. Suburban living is generally less expensive, and is likely to allow more readily for companionship. For some people the latter can be overdone, anonymity being more easily attained in a city. On the other hand nothing can be more lonely, for the less fortunate, than living in a city. A final score for the suburb is that it is free from slums.

It is customary to think of suburbanites as spending more time and money on transportation than do city dwellers. That is generally, but not always, true. It may be easier to reach downtown Toronto from a distance of twenty miles than from some point within or close to the city. Travel within Toronto is governed not only by distance but by the availability of facilities. No problem has, throughout the history of Toronto, more concerned citizens and visitors than the means of getting about, and none has been more difficult to solve. In each generation new techniques have helped but they are always a step behind the pressures of the day.

Arterial roads were advocated with cogent reasoning by virtually every group of planners from the beginning of the twentieth century, but not built when land was relatively cheap and large buildings fewer. After the second war some major ones were constructed. The Gardiner Expressway affords a much needed route to the Queen Elizabeth Way and at its eastern end connects with the Don Valley Parkway running north from the lakeshore. A start has been made on another north-and-south expressway by way of Spadina Avenue. Lesser roads throughout the boroughs have been widened and straightened.

The operation of public vehicles, other than steam railways and taxicabs, is, under the statute of 1953, the responsibility of metro. Its agent, the Toronto Transit Commission, a modified form of the earlier Toronto Transportation Commission, was appointed by the metropolitan council. An early step taken by the commission, indicative of the geographical range of its field, was to buy four privately owned bus lines. Buses continued to multiply within and beyond the city, so that in 1967 they were carrying 41 per cent of the total traffic. Unlike some other cities, however, Toronto did not lose its street cars for the commission concluded that they were efficient for heavy surface traffic and would continue to be so until they were superseded by a sufficiency of subways.

Subways had been talked of for forty years, but the bottlenecks on the main travelled routes became so serious that it was essential to go under-

Scarborough Bluffs and suburban dwellings, late 1960s

ground. In 1946 the city council agreed to proceed, a decision overwhelmingly ratified by popular vote. A Yonge Street line had obvious priority, as anyone struggling with the packed surface cars would agree, and construction began on it under the Toronto Transportation Commission which passed it as heritage to its successor when completed in 1954. Beginning at the Union Station the line ran 4.6 miles to Eglinton Avenue, about one-quarter of it being open cut. It had been intended that an east-west line should follow Queen Street, but as the centre of gravity of the city shifted northward Bloor Street was chosen instead. In its original form the Bloor-Danforth subway was eight miles long, extending from Woodbine Avenue to Keele Street, and was opened in 1966.

Meanwhile a link between the two lines was run northwestward from the Union Station to St George Street, it being designed to take a portion of the traffic off Yonge Street. The wisdom of that move has been debated, whether the effort should not have been put instead on carrying the Yonge

Interchange of the Spadina Expressway and Highway 401, 1966

Street subway into the heavily populated area north of Eglinton Avenue. It should be noted, however, that the long-range plan was to carry the University line considerably beyond Bloor Street. The next move was extension along the Danforth into Scarborough and along Bloor Street into Etobicoke; and, that being done, work began on lengthening the Yonge Street line. At some future time it is intended to build along Queen Street.[11]

The subway was essential within the distance which it could economically cover but was never intended to serve all the people of the spreading Toronto area. In the past Toronto had never had an adequate suburban rail service, partly because the steam railways made little effort to supply one and partly because the electric lines fell victim to the automobiles. A glance at some other cities, however, showed the value of fast local trains within an extensive urban region. In 1967 the provincial government moved to provide this facility through the Government of Ontario Transit, whose

Construction of the subway on Yonge Street

'GO trains' are operated for it by the Canadian National Railways. Rapid and frequent service was instituted between Oakville and Pickering, it being supposed that it, together with free parking at stations, would draw the public away from bumper-to-bumper driving and thus not only convenience themselves but reduce the unbearable demands on roads.

Neither within the city nor near it, however, can any fully effective defence be found against the human weakness for edging along in endless streams of traffic and polluted air. Metro has a ratio of persons to motor cars that is high even for North America. The police operate a computer network which regulates traffic signals throughout the metro area and is capable of covering eventually fifteen hundred intersections. The traffic at rush hours is watched from helicopters by men who, through radio stations, inform travellers of conditions on the various main arteries. On the whole it is a losing battle for new expressways seem only to generate more motor vehicles. Some people have given up the struggle, sold their cars, and depend on public transport; but even that is only partly successful as any one trying to board a bus or subway train in the rush hours will testify. Toronto shares with other large urban regions a problem to which no solution is in sight.[12]

Apart from agriculture, forestry, and mining few occupations are without a place in a big city, and even these three are found in miniature. The suburbanite may grow his vegetables; the civic authorities are kept busy removing dead elms, once the glory of many streets; and crews of men incessantly (and to the amateur mysteriously) dig and fill in holes, only to return to the attack a few weeks or months later.

Any attempt to make a complete list of occupations would be tedious and unprofitable, for in a large urban community a great array of goods and services is needed. A few generalizations, however, would be in order. One is the high proportion of females gainfully employed. That varies by type of work – for example, there are more women than men in personal services and fewer in industry – but it is in almost every case substantial. The largest part of the labour force is in industry, of which manufacturing forms a little less than one-quarter. Next comes trade of which the wholesale side has declined relatively. Then follow services of all kinds, transportation and communications, and construction in that order. Finance, however powerful, does not demand extensive personnel, nor do the professions. For the male labour force of the census metropolitan area in 1961 the percentage of those in professional and technical occupations was about eleven.

For most people income has increased and hours of work diminished. The range in the first is very wide. Hours of work can be found for most of the wage-earning categories, but not for some others such as small shop-keepers and other self-employed persons, lawyers, doctors, clergymen, artists, and non-union artisans.

The first responsibilities of a municipality, declared the Cumming Report, are provision and financing of public services; and it was the inability of some of the municipalities in the Toronto region to meet these responsibilities that was the major argument in favour of federation. In most respects the means of improvement existed in the mid-twentieth century as they had not done in earlier days. Throughout the span of the Town of York, and of the succeeding city for some decades, the struggle for sanitary conditions, water adequate in quantity and quality, control of fire with primitive equipment and amateur firemen, was often discouraging and unproductive. Gradually the worst difficulties were overcome but at the same time the acceptable standard rose. Citizens had come to expect that streets would be clean, water plentiful and safe to drink, sewers would work, policemen be readily available, and firemen prepared to rush to a burning building.

Defects remained, and some of them have been remedied by the metropolitan government. By substantially enlarging the water system it was able, as wholesaler, to supply sufficient water for the suburban municipalities to distribute. As wells were by this means largely eliminated, so were septic tanks by revised collection of sewage, as far as Markham and Woodbridge, for treatment and disposal. Sewage plants are designed to prevent pollution of the lake – or rather further pollution, since it and rivers leading into it have long been in a deplorable condition. Pollution is now – at last – a subject of wide concern; but it is ironic that it has taken 150 years to appreciate a menace so clearly pointed out in the Town of York.[13] Since that time, of course, new sources of pollution have arisen: oil and chemicals dumped into the waterways, fumes from motor vehicles and from industrial plants. It is one of the problems of urban society which, in part, could have been avoided by farsighted measures of control adopted long since, but which now threatens the health of the people of cities everywhere.

Maintenance of law and order is a public service the effectiveness of which depends on the combined efforts of government and public. Until 1957 each municipality in Toronto had its own police force, a situation which made co-operation difficult and gave uneven protection. The city, for example, had one police officer for each 450 residents while Scarborough had one for every two thousand. The Metropolitan Police Department, which took the place of the several local ones, is directed by a Board of Police Commissioners the membership of which is similar to that of the former city board. In addition to one county judge and two magistrates, all appointed by the provincial government, are the chairman of metro and another member elected by the council from its own ranks.

The task of the police in an age of violence and crime is a formidable one. Daily the press and radio report cases of armed robbery, arson, vandalism, drug peddling, and, not infrequently, of murder. The volume of crime continues to rise. Comparing 1966 and 1967, for instance, the total list went up by 9.6 per cent, caused primarily by sharp increases in murder and robbery. Frequently after dark, and even in the daytime, women are knocked down in the streets and their purses stolen, most commonly by young criminals. The attitude of the non-criminal portion of the public is mixed. The police commissioners seek to have the public regard the police as their friends and protectors, a relationship given substance by many acts of kindness and courage. They have also looked for positive aid by citizens, and in hundreds of cases information has been passed to the police which has led to the arrest of criminals. Individual citizens have displayed gallantry in subduing armed robbers and would-be murderers. On the other hand lone constables have been left unassisted when attacked by gangs, and the efforts of professional agitators to incite the police to retaliation in order to raise the cry of 'police brutality' are too seldom condemned by the public.[14]

Subject to breathing polluted air and the chance of being injured by a thug on the street, the health of the citizen may be as good as urban conditions ever permit. Skilled doctors are available, and both in the city and the other boroughs hospital capacity has been greatly enlarged. Those who enjoy good dwellings have in respect of health an advantage over the victims of slum conditions. Welfare is only in part a responsibility of metro, for the programmes of the federal and provincial governments include the main aspects of social security. These are the same in Toronto as anywhere else, but they afford a degree of protection against unemployment, the cost of bringing up children, poverty in old age, and the expenses of illness.

Shelter and warmth in winter, food and clothing, water supply and at least some degree of sanitation, means of travel to and from work, elementary education and perhaps some technical training – these are the basic needs for a town-dweller – what might be described in a school curriculum as compulsory subjects. To attain these most people have to work for the greater part of their lives. That occupies a good deal of their time, but not as much as formerly. For the remaining waking hours there is available a wide variety of forms of entertainment, recreation for the great majority and vocations for those professionally employed in them. Freedom of choice is restricted by financial considerations but is otherwise a matter of taste. Of the two broad categories of what may equally be called recreation and entertainment, the first has no collective name other than the imprecise word 'culture,' and the other is more simply described as sports and games. Two aspects must be borne in mind: what Toronto consumes and what it produces.

In spite of competition from other media reading remains as an interest for many people. They may find anything from detective stories to erudite monographs in the numerous public libraries, of which the reference ones were taken over by the Metropolitan Toronto Library Board and the remainder financially assisted. Toronto has long been the centre of Canadian publishing. Although publishing has serious problems connected with costs, a market still limited, and competition from abroad, it is on a much larger scale and can draw on a greater number of Canadian authors. A representative group of the latter live in Toronto. Because of the large universities in metro many of the books produced are for those who specialize in some subject or other, but a portion, such as biographies and studies of public affairs, are of more general interest. In the field of *belles lettres* Toronto's novelists and poets are included.

Drama, music, and art are necessarily centred in the city. The only surviving theatre of the professional type, the Royal Alexandra, was in danger of following the Grand Opera House and the Princess into oblivion when it was bought from the Mulock estate by Edward Mirvish, who restored it tastefully and within the bounds of its period style. The O'Keefe Centre is a newcomer, the great size of which is better adapted to music and dancing

263

than to intimate plays. Music and then television had cut so deeply into attendance at theatres that the procession of great actors and actresses in travelling companies had sadly dwindled. The opportunity then arose of filling some gaps with local productions. *Spring Thaw* has had long runs in the Alexandra, directed by Mavor Moore, whose mother, Dora Mavor Moore, has done so much to stimulate interest in the drama. In 1968 a new company, Theatre Toronto, also offered plays in the Alexandra under the artistic direction of Clifford Williams.

The little theatre movement has flourished since the war. Hart House Theatre and the small theatre in the Central Library were supplemented by others, including that in the restored St Lawrence Market building. Many others have had continuous or temporary existence: the Crest, Colonnade, Poor Alex, Toronto Workshop, and Coach House among them. Most types of plays are performed, some experimental and others more conventional. For those who cannot or do not wish to attend performances the CBC produces many kinds of plays on radio.

Some of the long-standing musical organizations have continued and others have been added. The *doyen* of choirs, the Mendelssohn, was joined by the Festival Singers. The Toronto Symphony, only less venerable, was happy in its Japanese conductor, Seiji Ozawa. The fact that a local opera company, the Canadian Opera Company, could be supported was another indication of Toronto's size and wealth. Many other concerts, instrumental or vocal, by residents or visiting artists, testify to the wide range of taste in listeners.

Ballet, combining drama and music, would, like opera, have been impracticable in a smaller place. In the late 1940s companies visited Toronto, and in 1951 the National Ballet, fortunate in securing Celia Franca as artistic director and dancer, gave its first performance. After struggling through characteristic financial crises it was able to give regular programmes in the Royal Alexandra from 1953, moving to the larger stage and auditorium of the O'Keefe Centre in 1964.[15]

The Art Gallery of Ontario, as it has been renamed, supplemented by a number of private galleries, affords opportunities for the display of paintings, old and new, imported or by local artists. The Painters Eleven, founded in 1953, exhibited until 1960 when it was disbanded. Among its members were Harold Town, Jack Bush, and Tom Hodgson. Their prime interest was in abstract impressionism. In some respects they could be compared to the Group of Seven a generation earlier but their inspiration was not peculiarly Canadian. More conventional forms of painting are found too, for example by Graham Coughtry who turned away from impressionism, or by Adrian Dingle whose landscapes bridged old and new. As had always been the case portrait painting in Toronto was not of international fame.

Many amateurs enjoy landscape painting as a hobby, and some of their work is more than creditable.

The Royal Ontario Museum, now administratively separated from the University of Toronto, has continued to build up its collections and has been fortunate in the addition of the Planetarium, the gift of R. S. McLaughlin. It attracts more and more visitors of all ages, including escorted groups of school children.

The extent of performance and patronage of music and the arts in Metropolitan Toronto is in proportion to its size, wealth, and variety of people; and the same could be said of the town or city from the time of its origin. In early days men and women collected great works of literature to read by candlelight; organized amateur and professional theatricals in makeshift quarters; imported pianos through crude means of transport and spent long evenings singing and playing. Residents and visitors, including officers of the Royal Engineers, built up a body of paintings and drawings. Immigrants, bringing talents, were mainly from Britain, but always some Europeans came too, men such as G. T. Berthon the Austrian painter, or the three Hambourg brothers from Russia, all distinguished musicians.

Since the last war the European contribution has grown with the greater number of immigrants: from the lands that held the glory that was Greece and the grandeur that was Rome; that gave birth to Rembrandt and Dürer; to Bach and Chopin; to Molière and Bernhardt. Most immigrants, at any time and to any place, are more concerned with the necessities of daily life than with the arts; but among them a minority have tastes or gifts in the cultural field. The change brought by the postwar immigrants was in degree and not in kind, and was concurrent with the development of native skills. That combination is a necessary and normal one as, for example, the membership of any symphony orchestra in the United States would indicate.

A very different form of recreation brought by immigrants, more especially by those from Italy, was enjoyment of soccer, a game new in its professional aspect to Toronto. Spectators of the Canadian version of rugby football have not yet reached the astronomical figures current in the United States, but some thirty thousand people will trek to the stadium in the grounds of the Canadian National Exhibition to watch it. Daily the newspapers report on the critical state of a quarterback's right hand or the knee of a split end. Professional hockey, too, has long been a major attraction through attendance in the Maple Leaf Gardens or on television. As the final games approach young people camp outside the building in a scramble for tickets. Horse racing, one of the oldest sports in Toronto, has become a large-scale enterprise. For amateurs curling continues to provide exercise in the winter, as do bowling and skiing.

Public parks and playgrounds are still inadequate. In 1920 the city had about eighteen hundred acres of parks for some half million people and in

Toronto City Hall, erected 1961–5

the next ten years only about two hundred were added. That lowered the ratio to 3.3 acres per thousand people, and twenty years later the figure was about the same although the planners had set the target at 4.6 acres per thousand. In the existing open spaces are tennis courts and hockey rinks, with swings and slides for the small children. The serious shortage is of neighbourhood parks and playgrounds in the poorer and thickly populated districts where they are most needed. Forcing children to play on narrow streets or in cluttered backyards is simply asking for trouble.

For those in the newer parts of metro and for those with automobiles the prospect is much brighter. Metro parks are progressing well, and if the scheme for the waterfront is followed up the whole width of metro will be benefited. Beyond are the conservation areas under the direction of a provincial body, the Metropolitan Toronto and Region Conservation Authority. Areas of considerable size are being kept in their natural state, and in them a family may spend a day or longer enjoying the unspoiled outdoors.

In summer and winter many people go further afield on weekends or holidays, as they have always done. Many places within a hundred miles of Toronto afford excellent skiing even when Toronto has little snow. Bus lines advertise trips by the day or weekend for those who are without cars or choose not to use them. In the summer Muskoka, Georgian Bay, and the Kawartha Lakes continue to draw cottagers although the simple life of thirty or forty years ago is more elusive in the midst of speed boats and cocktail parties. A substantial number of people, too, take their winter holidays in the American south or the West Indies, and others travel to any part of the world or around it.

Within the city the Department of Parks and Recreation has established community centres which hold classes in leatherwork, woodwork, art, dressmaking, and other crafts. Dances and movies provide entertainment in a lighter vein. At Senior Citizens' Clubs older people may play chess and other games or join in singing. In some districts citizens have organized community clubs which also have crafts and games.

The only generalization that can safely be made about life in Metropolitan Toronto is that generalizations are unsafe; for the urban complex that has grown out of the bush town of York is a great city, and as such is full of variety and contradictions. People of all origins, incomes, occupations, and interests are to be found in it, as the human senses will testify.

Driving about the city (to walk would take a lifetime) a persistent observer would see fine streets and mean ones; great office buildings breathing confidence and little commercial establishments tucked away in obsolete structures; fine houses, medium houses, and broken-down tenements; apartment houses and interminable stretches of small new houses. He would see shops of all kinds: great department stores, high-class specialty shops, shopping centres; old-fashioned family groceries and shops specializing in dress, commodities, or foods from most parts of the world. Clothes of passers-by would deny any single type: business executives dressed in the mode of Savile Row; women from India or Pakistan in saris, and other women in Paris models or ill-cut slacks and hair-curlers; individuals who seem to be en route from a rummage sale to a fancy dress party.

The sense of taste may have full play in a host of restaurants having menus from the roast beef of old England to the dishes of southern Europe and the far east. With some determination (and a full pocket-book) anyone in Toronto can gastronomically tour the world. The sense of smell is less rewarded by smoke and fumes, unattractive evidence of any large city. The obvious sound is of traffic, but more indicative of Toronto's character are the many languages and accents heard everywhere – on the street, in subways, in shops, and in offices. Returning now from his pilgrimage our observer might conclude that Toronto followed no set pattern, except to the extent that it resembled any other large North American city. Such impressions would be not so much wrong as incomplete, based as they would be on superficial evidence. To reach any understanding of the ethos one has to dig deeper.

Metropolitan Toronto is not explained by multiplying the population and area of the prewar city, but the greater size is an important component. Others, associated with it, are ethnic variety and economic strength. The remaining principal factor, mentioned at the beginning of this chapter, is the body of changed social thought and behaviour that developed in western countries after the war and against which Toronto could hardly have been insulated. From that point of view Toronto would have been different even if it had remained the same size.

To one or some combination of the above circumstances can be attributed most of those characteristics of the present urban region that are new. The 'city of homes' (a phrase which, however hackneyed, was descriptive of the place and illuminates the attitude of those who used the words) retreated before the invasion of commercial and other institutions to the extent that it ceased to house the majority of its own workers. There developed a concentrated centre surrounded on three sides by widely spread districts in the main residential. Throughout the whole area a population no longer predominantly British by origin was distributed; but the distribution was uneven, the city itself being more affected by European immigration than were most of the other parts of metro, and within the city some ethnic groups being mainly in a few sections.

The majority of the people enjoy a high standard of living. Comparisons are to some extent distorted by the depression of the 1930s, but if made over a longer period will show a distinct improvement. The large numbers of motor cars, television sets, and electric household appliances, and the use of processed foods, are illustrative of the new order. An essential part of it is the extensive use of credit, a practice which is sometimes viewed with alarm, but the risk is in part cushioned by insurance against illness and unemployment.

Such are deductions to be drawn from the principal causes of change; but neither category covers the whole life of the city and its environs, nor do they affect everybody or in the same degree. Old modes and traditions jostle with new ones, and many people live and think not essentially differently from what they would have done one or two generations ago. The great size of metro does not necessarily affect those who live in any one part of it, and indeed great sections may be *terra incognita* to them. The single 'society' of Toronto has long since faded, for a big city cannot be socially stratified like a small one. Various groups emerge instead and have for two excellent reasons limited relations with each other. One is that they have developed around similar attitudes and interests, and the other is that it is not humanly possible to spend time with more than a limited number of people.

There have been great changes, conspicuous and real. It is a cosmopolitan place now, and the more interesting for it. And yet to the perceptive it is, while very different, recognizable. Underneath the surface, and only sometimes detected, old Toronto slumbers.

# 12

# *Toronto's realm*

Toronto had become metropolitan: in name and, more important, in fact. The word is applied to a principal city within a country or region. In modern times especially it has about it an urbanized or semi-urbanized area, dependent on and complementary to itself. A metropolis may be, but is not necessarily, a seat of government. It must be of a size (in terms of the scale of population in any era) to encompass men and women engaged in a great variety of activities, mental and physical. It is not self-contained – no urban community is – but comprehensive in its interests and its productivity. It is something more than a large collection of human beings: or, rather, it is the result of such concentration. In maturity it is cosmopolitan and sophisticated, with a character of its own, built up, perhaps, over centuries. A city of this kind may be examined in three related aspects: its internal life; how it draws visitors, migrants, and organizations to itself; and in the kind and degree of influence it exerts in its neighbourhood and beyond.

The story of the great city in older civilizations is a long one, but in the new world urban concentration is relatively new. Perhaps for that reason an American scholar, N. S. B. Gras, turned to early days in Britain and Europe to analyse long-term patterns of urban growth.[1] His pioneer study has influenced thinking in Canada where the large city is a phenomenon even more recent than in the United States. Some preliminary attention has been paid by Canadian historians to this subject,[2] and more is due in view of the transition from a rural to an urban country. Gras unwittingly led his successors to equate influence with economic influence in spite of his warning that his own treatise was confined to economic history. Over the centuries, however, the role of the city has been many-sided as a few examples will show. They are drawn from Britain and Europe whence came the colonists of North America.

At its zenith the empire ruled from Rome covered all western Europe, England, the middle east, and North Africa. When the political structure collapsed the standards set in jurisprudence, in engineering, and in architecture continued as guides to other peoples. Athens was a principal inspiration of the renaissance, an attitude toward man and the world that constituted one of the great milestones in European history. As a continuing treasure house of the arts Florence has probably drawn more admirers to it than has any other city of the same size. In the middle ages Venice, taking advantage of the assets and overcoming the liabilities of its environment, built up for a time a mastery of commerce, protected by sea and land forces. The wealth and confidence that came from such worldly success can be seen reflected in the buildings, glass, and painting which outlasted the politico-economic power that had given birth to them.

As a governmental and financial centre of the Habsburg lands in the valley of the Danube Vienna was the focal point of a region of different tongues and races. While adding to the baroque beauty of the city in which they held court the Habsburg emperors failed to arrest the centrifugal forces inherent in their diverse domains, but they drew to themselves the best in science and the arts. Students in specialized fields of medicine long came from distant lands. Mozart and Haydn lived in a city which counted music as a part of its being. Of Beethoven, who did some of his best work there, it has been said that of the men of the early nineteenth century it was he, rather than Napoleon, who most influenced mankind.

While some western cities have seen their greatest days Paris and London remain unique within their own countries and to the rest of the world. To tell their story would be to recount much of the history of Europe and beyond. Eighteenth-century Paris was a laboratory for social and political philosophy and arbiter of social modes. The revolution of 1789 introduced the nineteenth century, and after it Paris was the touchstone of political controversy. 'When Paris sneezes,' it was said, 'all Europe catches cold.' London is marked by its own unmistakable character and as being a haven for all manner of men and ideas. It was the base of the industrial revolution and the financial capital of the world. Once the centre of a vast empire it has watched the parliamentary system born in it used and misused elsewhere.

It is not intended to suggest a comparison between old cities of Europe and the youthful Toronto, but rather to indicate some of the roles that a city can play in the circumstances of its day. If parallels were sought they would best be found in the United States: not with New York or Boston, venerable and majestic, but with middle-sized cities such as Detroit or Cleveland. In such company Toronto could compete successfully; but the factors to consider are too many, and some of them are too nebulous, to allow for much meaning in an overall comparison.

For the majority of those who visit Toronto the motive is not to take advantage of particular qualities which they know it to possess. Many tourists include it on a motor tour because they have not seen it before or because it is on their route. Large numbers of men and women attend conventions in Toronto as they do in a hundred other North American cities, staying in hotels which could be almost anywhere on the continent. Some of the former, but infrequently the latter, will, while in the city, direct their steps to buildings they are told are of interest. A smaller number of people come with specific objects in mind. The federal government of Metropolitan Toronto, a unique experiment, has attracted the attention of those concerned with the problems of similar urban areas. Thousands of Canadians and Americans attend the Canadian National Exhibition. The city hall has international fame, and university administrators have long studied Hart House as a successful club for undergraduates. The Royal Ontario Museum, with its great oriental collection, is known far and wide. Many businessmen have occasion to visit Toronto.

Toronto has long been a respected centre of higher education, and to its universities come young men and women from most parts of the world, returning to their native countries or to other parts of Canada as, it may be hoped, sympathetic interpreters of Toronto as a whole or one or other of the universities in particular. Doctors, dentists, teachers, engineers, and other trained men and women fan out from the universities, sometimes to great distances. Advanced studies, including, for example, research in medicine and physics, have drawn experts from far afield.

Nearly a century ago it was said that Ned Hanlan, the oarsman, had done more than any other individual or institution to make Toronto known in other parts of the world. Fifty years later that honour would probably have fallen on the inventors of insulin, Sir Frederick Banting and Dr Charles Best. At the present time the flag is carried by more people, but among them are musicians and artists. The singer Lois Marshall has been acclaimed in Britain, the United States, the Soviet Union, Holland, Australia, New Zealand, and other countries. Glenn Gould, the pianist, has played with many of the great orchestras of the world and made concert tours of Europe. The Toronto Symphony and the Mendelssohn Choir have travelled widely and successfully. On the whole Toronto painters have made less impact, but one of the moderns, Harold Town, has exhibited all over the world and won many awards. Scholarly writing has probably made more impression than has fiction. Northrop Frye, for example, is well known for his volumes of literary criticism.

The works of the mind and the spirit are subject to individual judgment except when they are recognized as supreme, and that is frequently after the death of the individuals concerned. No one is now likely to question the greatness of Michelangelo, Shakespeare, or Beethoven; but modern forms of art, poetry, and music are not immune from extravagant praise or carping criticism. There must, therefore, be a degree of uncertainty in these fields of a kind that is not found when examining the economy of an urban area. The wealth and economic power of a city do not necessarily bring comparable strength in learning, music, and the arts,but they do make possible a broader advance than would otherwise be the case.

In the case of Toronto – or, rather, of York – the first two groups of those gainfully employed were the personnel of the provincial government and the artisans who erected houses, shops, and public buildings where there had been only forest. The demands of such people brought the corresponding supply: of innkeepers to furnish accommodation for the workers, for those attending the legislature, and others involved in the courts; of shopkeepers to provide goods; and of those who minister to others. Among the last were doctors, lawyers, school teachers, hairdressers, shoemakers, blacksmiths, and so on. All this was miniature in comparison with present dimensions, and the same sort of process was going on in other little towns of a pioneer province. York, however, began to forge ahead with trade as the principal means.

All that is known of the misty days of the prologue at the mouth of the Humber is the trade in furs that was intermittently conducted there; and that was followed by the merchants of York who struggled over the unspeakable roads of their day to sell goods to the settlers of York County. Their ambitions spread to what is now western Ontario and then to drawing off the commerce of the American middle west through Toronto. When railways supplemented canals the traders reached into the new mining towns in the north of the province and catered to the pioneer farmers of the western prairies. When wholesale trade was separated from retail it became a powerful branch of business.

Early shopkeepers, obliged to import and to sell on long credit, were aided by the introduction of banks, which were the centre of a growing financial network that came to include insurance agents and then local companies, building and loan societies, stock brokers and the stock exchanges, and trust companies. Manufacturing, except in a few light lines, was not as prominent in early decades.

In such conventional ways the economy of Toronto developed. How the city outpaced its rivals, shed most of its dependence on Montreal, and extended its financial and trading interests far beyond its own boundaries has been recounted in earlier chapters. To have called the Toronto of the early twentieth century a metropolis would have evoked derisive laughter without its walls and even within them, and yet all the elements were there, but not on a scale to allow the city to be called metropolitan. After the depression of the 1930s had slowed all development the war stimulated it again, and at that time the city reached what may prove to have been its maximum population. The changes that came over Toronto after the second world war were both in degree and in kind, the total effect being to produce a great urban area of a type not previously known in Canada.

Not only was the population of all Canada becoming predominantly urban – about 70 per cent in 1961 – but disproportionately concentrated in and around the larger cities. Toronto is a prime example of the results of that process. Because there was not enough space in the city for the newcomers, or even for all the economic operations with which they were to be concerned, one has to think in terms of a region rather than just a city.

For such a region to be viable within itself and in effective contact with its wider economic constituency presupposes adequate means of transportation. Those within Metropolitan Toronto have been described in the previous chapter.[3] For longer distances, too, methods have been modified. That the railways carry a great deal of freight is indicated by the long trains and the extensive new marshalling yards; but much of the passenger business has been lost to aeroplanes and motor vehicles. The international airport at Malton, seventeen miles from downtown Toronto, and completed in 1964, carries more traffic than any other airport in Canada, amounting in 1967 to about fifty-seven hundred aircraft a month and three and a quarter million passengers in a year. Roads and motor vehicles have improved to such an extent that they are much more extensively used for passengers, and also for a portion of the freight, particularly for local freight.

Whatever else happens in Toronto the harbour always holds its own. Ever since the St Lawrence had been first canalized a few ships had sailed between Toronto and salt water, but as the size of vessels increased the shallow canals became decreasingly useful for that purpose. The opening of the St Lawrence Seaway in 1959 made Toronto an ocean port, and international shipping is now much the larger part of the business of the port. As has always been the case incoming cargoes are far greater than outgoing. Among the largest commodities unloaded is coal, with fuel oil as a poor second. Soybeans, wheat, and barley enter in fairly substantial amounts. In 1967 the total tonnage of cargo handled by the port was 5,758,745, a figure very much below that for Hamilton which imports large quantities of iron ore concentrates and coal.

As well as facilitating movement of people and goods transportation is an important business in itself. Sale and servicing of cars and trucks, making and repairing roads, maintenance and operation of the harbour, and staffing the railway station and trains all call for a considerable number of personnel. Financial institutions require few employees but are, like transportation, essential to the operation of the whole economy. From one point of view

275

they are highly centralized, being for the most part in a small area of the city; but from another they have the widest range of any section of the economy. Banks, insurance companies, and loan organizations do business all over Canada and in other countries.

It would not be practicable to measure the value of the financial institutions in the same way as can be done for other branches of the economy, but other tests can be applied which will indicate the financial strength of Metropolitan Toronto. Taxable assessment shows both totals and the change in distribution. Between 1954 and 1966 the taxable assessment rose from some $2.5 billion to more than $5 billion. When metro began the city contributed more than half of the total value, but as the outer boroughs – North York, Etobicoke, and Scarborough – developed industrially as well as in dwellings their shares increased. Another approach is to examine the figures for cheques. In 1939 the total value of cheques cashed in Toronto against individual accounts was a little more than $10 billion, and in 1968 had multiplied to well over $230 billion. This latter amount was 37.31 per cent of the Canadian total, the only competitor being Montreal at 26.49 per cent.[4] The Toronto Stock Exchange is exceeded in its operations in North America only by the exchanges in New York, and in 1969 reached a new high point of shares traded.

The construction industry is large, both in capital expenditures and personnel, but the largest employer is manufacturing. Accuracy of comparisons with the past is limited by changes in the value of money, the size of the city, and the effects of mechanization, but some general differences are apparent. One is that the proportion of the population engaged in manufacturing is smaller. During the second war the number of employees rose to a very high point, but by the 1960s was somewhat lower than it had been in the 1920s. The situation is probably explained in part by the greater choice of occupations and largely by the withdrawal of industry to the suburbs. At the present time about two-thirds of the manufacturing in the census metropolitan area, whether measured by personnel or value, is outside the city. Some factories had always been located outside the city limits, but as late as 1951 the only parts of York County which had a serious industrial tinge were Leaside and New Toronto and together they made up only a small part of the whole.

The total value of manufacturing in the metropolitan area is very large, with shipments and other revenues approaching the $8 billion mark. Types of manufacturing are many. Food and beverage industries are first in number of employees, followed by metal fabricating, printing and publishing, electrical products, machinery, transportation equipment, and chemicals. A glance over the whole list suggests few forms of manufacturing that are not included.[5]

Wholesale trade is distinctly urban, more than half of it being conducted in nine cities of Canada. Toronto comes third in the list, after Winnipeg (because of the grain trade) and Montreal. A general rise in the value of wholesaling in Canada through the 1950s was not reflected in Toronto, which saw on the contrary a marked decline. Nevertheless it is still a very large business, although not a great employer of labour. Net sales in the City of Toronto in 1961 amounted to about $1.75 billion.[6] Retail trade, on the other hand, engages some hundred thousand persons throughout the census metropolitan area. Of sales of about $3 billion somewhat more than a third are in the city. Grocers and butchers have together first claim on the public purse, followed by dealers in motor vehicles and service stations. It is a sobering thought that the last had in 1966 a revenue of about $200 million.[7]

The remaining large category of business, embracing the 'service trades,' claimed nearly eighty thousand workers in 1966 and accounted for an income of more than $850 million. The service trades are not self-explanatory as are manufacturing or retail trade, and, moreover, a study of their branches throws a good deal of light on the complications of modern urban society. Of the several groups of service trades that with the largest receipts is made up of hotels and other places in which to eat and drink. The many millions spent in alcoholic beverages suggests that an old habit has not died. The business services group, next in order of revenue, has advertising organizations as much the largest component, followed by chartered accountants. The public pays for close to seven thousand persons to provide it with recreation. Many of these are connected with the legitimate theatre or with motion pictures. But the public of metro exercises too: in thirty-eight dance halls, on fifty golf courses, at twenty-five riding academies, and on skating rinks. To the extent that billiards afford exercise 151 parlours are open.

The personal services group is largely devoted to cleaning and dyeing people and household equipment. Maintenance of the appearance of females costs annually more than $25 million. The theory that the male hair is now uncut was refuted in 1966 by a bill of $10 million from barber shops. Laundry and dry cleaning on inanimate objects account for the largest expenditure. A group properly described as miscellaneous includes window cleaning, disinfecting and exterminating, funeral directors, and photographers.[8] The types of work which have been noted cover a large part of the population but the total list is longer, including, for example, the professions, domestic servants, artisans not otherwise mentioned, and those engaged in small crafts and trades.

The economic structure of Metropolitan Toronto is comprehensive, and the few figures that have been quoted show that it is measured in billions of dollars. Having about one-tenth of the population of all Canada

Downtown Yonge Street today, the jumbled confusion enhanced by double exposure

(which itself has greatly increased in numbers) it readily attains to the status of a metropolis. With such riches, population, and productive capacity Toronto might be expected to cast some shadow over the country as a whole and be not unknown beyond it. In the political field it is the seat of a provincial government the responsibilities of which have grown; but in the relationship between the two protest is not of undue influence by the great city of Toronto but rather by the city on the ground that municipalities are kept by the province in leading strings. Because of the number of federal constituencies within the metro area and because of ability to support political parties financially Toronto would seem to have openings to exert considerable influence in Ottawa. If, as was once the case, Toronto voted solidly for one political party it might in a close election hold a casting vote; but variety has entered politics as it has other fields.

No urban community, however large, is self-sufficient. As Toronto has grown so it has accumulated greater resources within itself, as, for example, in what is for sale in the shops, in medical skills, or in entertainment. It must still, however, buy and sell beyond its boundaries. Food in great quantities, lumber, raw materials for factories, some lines of goods for wholesale or retail trade are imported from Canada and abroad. Equally the city must sell the commodities which it produces and the financial and other services which it has developed, for both are in excess of local needs and are exported to pay for imports.

A city is sometimes described as dominating the regions to which its influence extends, and more especially its immediate neighbourhood. In the case of Toronto it is sometimes represented that in an area of about fifty miles the towns and villages have lost their identity and are economically in the grip of the city. To some degree this is true. Large-scale business in Toronto, combined with ease of access by road, has cut into the business of local stores or drawn them into networks controlled in the city. The little town is not independent but neither is it wholly dependent. Local shops survive, although fewer in number. Artisans, professional men, and service organizations are of the town. Municipal government is usually in the hands of established residents. Churches, fairs, and community entertainments are directed by the people on the spot. The towns are semi-detached.

Further afield are department stores, branches of Toronto organizations, and the mail order business which has long been on the one hand criticized as damaging local shops and on the other praised as offering better value. Goods manufactured in Toronto are sold in most parts of Canada and exported outside the country. Customers of Toronto banks and insurance companies are spread throughout the country and beyond. Mining in northern Ontario continues to be an important factor in the development of Toronto in respect of finance, trade, and manufacturing. From small beginnings early in the century it has become a large industry. Without the management and financial support largely located in Toronto it is unlikely that the mines would have advanced so well; without the mines Toronto would have been poorer.

Viewed from outside, a great and rich city like Toronto may appear as monolithic, the centre of the 'big interests,' exploiting the weak beyond its boundaries. To some unfriendly eyes it is 'hogtown' (a phrase which originally may have referred to an early inhabitant with a similar name). A more kindly picture brings out the graceful arts which it encourages and sustains and the comfortable life it provides for tens of thousands of families. All such generalizations are misleading, not necessarily because they are wholly untrue in themselves but because among two million people every approach to life will be found. That comment in turn recalls two of the principal characteristics of a metropolis: that it is large and powerful; and that within it may be found a diversity of creatures, who – if obliged to do so – would describe the city in a hundred different ways.

As the second-century milestone comes within sight Toronto is in a state of transition, with old features clinging on and new ones not fully assimilated. By 1993 it will have had time to shake down, to find a definite character, and become more sophisticated. It will, too, be the hub of an increasingly populated urban area. One sweeping plan for development which is under provincial study envisages a 'Toronto-centred region' for which a population of eight million people is envisaged by the year 2000.[9] What a contrast with Peter Russell's apprehension that York would lack a hinterland producing food, that the body would be too small for the head!

Anything on that scale would be a remarkable growth from a beginning not so far in the past. When the Simcoes arrived from Niagara in 1793 they found one white trader who piloted their vessel into a natural harbour innocent of shipping. All about them was forest with hardly a break in a province virtually unoccupied. Toronto started from nothing. Generation after generation of its people have brought it from clearing to town, from town to city, from city to metropolis.

# Notes

## 1 A place in search of a purpose 3–12

1 The principal source of information on the portage and all that relates to it is Percy J. Robinson, *Toronto during the French Régime: a history of the Toronto region from Brûlé to Simcoe, 1615–1793* (Toronto, 1965). On the posts at Toronto there is some information in Frank H. Severance, *An Old Frontier of France: the Niagara region and adjacent lakes under French control* (2 vols., New York, 1917)

2 Metropolitan Toronto Central Library, Memorials of the North West Company

3 For the treaties and reservations see J. L. Morris, *Indians of Ontario* (Toronto, 1943)

4 Collins' report is printed in *Report of the Bureau of Archives for the Province of Ontario, 1905*, p. 379

5 The correspondence reflecting Simcoe's thinking will be found in E. A. Cruikshank, ed., *The Correspondence of Lieutenant-Governor John Graves Simcoe, with allied documents relating to the administration of the government of Upper Canada* (5 vols., Toronto, 1923–31)

## 2 The birth of a town 13–41

1 Mary Quayle Innis, ed., *Mrs. Simcoe's Diary* (Toronto, 1965)

2 Edith G. Firth, ed., *The Town of York, 1793–1815: a collection of documents of early Toronto* (Toronto, 1962), p. lxxviii. Throughout this chapter I have been aided by this valuable book.

3 Some of William Jarvis' letters were printed in the *Women's Canadian Historical Society of Toronto* in 1922. Others will be found in manuscript in the William Jarvis Papers in the Metropolitan Toronto Central Library.

4 Metropolitan Toronto Central Library, Elizabeth Russell Papers

5 Cruikshank, *The Correspondence of Lieutenant-Governor John Graves Simcoe*, IV, 233. For pictures and descriptions of early houses see Eric Arthur, *Toronto: no mean city* (Toronto, 1964)

6 Ontario Archives, John Macaulay Papers

7 Metropolitan Toronto Central Library, Jarvis Papers. Agreement with Abner Miles, 26 August 1794

8 Ontario Archives, J. B. Robinson Papers. An undated list, by streets, of houses and other buildings erected before 1812

9 'Minutes of the Court of General Quarter Sessions of the Peace for the Home District, 1800–1811' (*Twenty-first Report of the Department of Public Records and Archives of Ontario*, 1932)

10 Extensive lists of goods advertised for sale are printed in J. Ross Robertson, *Landmarks of Toronto* (Toronto, 1894–1914), I and III

11 In the Thirteen Colonies the dollar (which came from the Spanish West Indies) was officially rated at six shillings. In practice, however, it was rated at five shillings in Massachusetts, and this, under the name of Halifax, was introduced into Nova Scotia. In Upper and Lower Canada the dollar was rated at eight shillings as in New York, and the name was abbreviated to 'York.' At a later date, however, the Halifax rating became the common one in Upper Canada.

12 Henry Scadding, *Toronto of Old*, ed. F. H. Armstrong (Toronto, 1966), p. 275 ff. For documents concerning lower Yonge Street see also Firth, *Town of York, 1793–1815*

13 The text of the memorial is in Firth, *Town of York, 1793–1815*, p. 154; see also Percy J. Robinson, 'Yonge Street and the North West Company' (*Canadian Historical Review*, XXIV, no. 3)

14 One of the few exceptions is the chatty diary of Ely Playter who managed a tavern and jotted down large and small events in the town. The original is in the Public Archives of Ontario and extracts are printed in Firth, *Town of York, 1793–1815*.

15 Elizabeth Collard, *Nineteenth-century Pottery and Porcelain in Canada* (Montreal, 1967)

## 3 War and reconstruction   43–74

1 J. Mackay Hitsman, *The Incredible War of 1812: a military history* (Toronto, 1965), p. 123. This book is a modern and general account of the war.

2 William Wood, ed., *Select British Documents of the Canadian War of 1812* (4 vols., Toronto, 1920–6), I, 258

3 There is no single and detailed study of the capture of York. Brief accounts are in Hitsman, *The Incredible War of 1812*; in Charles W. Humphries, 'The Capture of York' (*Ontario History*, LI, no. 1); and in Firth, *Town of York, 1793–1815*. The last also has relevant documents. An important source is E. Cruikshank, ed., *The Documentary History of the Campaign upon the Niagara Frontier in the Year 1813*, part 1 (Welland, 1902). Some short documents in the Metropolitan Toronto Central Library are of interest: 'Description of York ... written at the time of capture and occupation by General Dearborn ... '; (United States) 'General Orders, 30 April 1813'; 'Statement by Citizens of York, 30 April 1813.'

4 The draft letter is in the Metropolitan Toronto Central Library. Throughout the war Strachan was useful in rallying the loyal and arranging for the comfort of troops, but unfortunately his self-confidence led him to regard himself as an authority on military strategy. Others of his utterances are in J. L. H. Henderson, ed., *John Strachan: documents and opinions* (Toronto, 1969), p. 40 ff.

5 The text is in Edith G. Firth, ed., *The Town of York, 1815–1834: a further collection of documents of early Toronto* (Toronto, 1966), p. 4

6 Helen I. Cowan, *British Emigration to British North America: the first hundred years* (Toronto, 1961)

7 *Authentic Letters from Upper Canada, including an account of Canadian field sports by Thomas William Magrath: the whole edited by the Rev. Thomas Radcliff: illustrated by Samuel Lover and introduced by James John Talman* (Toronto, 1953), p. 67

8 Audrey Saunders Miller, ed., *The Journals of Mary O'Brien, 1828–1838* (Toronto, 1968). This remarkable woman's diary is a mine of information.

9 Firth, *Town of York, 1815–1834*, p. 36

10 Weller is not a common name and it would be interesting to know whether Charles Dickens' Tony Weller had a literary relationship to William of Upper Canada. *Pickwick Papers* was published before Dickens visited North America but he might have noticed the name in one of the many guides to immigrants that were published in England.

11 Ontario Archives, Robinson Papers

12 T. W. Acheson, 'John Baldwin: colonial entrepreneur' (*Ontario History*, LXI, no. 3)

13 On early banks see Gerald M. Craig, *Upper Canada: the formative years, 1784–1841* (Toronto, 1963); R. Craig McIvor, *Canadian Monetary, Banking and Fiscal Development* (Toronto, 1958); and Victor Ross, *A History of the Canadian Bank of Commerce, with an account of the other banks which now form part of its organization* (2 vols., Toronto, 1920–22), I

14 For location and description of buildings see Scadding, *Toronto of Old*; Robertson, *Landmarks of Toronto*; *York Commercial Directory, street guide and registry, 1833–34 ... compiled and arranged by George Walton* (York, UC, [1834]); and Arthur, *Toronto: no mean city*

15 Ontario Archives, Robinson Papers. Policy dated 27 October 1830, Phoenix Assurance Company of London, England

16 One question put to a select committee of the House of Assembly in 1828 was the proportion of Anglicans to all Christians in Upper Canada. The answers ranged from one-sixth to one–one-hundredth. J. B. Robinson said he did not know and did not think that anyone else did. George W. Spragge, ed., *The John Strachan Letter Book, 1812–1834* (Toronto, 1946), p. 536n.

17 In addition to Spragge, *Letter Book*, see Henderson, *John Strachan: documents and opinions*, and *John Strachan, 1778–1867* (Toronto, 1969). For a general study of the churches see S. D. Clark, *Church and Sect in Canada* (Toronto, 1948)

18 The original indenture is in the Metropolitan Toronto Central Library.

19 J. Ross Robertson, *The History of Freemasonry in Canada, from its introduction in 1749* (2 vols., Toronto, 1900); Henry T. Smith, *History of St. Andrew's Lodge A.F. and A.M. No. 16, G.R.C., 1822–1922* (Toronto, 1922)

20 W. B. Kerr, *The Orange Order in Upper Canada* (articles in the *Sentinel* in 1939); Firth, *Town of York, 1815–1834*

21 J. George Hodgins, *The Establishment of Schools and Colleges in Ontario, 1792–1910* (3 vols., Toronto, 1910)

22 Examples are printed in Firth, *Town of York, 1815–1834*.

23 R. I. Harris, 'Christopher Widmer, 1780–1858, and the Toronto General Hospital' (*York Pioneer*, 1965). On the medical profession see also William Canniff, *The Medical Profession in Upper Canada, 1783–1850* (Toronto, 1894); and H. B. Anderson, 'An Historical Sketch of the Medical Profession of Toronto' (*Canadian Medical Association Journal*, XVI, 446)

24 On health and medicine see John J. Heagerty, *Four Centuries of Medical History in Canada, and a sketch of the medical history of Newfoundland* (2 vols., Toronto, 1928); and 'Toronto Papers, Board of Health,' manuscripts in the Metropolitan Toronto Central Library

[25] Ontario Archives, Macaulay Papers. Robert Stanton to Macaulay, 10 June 1826

[26] Edith G. Firth, ed., *Early Toronto Newspapers, 1793–1867* (Toronto, 1961)

[27] S. A. Heward and W. S. Wallace, eds., 'An American Lady in Old Toronto: the letters of Julia Lambert, 1821–1854' (*Royal Society of Canada, Proceedings and Transactions,* 1946)

[28] E. S. Dunlop, ed., *Our Forest Home: being extracts from the correspondence of the late Frances Stewart.* 2nd ed., ed. Frances Brown (Montreal, 1902)

[29] The quotations from Duncan, Elmsley, Henry, and Jackson are in Firth, *Town of York, 1815–1834.*

## 4 Government and governed 75–98

[1] E. A. Cruikshank and A. F. Hunter, eds., *The Correspondence of the Honourable Peter Russell, with allied documents relating to the administration of the government of Upper Canada during the official term of Lieutenant-Governor Simcoe* (3 vols., Toronto, 1932–6), I, 229. Russell to Elmsley, 12 June 1799

[2] Firth, *Town of York, 1815–1834,* p. lxxii ff.

[3] F. H. Armstrong, 'Toronto in Transition: the emergence of a city, 1828–1838' (unpublished PH D thesis, University of Toronto, 1965); 'William Lyon Mackenzie, First Mayor of Toronto: a study of a critic in power' (*Canadian Historical Review,* XLVIII, no. 4)

[4] Ontario Archives, Macaulay Papers

[5] Metropolitan Toronto Central Library, 'Sketch of events in Toronto and vicinity during the months of October, November and December,' by James Fitzgibbon, dated 13 December 1837; William Kilbourn, *The Firebrand: William Lyon Mackenzie and the rebellion in Upper Canada* (Toronto, 1956). Bond Head's own account, *A Narrative,* was published early in 1839. It was republished in 1969, edited by S. F. Wise and with Mackenzie's comments added. It throws more light on the characters of Head and Mackenzie than on the events of the rebellion.

[6] City of Toronto Archives, Toronto City Council Papers (in manuscript until 1859)

[7] C. R. Sanderson, ed., *The Arthur Papers: being the Canadian papers mainly confidential, private and demi-official of Sir George Arthur in the manuscript collection of the Toronto Public Libraries* (3 vols., Toronto, 1957–9), I, 254. Arthur to the Archbishop of Canterbury, 11 August 1838

[8] J. O. Coté, ed., *Political Appointments and Elections in the Province of Canada from 1841 to 1865* (Ottawa, 1866)

[9] H. E. MacDermot, *One Hundred Years of Medicine in Canada, 1867–1967* (Toronto, 1967)

[10] Henderson, *John Strachan: documents and opinions,* p. 177

[11] W. H. Pearson, *Recollections and Records of Toronto of Old* (Toronto, 1914)

[12] Sigmund Samuel, *In Return: the autobiography of Sigmund Samuel* (Toronto, 1963); David Eisen, 'Jewish Settlers of Old Toronto' (*Jewish Standard,* December 1965 – April 1966); Albert Rose, ed., *A People and Its Faith: essays on Jews and reform Judaism in a changing Canada* (Toronto, 1959)

[13] Ontario Archives, Robinson Papers. 'Number of coloured persons resident in Toronto and liberties, July 25, 1840.' See also Daniel G. Hill, 'Negroes in Toronto, 1763–1865' (*Ontario History,* LV, no. 2), and F. H. Armstrong, 'The Toronto Directories and the Negro Community in the Late 1840's' (*Ontario History,* LXI, no. 2)

14 *Report of the past history and present conditions of the Common or Public Schools of the City of Toronto* (Toronto, 1859)

15 The original minutes with newspaper clippings are in the Metropolitan Toronto Central Library.

16 Frank Norman Walker, *Sketches of Old Toronto* (Toronto, 1965), chap. 13

17 J. Russell Harper, 'Landscape Painting in Upper Canada,' in Ontario Historical Society, *Profiles of a Province: studies in the history of Ontario* (Toronto, 1967)

18 Murray D. Edwards, *A Stage in Our Past: English-language theatre in Eastern Canada from the 1790s to 1914* (Toronto, 1968)

19 Metropolitan Toronto Central Library, Diary of Larratt Smith


## 5 *Urban supremacy*  99–133

1 Edward M. Hodder, *The Harbours and Ports of Lake Ontario* (Toronto, 1857)

2 For descriptions and history of the harbour and waterfront see V. M. Roberts, 'Memorabilia, being a collection of extracts relating to the origin of the name Toronto and history of the waterfront of the city, its harbour and shipping from 1669 to 1912, gathered from standard authorities and newspapers.' This valuable collection, in typed form, is in the Metropolitan Toronto Central Library.

3 *The Port and Harbour of Toronto, 1834–1934, centennial year* [Toronto, 1934]. Probably written by V. M. Roberts

4 F. H. Armstrong, 'Toronto's First Railway' (*Ontario History*, LVIII, no. 1)

5 G. R. Stevens, *Canadian National Railways* (2 vols., Toronto, 1960–2), I, chap. 12

6 *Preliminary report of the engineer on the survey of the various routes for the proposed ship canal to connect the waters of Lakes Huron and Ontario at Toronto, to the President of the Board of Trade.* 22 January 1857

7 *Provincial Exhibition, 1858. Facts for the people about the Toronto and Georgian Bay Ship Canal* (broadside to accompany a topographical model)

8 *Report of Thomas C. Keefer of survey of Georgian Bay canal route to Lake Ontario by way of Lake Scugog* (Whitby, 1863)

9 *Report of select committee on Georgian Bay and Lake Ontario Ship Canal, 1864; Report of select committee on the Georgian Bay Ship Canal through the west of Ontario, 1864; Second report of the select committee on the Huron and Ontario Ship Canal, 1869*

10 Canada, *Sessional Papers*, 1871 (no. 54)

11 On transportation generally see G. P. de T. Glazebrook, *A History of Transportation in Canada* (2 vols., Toronto, 1964)

12 Douglas McCalla, 'The Commercial Politics of the Toronto Board of Trade, 1850–1860' (*Canadian Historical Review*, L, no. 1)

13 Annual Tables of Trade and Navigation (appendices to the *Journals of the Legislative Assembly*)

14 Metropolitan Toronto Central Library, James Lesslie, 'Résumé of Events in Toronto.'

15 Joseph Schull, *100 Years of Banking in Canada: a history of the Toronto-Dominion Bank* (Toronto, 1958)

16 Ross, *A History of the Canadian Bank of Commerce*

17 *The Western of Toronto: a century of insurance* (Toronto, [1950])

18 G. R. Stevens, *The Canada Permanent Story* (n.p., 1955)

19 Lyndhurst Ogden, *Sketch of the Toronto Stock Exchange, 1852–1913* (Toronto, 1913)

20 The censuses for 1850–1 and 1860–1 include statistics on all manufacturing firms in Toronto.

21 S. D. Clark, *The Canadian Manufacturers' Association: a study in collective bargaining and political pressure* (Toronto, 1939)

22 Firth, *Town of York, 1815–1834,* pp. 31–5

23 Sanderson, *The Arthur Papers,* II, 390

24 V. M. Roberts, *The Trail of the Canadian National Exhibition: an illustrated historical souvenir* (Toronto, 1925)

25 Documents concerning the esplanade are in Roberts, 'Memorabilia'

26 Arthur, *Toronto: no mean city*

27 A Member of the Press [George P. Ure], *The Hand-Book of Toronto, containing its climate, geology, natural history, educational institutions, courts of law, municipal arrangements, etc., etc.* (Toronto, 1858)

28 Loris S. Russell, *A Heritage of Light: lamps and lighting in the early Canadian home* (Toronto, 1968)

29 *Toronto Police Force: a brief account of the force since its reorganization in 1859 up to the present date* (Toronto, 1886)

30 *Toronto City Council Minutes,* 1859

31 W. H. Pearson, who was for some years an employee of the Post Office, describes it in his *Recollections and Records of Toronto of Old.*

## 6 Provincial capital 135–60

1 *First report of the commission on municipal institutions appointed by the government of the Province of Ontario* (Ontario Sessional Paper no. 42, 1888); *Second report ...* (Ontario Sessional Paper no. 13, 1889)

2 For lists of those concerned with local government see *By-laws of the City of Toronto of general application and showing those passed since 13th January 1890 to 22nd February 1904 ... together with the names of the members of the municipal council and principal officials ...* (Toronto, 1904)

3 The readiest guides to the history of annexations are a map hung in the City of Toronto Archives and a list prepared by the archivists.

4 On the printers' strike see H. A. Logan, *Trade Unions in Canada: their development and functioning* (Toronto, 1948); J. M. S. Careless, *Brown of the Globe* (2 vols., Toronto, 1959–63); D. G. Creighton, 'George Brown, Sir John Macdonald, and the "Workingman": an episode in the history of the Canadian labour movement' (*Canadian Historical Review,* XXIV, no. 4); University of Toronto Archives, Minutes of the Toronto District Trades and Labor Council

5 *Report of the commissioners appointed to enquire into the working of mills and factories of the Dominion, and the labor employed therein* (Sessional Paper no. 42, 1882)

6 *Report of the royal commission on the relations of labor and capital in Canada* (Ottawa, 1889)

7 Ruth Elizabeth Spence, *Prohibition in Canada: a memorial to Francis Stephens Spence* (Toronto, 1919)

8 Mary Quayle Innis, *Unfold the Years: a history of the Young Women's Christian Association in Canada* (Toronto, 1949)

9 *Papers relating to the estate of the late Andrew Mercer, of the City of Toronto, Esquire, who died unmarried, intestate, and without heirs* (Ontario Sessional Paper no. 38, 1878)

10 Most of the Toronto papers are touched on in W. H. Kesterton, *A History of Journalism in Canada* (Toronto, 1967).

11 Elisabeth Wallace, *Goldwin Smith: Victorian liberal* (Toronto, 1957)

12 See Careless, *Brown of the Globe*; Hector Charlesworth, *Candid Chronicles: leaves from the note book of a Canadian journalist* (Toronto, 1925), and *More Candid Chronicles* (Toronto, 1928); Sir John Willison, *Reminiscences, political and personal* (Toronto, 1919)

13 Ontario Archives, Thomas Charles Patteson Papers

14 F. H. Brigden, 'The Ontario Society of Artists' (*Canadian Review of Music and Art*, VI, nos. 1–4)

15 Roberts, *The Trail of the Canadian National Exhibition*

16 Metropolitan Toronto Central Library, J. G. Howard Papers

17 Drawings and descriptions of Hanlan's and Duck's hotels are in J. Clarence Duff, *Pen Sketches of Historic Toronto* (Toronto, 1967)

7 *Pride and prejudice*   161–87

1 A detailed account is in Roy C. Dalton, *The Jesuits' Estates Question, 1760–1888: a study of the background for the agitation of 1889* (Toronto, 1968)

2 Jesse Edgar Middleton, *The Municipality of Toronto: a history* (3 vols., Toronto, 1923), II, 788

3 Public Archives of Canada, Laurier Papers. Letter dated 17 June 1889

4 The views of McCarthy and Archbishop Lynch are well illustrated in the newspapers and also in correspondence with J. A. Macdonald (Public Archives of Canada, Macdonald Papers).

5 The *Globe*, 17 January 1889

6 Ontario Archives, J. P. Whitney Papers. Letter dated 5 September 1890

7 Metropolitan Toronto Central Library, Diary of Helen Sarah Grant Macdonald

8 W. G. Larder, 'Controversy in the Baptist Convention of Ontario and Quebec, 1903–1929' (unpublished BD thesis, McMaster University, 1950); Alan Wilson, *John Northway: a blue serge Canadian* (Toronto, 1965)

9 J. V. McAree, *Cabbagetown Store* (Toronto, 1953)

10 In *Candid Chronicles* and *More Candid Chronicles* Charlesworth wrote of music and the stage in the nineties.

11 The readiest guides are the city directories.

12 For accounts and pictures of the buildings mentioned above and of others of the same period, see Eric Arthur, *Toronto: no mean city*.

13 Toronto Transportation Commission, *Wheels of Progress* (Toronto, 1953); Toronto Transit Commission, *Transit in Toronto, 1849–1967* (Toronto, 1967)

14 John F. Due, *The Intercity Electric Railway Industry in Canada* (Toronto, 1966)

15 W. Sanford Evans, *The Canadian Contingents and Canadian Imperialism: a story and a study* (London, 1901)

8 *Progress and poverty*   189–210

1 Roland Wilson, 'Migration Movements in Canada, 1868–1925' (*Canadian Historical Review*, XIII, no. 2)

2 Harold A. Innis, 'Settlement and the Mining Frontier' in W. A. Mackintosh and W. L. G. Joerg [eds.], *Canadian Frontiers of Settlement*, IX (Toronto, 1936); L. Carson Brown, *Ontario's Mineral Heritage* (Toronto, 1965); Canadian Pulp and Paper Association, *From Watershed to Watermark* (n.p., 1967); Fred W. Field, *The*

*Resources and Trade Prospects of Northern Ontario: a special report made on behalf of the Toronto Board of Trade* (Toronto, 1911). Apart from its intrinsic interest the latter volume is revealing of the awareness of Toronto of the new possibilities of the north.

3 Department of External Affairs, *Documents on Canadian External Relations*, I, 1909–18 (Ottawa, 1967), pp. 59, 61

4 See above, p. 106

5 The Toronto Board of Trade's pamphlet, *Canada's Canal Problem and Its Solution*, is undated but was evidently published in 1910 or 1911. The Canadian Federation of Boards of Trade and Municipalities launched into an indignant defence of the Ottawa waterway in *Canada's Canal Problem and Its Solution: a reply to the Toronto Board of Trade* (also undated but probably published in 1912).

6 Toronto Harbour Commissioners, *Toronto's Waterfront Development, 1912–1920*; *Toronto Municipal Handbook*, 1927, p. 142

7 G. de T. Glazebrook, Katharine B. Brett, and Judith McErvel, *A Shopper's View of Canada's Past: pages from Eaton's catalogues, 1886–1930* (Toronto, 1969)

8 Ross, *A History of the Canadian Bank of Commerce*

9 Donald Kerr and Jacob Spelt. *The Changing Face of Toronto: a study in urban geography* (Ottawa, 1965), p. 80

10 *Census of Canada*, 1901 and 1911

11 *Casa Loma: Canada's famous castle*, published by the Toronto Kiwanis Club about 1939

12 *Board of Inquiry into the Cost of Living in Canada: report of the board* (2 vols., Ottawa, 1915)

13 I was given the privilege of examining the working papers which are in private hands.

14 But curiously little has been written on the impact of the depression on Toronto or on Ontario generally. The principal work is H. M. Cassidy, *Unemployment and Relief in Ontario, 1929–1932: a survey and report* (Toronto, 1932).


9 *The end of an era*   211–34

1 *Report of the lieutenant-governor's committee on housing*, 1934

2 Lewis Duncan, *Report on housing for the City of Toronto*, 1942

3 Examples of household appliances and furniture may be found in Glazebrook, Brett, and McErvel, *A Shopper's View of Canada's Past.*

4 Metropolitan Toronto Central Library, Diary of Mrs Mary Robertson

5 C. T. Currelly, *I Brought the Ages Home* (Toronto, 1956); G. P. de T. Glazebrook, *Sir Edmund Walker* (London, 1933)

6 Leo Smith, 'Music' (*Encyclopaedia of Canada*, IV, ed. W. S. Wallace); Ernest MacMillan, ed., *Music in Canada* (Toronto, 1955); *A Responsive Chord: the story of the Toronto Mendelssohn Choir, 1894–1969* (Toronto, n.d.)

7 R. H. Hubbard, *The Development of Canadian Art* (Ottawa, n.d.); J. Russell Harper, *Painting in Canada: a history* (Toronto, 1966)

8 K. G. Crawford, *Canadian Municipal Government* (Toronto, 1954); R. K. Ross, *Local Government in Ontario* (Toronto, 1962)

9 *Annual Report of the Toronto Board of Trade*, 1905; H. C. Goldenberg, *Municipal Finance in Canada: a study prepared for the Royal Commission on Dominion-Provincial Relations* (Ottawa, 1939); H. E. Manning, *Assessment and Rating: municipal taxation in Canada* (Toronto, 1962)

10 *Toronto Municipal Handbook*, 1927

11 John H. Dales, *Hydroelectricity and Industrial Development, Quebec, 1898–1940* (Cambridge, Mass., 1957); C. A. S. Hall, 'Electric Utilities in Ontario under Private Ownership, 1890–1914' (unpublished PH D thesis, University of Toronto, 1968); E. M. Ashworth, *Toronto Hydro Recollections* (Toronto, 1955)
12 Toronto Guild of Civic Art, *Report on a comprehensive plan for systematic civic improvements in Toronto* (Toronto, 1909)
13 *Report of the Civic Improvement Committee for the City of Toronto*, 1911
14 *Report of Messrs Jacobs and Davies on street railway transportation in the City of Toronto* (New York, 1910)
15 For the radial scheme proposed by Beck and the Ontario Hydro see Due, *The Intercity Electric Railway Industry in Canada*, chap. 5.
16 *Report to the Civic Transportation Committee on radial railway entrances and rapid transit for the City of Toronto* (2 vols., Toronto, 1915). Tne maps in the second volume are of exceptional value.
17 Toronto Transit Commission, *Transit in Toronto, 1849–1967*
18 Civic Guild, *Report on widening College Street*, 1911
19 *Street and bridge problems of the Reservoir Park District of Toronto: plan of treatment devised by the Civic Guild*, 1917
20 *Report of the Advisory City Planning Commission and recommendations for the improvement of the central business section of the City of Toronto*, 1929
21 *Report of civic department heads re the Advisory City Planning Commission report for the improvement of the City of Toronto*, 1929
22 Toronto Civic Guild, *Two suggested additions to Toronto highways*, 1930
23 *City of Toronto: report on a survey of the treasury, assessment, works, fire, and property departments*. Prepared for the City Survey Committee by the New York Bureau of Municipal Research, 1913
24 *Annual Report of Toronto Bureau of Municipal Research*, 1915
25 *Official master programme, Toronto centennial celebrations*
26 Suzanne M. Skebo, 'Liberty and Authority: civil liberties in Toronto, 1929–1935' (unpublished MA thesis, University of British Columbia, 1968)
27 J. de N. Kennedy, *History of the Department of Munitions and Supply: Canada in the second world war* (2 vols., Ottawa, 1950); Department of Reconstruction and Supply, *Location and Effects of Wartime Industrial Expansion in Canada, 1939–1944*


*10 Problems of greatness* 235–45

1 A. F. W. Plumptre, 'Report on the government of the metropolitan area of Toronto' (typed, 1935). A copy is in the library of the University of Toronto.
2 Leroy O. Stone, *Urban Development in Canada: an introduction to the demographic aspects* (1961 Census Monographs, Ottawa, 1967); and the article 'Recent Trends in Urbanization and Metropolitan Growth' in the *Canada Year Book*, 1969, by the same author
3 Civic Advisory Council of Toronto, *First Report*, 1949; *Final Report*, 1951
4 This body was composed of five members appointed by the city and four by the county. It superseded the Toronto and Suburban Planning Board.
5 *Ontario Municipal Board: decisions and recommendations of the Board*, 1953
6 John C. Bollens, *Special District Governments in the United States* (Berkeley and Los Angeles, 1957); John J. Clarke, *A History of Local Government of the United Kingdom* (London, 1955); W. Eric Jackson, *The Structure of Local Government in England and Wales* (London, 1966)

[7] *Metropolitan Toronto Commission of Inquiry: first report,* 1958

[8] Ontario Department of Economics, *A Report on the Metropolitan Toronto System of Government.* Prepared for the special committee of the metro council on metro affairs, 1961. On the early years of metro see also John G. Grumm, *Metropolitan Area Government: the Toronto experience* (University of Kansas, 1959); Frank Smallwood, *Metro Toronto, a decade later* (Bureau of Municipal Research, Toronto, 1963); and Harold Kaplan, *Urban Political Systems: a functional analysis of Metro Toronto* (New York, 1967)

[9] H. Carl Goldenberg, *Report of the Royal Commission on Metropolitan Toronto,* 1965

[10] Nathan Phillips, *Mayor of All the People* (Toronto, 1967)

[11] City of Toronto Planning Board, *Proposed Revision of Standards,* 1956. The full report, of which this is an abstract, is entitled *Report on Residential Zoning Standards,* 1956.

[12] City of Toronto Planning Board, *The Changing City: a forecast of planning issues for the City of Toronto, 1956–1980,* 1959

[13] City of Toronto Planning Board, *Plan for the Annex,* 1959

[14] City of Toronto Planning Board, *Plan for the Don,* 1963

## 11 *Life in Metropolitan Toronto*   247–69

[1] Two sections of the Canadian census for 1966 are of particular interest in this connection. Statistics are broken down by small districts, these being shown on maps. They are 'Retail Trade, metropolitan areas by census tracts' and 'Service Trades, metropolitan areas by census tracts.' On the downtown area generally see also Kerr and Spelt, *The Changing Face of Toronto,* chap. 7

[2] See the bulletin in the 1966 census on 'Population characteristics by census tracts'

[3] S. D. Clark emphasizes the latter motive in *The Suburban Society* (Toronto, 1966).

[4] *Ontario Economic Review,* VII, no. 6, pp. 4, 12

[5] The census of 1961 remains the authoritative source since that of 1966 did not cover ethnic origin, birthplace, or language. Later figures of immigration for all Canada are in Department of Manpower and Immigration, *1969 Immigration, Canada.* Unofficial calculations help to fill the gaps.

[6] By Anthony H. Richmond in *Immigrants and Ethnic Groups in Metropolitan Toronto* (York University, 1967). An earlier study was made by the Toronto Planning Board, *A report on the ethnic origins of the population of Toronto,* 1960.

[7] *Census of Canada,* 1961: 'Population, ethnic groups.'

[8] On this point see Anthony H. Richmond, *Post-War Immigrants in Canada* (Toronto, 1967).

[9] Metropolitan Toronto Council, *Metropolitan Toronto, 1967.* This report includes information on all aspects of the council's responsibilities.

[10] Dominion Bureau of Statistics, *Directory of Private Schools,* 1969–70

[11] Toronto Transit Commission, *Transit in Toronto, 1849–1967*

[12] The Metropolitan Department of Roads has issued biennial reports.

[13] See above, p. 68.

[14] The Metropolitan Board of Commissioners of Police publishes annual reports.

[15] Herbert Whittaker, *Canada's National Ballet* (Toronto, 1967)

## 12  Toronto's realm  271–80

1 N. S. B. Gras, *An Introduction to Economic History* (New York, 1922)
2 J. M. S. Careless, 'Frontierism, Metropolitanism, and Canadian History'
  (*Canadian Historical Review*, XXXV, no. 1)
3 See above, pp. 257–60
4 Dominion Bureau of Statistics, *Cheques Cashed in Clearing Centres, 1968*
5 Dominion Bureau of Statistics, *Preliminary Bulletin: manufacturing industries*, 1967;
  Dominion Bureau of Statistics and Department of Trade, Industry and Commerce,
  *Private and Public Investment in Canada, outlook 1970; Census of Canada*, 1961:
  'Labour force, metropolitan areas'
6 *Census of Canada*, 1961: 'General review, merchandising: wholesale trade'
7 *Census of Canada*, 1966: 'Retail trade: provinces and cities by kind of business'
8 See three publications in the 1966 Census on service trades: 'Metropolitan areas
  by census tracts,' 'Counties or census divisions  cities and towns,' and
  'Provinces and cities by kind of business.'
9 *Ontario Economic Review*, VIII, no. 4

# Bibliography

MANUSCRIPTS

*Metropolitan Toronto Central Library*

Allan Papers

Baldwin Papers

John Elmsley Letter Book

Toronto Papers, Board of Health

J. G. Howard Papers

William Jarvis Papers

Diary of Helen Sarah Grant Macdonald

Letters and Accounts, North West Company

Memorials of the North West Company

William Dummer Powell Papers

T. A. Reed Papers

Diary of Mrs Mary Robertson

Elizabeth Russell Papers

Goldwin Smith Papers

Diary of Larratt Smith

Diary of a Soldier, 1838–40

Toronto Literary Debating Society

Minutes of Town Meetings and Lists of Inhabitants of York, 1797–1822

Alexander Wood Papers

Papers relating to the capitulation of York

*Ontario Archives*

Minutes of the General Quarter Sessions of the Peace, Home District
John Macaulay Papers
Thomas Charles Patteson Papers
Diaries of Ely Playter
J. B. Robinson Papers
John Strachan Papers
J. P. Whitney Papers

*City of Toronto Archives*

Assessment Rolls, 1834–
Toronto City Council, Minutes and Journals, 1834–58

*University of Toronto Library*

Blake Papers
Land Account Books
Minutes of the Toronto District Trades and Labor Council

*Public Archives of Canada*

Laurier Papers
Macdonald Papers

PRINTED DOCUMENTS

*General*

Firth, Edith G., ed., *The Town of York, 1793–1815: a collection of documents of early Toronto.* Toronto, 1962
— *The Town of York, 1815–1834: a further collection of documents of early Toronto.* Toronto, 1966
Doughty, Arthur G., and McArthur, Duncan A., eds., *Documents Relating to the Constitutional History of Canada, 1791–1818.* Ottawa, 1914
Cruikshank, E. A., ed., *The Correspondence of Lieutenant-Governor John Graves Simcoe, with allied documents relating to the administration of the government of Upper Canada.* 5 vols., Toronto, 1923–31
Cruikshank, E. A., and Hunter, A. F., eds., *The Correspondence of the Honourable Peter Russell, with allied documents relating to the administration of the government of Upper Canada during the official term of Lieutenant-Governor J. G. Simcoe.* 3 vols., Toronto, 1932–6

Sanderson, Charles R., ed., *The Arthur Papers: being the Canadian papers mainly confidential, private and demi-official of Sir George Arthur in the manuscript collection of the Toronto Public Libraries.* 3 vols., Toronto, 1957–9

Hodgins, J. George, *Documentary History of Education in Upper Canada from the Passing of the Constitutional Act of 1791 to the Close of the Reverend Doctor Ryerson's Administration of the Education Department in 1876.* 28 vols., Toronto, 1894–1910

Powell, A. M., 'Letters of Mrs. William Dummer Powell, 1807–1821' (*Niagara Historical Society*, no. 14)

'Letters from William Jarvis, Secretary for Upper Canada and Mrs. Jarvis to the Rev. Samuel Peters' (*Women's Canadian Historical Society of Toronto*, no. 23)

*A Submission to the Royal Commission on Canada's Economic Prospects*, presented by the mayor of Toronto, 1956

*Provincial publications*

Statutes of Upper Canada, the Province of Canada, and Ontario

Journals and appendices (later sessional papers) of the legislatures. These are not all preserved. See Elaine Allan Mitchell, 'The "Sessional Papers" of Upper Canada, 1792–1840' (*Canadian Historical Review*, XXII, no. 3)

'Minutes of the Court of General Quarter Sessions of the Peace for the Home District, 1800–1811' (*Twenty-first Report of the Department of Public Records and Archives of Ontario*, 1932). For other years see manuscripts.

'Grants of Crown Lands in Upper Canada, 1792–96' (*Report of the Department of Public Records and Archives of Ontario*, 1929)

*The Municipal Manual for Upper Canada*, fifth edition, 1855

*Municipal publications*

*Statutes especially relating to the City of Toronto.* Toronto, 1894

*Additional statutes especially relating to the City of Toronto since 1894 (including some previously omitted).* Toronto, 1908

*By-laws of the City of Toronto of practical utility and general application ...* Toronto, 1870

*By-laws of the City of Toronto from the date of its incorporation in 1834 to the 13th January, 1890 ...* Toronto, 1890

*By-laws of the City of Toronto of general application and showing those passed since 13th January, 1890 to 22nd February, 1904 ... together with the names of the members of the Municipal Council and principal officials, also the police commissioners' by-laws.* Toronto, 1904

*Toronto City Council Minutes,* 1859 to the present. For earlier ones see
manuscripts.

*Municipal Handbook, City of Toronto.* Annual from 1904

ATLASES AND MAPS

Boulton, William Somerville, *Plan of Toronto surveyed and compiled
by H. C. Boulton.* 1858 (?)

*Atlas of the City of Toronto and suburbs from special survey and registered plans
showing all buildings and lot numbers.* Charles E. Goad, civil engineer.
Published in 1884, 1890, 1899, 1910, and 1923

Maps or plans are contained in several books about Toronto. Collections of
maps are in the Metropolitan Toronto Central Library, the Ontario Archives,
the City of Toronto Archives, and the Public Archives of Canada in Ottawa.

NEWSPAPERS

Newspapers are invaluable for the history of a city, but over the nearly two
centuries so many have been published in and near Toronto that it will be best
to give only the directories to them. For many purposes one paper will be found
as useful as another of the same period.

*American Newspaper Directory, containing accurate lists of all the newspapers
and periodicals published in the United States, territories, Dominion of
Canada and Newfoundland, together with a description of the towns
and cities in which they are published.* New York, 1869–1908.
Incorporated with Ayer's directory in 1910

*American Newspapers, 1821–1936; a union list of files available in the
United States and Canada.* Edited by Winifred Gregory.
New York, 1937. Reprinted in 1967

*N. W. Ayer & Son's Directory of Newspapers and Periodicals: a guide to
publications printed in the United States and its possessions, the Philippine
Commonwealth, and the Dominions of Canada and Newfoundland ...*
Philadelphia, 1880 to the present. The title varies.

Canadian Library Association, microfilm committee, *Canadian Newspapers
on Microfilm.* Ottawa, 1959 to the present. Revised at intervals.

Chesman, Nelson and Co., *Newspaper Rate Book, including a catalogue
of newspapers and periodicals in the United States, Canada ...* St Louis
[c. 1913]

*Desbarats Newspaper Directory.* Montreal, 1904–17 (?)

*Directory of Canadian Newspapers for 1900, being a catalogue of all newspapers and periodicals published in Canada and Newfoundland ...* Toronto, 1900

Firth, Edith G., *Early Toronto Newspapers, 1793–1867.* Toronto, 1961

*McKim's Directory of Canadian Publications ... a complete list of the newspapers and periodicals published in the Dominion of Canada and Newfoundland with full particulars.* Montreal, 1892–1942. From 1892 until 1923 the title was *Canadian Newspaper Directory.*

Meikle, William, comp., *The Canadian Newspaper Directory; or, advertiser's guide, containing a complete list of all the newspapers in Canada ...* Toronto, 1858

Myers, R. Haltby and Co., *Complete Catalogue of Canadian Publications, containing carefully prepared lists of all the newspapers and periodicals published in the Dominion of Canada.* Toronto, 1890

United States, Library of Congress, Union Catalog Division, *Newspapers on Microfilm.* 6th ed., Washington, 1967

DIRECTORIES AND GUIDE BOOKS

*City directories*

*York Commercial Directory, street guide and register, 1833–34 ...* compiled and arranged by George Walton. York, UC, [1834]

*City of Toronto and the Home District Commercial Directory and Register with Almanack and Calendar for 1837 ...* By George Walton. Toronto, [1837]

*Toronto Directory and Street Guide for 1843–44.* By Francis Lewis. Toronto, 1843

*Brown's Toronto City and Home District Directory, 1846–47.* Toronto, 1847

*Rowsell's City of Toronto and County of York Directory for 1850–51.* Toronto, 1851

*Brown's Toronto General Directory, 1856.* Toronto, 1856

From 1859 directories, mainly published by Chewett and Might, were issued regularly. They were at first biennial and then annual.

*Suburban directories*

Scott, John G., comp., *The Parkdale Register ...* Toronto, 1881

*Sloane and Purves' Directory of the Village of Yorkville.* Toronto, 1876

*Toronto East and North-east Suburban Directory.* Toronto, Might Directories, Ltd., 1958–65

*Toronto West and North-west Suburban Directory.* Toronto, Might Directories, Ltd., 1958–65

## Business directories

*City of Toronto Illustrated Business Directory.* Toronto, A. S. Irving, 1865

*County of York Gazetteer and Directory ... including a full business directory of the City of Toronto.* Toronto, McEvoy and Co., 1870

*Toronto Business Directory and Historical Sketch.* Toronto, Bell, Hawkins and Co., 1877

*Might and Taylor and Co.'s Classified Business Directory of Toronto.* 1879

*Toronto Business and Professional Directory.* Ingersoll, Union Publishing Co., [1890]

*Classified Business Directory of the Cities of Hamilton, London, Montreal, Ottawa and Toronto.* Toronto, Might Directory Co., 1895

*Toronto Classified Business Directory.* Toronto, Stevenson and Hovey, [c. 1912]

## Guide books

Sylvester, Alfred, *Sketches of Toronto, comprising a complete and accurate description of the principal points of interest in the city.* 1858

A Member of the Press [George P. Ure], *The Hand-Book of Toronto, containing its climate, geology, natural history, educational institutions, courts of law, municipal arrangements, etc., etc.* 1858

*The City of Toronto: illustrated with oil-colours taken from photographs.* Nelson and Sons' Hand-Books, 1860

*Chisholm's Hand-Book of Toronto and Tourists' Guide through Canada and the United States.* 1866

Timberlake, J., *Illustrated Toronto Past and Present, being an historical and descriptive guide book.* 1877

*Illustrated Toronto, the Queen city of Canada; its past, present and future, its growth, its resources, its manufactures, its financial interests, its public institutions and its prospects.* Toronto, 1890

*Toronto Illustrated, 1893: its growth, resources, commerce, manufacturing interests, financial institutions, educational advantages and prospects, also sketches of the leading business concerns which contribute to the city's progress; a brief history of the city from foundation to the present time.* Toronto, [1893]

## GENERAL ACCOUNTS

Craig, Gerald M., *Upper Canada: the formative years, 1784–1841.* Toronto, 1963

Careless, J. M. S., *The Union of the Canadas: the growth of Canadian institutions, 1841–1857.* Toronto, 1967

Scadding, Henry, *Toronto of Old.* Edited by F. H. Armstrong. Toronto, 1966

— *Memories of Four Decades of York, Upper Canada.* Toronto, 1884

Robertson, J. Ross, *Landmarks of Toronto, a collection of historical sketches of the old Town of York from 1792 until 1833 and of Toronto from 1834 to 1893.* 6 vols., Toronto, 1894–1914. Articles reprinted from the Toronto *Telegram*

Middleton, Jesse Edgar, with the co-operation of a group of special writers, *The Municipality of Toronto: a history.* 3 vols., Toronto, 1923

Middleton, Jesse Edgar, *Toronto's 100 Years.* Toronto, 1934

Guillet, Edwin C., *Toronto from Trading Post to Great City.* Toronto, 1934

Masters, D. C., *The Rise of Toronto, 1850–1890.* Toronto, 1947


FOR REFERENCE

Chadwick, Edward Marion, *Ontarian Families: genealogies of United-Empire-Loyalist and other pioneer families of Upper Canada.* 2 vols., Toronto, 1894

*Commemorative Biographical Record of the County of York, Ontario: containing biographical sketches of prominent and representative citizens and many of the early settled families.* Toronto, 1907

Davin, Nicholas Flood, *The Irishman in Canada.* London and Toronto, 1877

*Greater Toronto and the Men Who Made It.* Toronto, 1911

Roberts, C. G. D., and Tunnell, Arthur L., *A Standard Dictionary of Canadian Biography.* 2 vols., Toronto, 1934–8

Rattray, W. J., *The Scot in British North America.* 4 vols., Toronto, 1880–3

Wallace, W. Stewart, *The Macmillan Dictionary of Canadian Biography.* London and Toronto, 1963

— *The Encyclopaedia of Canada.* 6 vols., Toronto, 1936

*Encyclopaedia Canadiana.* 10 vols., Ottawa, 1957

*Morang's Annual Register of Canadian Affairs for 1901*

*Canadian Annual Review of Public Affairs*, 1903 to 1937–8

*Canadian Annual Review*, 1960 to the present

*Census of Canada*

*Canada Year Book*

Urquhart, M. C., and Buckley, K. A. H., eds., *Historical Statistics of Canada.* Cambridge and Toronto, 1957

Armstrong, Frederick H., *Handbook of Upper Canadian Chronology and Territorial Legislation.* London, Ontario, 1967

Coté, J. O., ed., *Political Appointments and Elections in the Province of Canada from 1841 to 1865.* Ottawa, 1866

Coté, N. Omer, ed., *Political Appointments, Parliaments, and the Judicial Bench in the Dominion of Canada, 1867–1895.* Ottawa, 1896

# PICTURE AND MAP CREDITS

**6**
T. A. Reed Collection, Metropolitan
Toronto Central Library (MTCL)

**14**
Toronto and Early Canada Collection,
MTCL (top)
T. A. Reed Collection, MTCL (bottom)

**20**
John Ross Robertson Collection, MTCL

**33**
Mr C. Ross Anderson, Quebec; Eric Arthur
Collection, MTCL

**Facing 52**
MTCL

**57, 59**
John Ross Robertson Collection, MTCL

**61**
Robertson's *Landmarks of Toronto*
(Toronto, 1894), I, 560, MTCL

**63**
John Ross Robertson Collection, MTCL

**82**
C. P. Mulvany, *Toronto Past and Present:
a handbook of the city* (Toronto, 1884),
p. 27, MTCL

**87**
*Brown's Toronto General Directory, 1856*,
p. xxv, MTCL

**91**
John Ross Robertson Collection, MTCL

**105**
*Canadian Illustrated News*, July 25, 1863,
p. 127; John Ross Robertson Scrapbooks,
MTCL

**111**
*Brown's Toronto City and Home District
Directory, 1846–7*, p. 136, MTCL

**112, 115**
*Rowsell's City of Toronto and County of
York Directory for 1850–1*, pp. 186, 154,
MTCL

**116**
*Canadian Illustrated News*, October 17,
1863, p. 272, MTCL

**118**
City of Toronto Department of Parks and
Recreation

**119**
*Canadian Illustrated News*, November 22,
1862, p. 18; Eric Arthur Collection, MTCL

**122, 124**
T. A. Reed Collection, MTCL

**126**
E. Hutchison, Toronto

**128**
*City of Toronto Directory for 1867–8*, opp.
p. 361, MTCL

**130**
Robertson's *Landmarks of Toronto*
(Toronto, 1908), v, between pp. 578 and
579, MTCL

**133**
*Rowsell's City of Toronto and County of
York Directory for 1850–1*, p. 187, MTCL

**139**
J. Timberlake, *Illustrated Toronto: Past and
Present* (Toronto, 1877), opp. pp. 300, 270,
MTCL

**147**
*Canadian Illustrated News*, January 25,
1879, p. 53, MTCL

151
*Illustrated Historical Atlas of the County of York, 1878*, p. 13, MTCL

156
T. A. Reed Collection, MTCL

159
*Illustrated Historical Atlas of the County of York, 1878*, p. 9, MTCL

168
MTCL

171
*Canadian Illustrated News*, August 29, 1874, p. 129, MTCL

173
Carre's *Art Work on Toronto*, 1898, MTCL

174
J. Timberlake *Illustrated Toronto: Past and Present*, opp. p. 256, MTCL

176
Carre's *Art Work on Toronto*, MTCL

179
MTCL

181
*Industries of Canada: historical and commercial sketches of Toronto and environs* (Toronto, 1886), p. 181, MTCL

185, 187
Carre's *Art Work on Toronto*, MTCL

190, 191, 199, 201
Archives, Eaton's of Canada

202, 203
Michel Lambeth, Toronto

206
Archives, Eaton's of Canada

213
MTCL

216
Courtesy of E. Hutchison, Toronto

220
City of Toronto Department of Parks and Recreation

222
Archives, Eaton's of Canada

239
T. A. Reed Collection, MTCL (top)
Michel Lambeth, Toronto (bottom)

248
Jack Mitchell, Toronto

258
Toronto Star Syndicate

259
Department of Highways, Ontario

260
Toronto Transit Commission

266
City of Toronto Fire Department

278
John Reeves, Toronto

281
Metropolitan Toronto Planning Board

Jacket
John Reeves, Toronto

Inside jacket
MTCL

# Index

This book
was designed by
ELLEN HUTCHISON
under the direction of
ALLAN FLEMING
University of
Toronto
Press